Discover the Career within You
THIRD EDITION

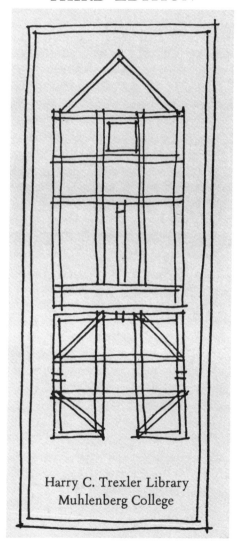

Discover the Career within You

THIRD EDITION

Clarke G. Carney
Kenyon College

Cinda Field Wells

Brooks/Cole Publishing Company
Pacific Grove, California

Brooks/Cole Publishing Company
A Division of Wadsworth, Inc.

The previous editions of this book were published under the title
Career Planning: Skills to Build Your Future.

Printed in the United States of America

10   9   8   7   6   5   4   3   2

Library of Congress Cataloging-in-Publication Data
Carney, Clarke G.
    Discover the career within you / Clarke G. Carney,
Cinda Field Wells. — 3rd ed.
        p.   cm.
    Includes bibliographical references and index.
    ISBN 0-534-14952-9
    1. Vocational guidance.   2. Job hunting.   I. Carney, Clarke G.
Career planning.   II. Title.
HF5381.C315   1991   90-45307
331.7′02—dc20   CIP

Sponsoring Editor: Claire Verduin
Editorial Associate: Gay C. Bond
Production Coordinator: Fiorella Ljunggren
Production: Greg Hubit Bookworks
Manuscript Editor: Pat Harris
Interior Design: Nancy Benedict
Cover Design and Illustration: Lisa Berman
Interior Illustration: John Foster and Lotus Art
Typesetting: Bookends Typesetting
Cover Printing: Phoenix Color Corporation
Printing and Binding: The Maple-Vail Book Manufacturing Group

Chapter opening quotes:

Chapter 1. Courtesy of Piet Hein, "Living is," in *Grooks*, Doubleday and Company,
        originally the M.I.T. Press, 1966. © by Piet Hein.
Chapter 2. Courtesy of Piet Hein, "A Psychological Tip," in *Grooks*, Doubleday
        and Company, originally the M.I.T. Press, 1966. © by Piet Hein.
Chapter 3. Boardman.
Chapter 4. From "Embrace Fleeting Time with Care, Tenderness" by C. W.
        Gusewelle, 1989, *Kansas City Star*, Friday, July 7, p. 2A. Copyright
        1989 by the *Kansas City Star*. Reprinted by permission.
Chapter 5. From "Getting Lost: The Case for Creative Ineptitude" by Tim Cahill.
        Reproduced by permission from *Outside* magazine. Copyright © 1986,
        Mariah Publications Corporation.
Chapter 6. John Schaar.
Chapter 7. Jacob A. Riis.
Chapter 8. Henry J. Kaiser. From *Good Advice*, compiled by Leonard Safir and
        William Safire (Random House, 1982). Copyright © 1982 by William
        Safire and Leonard Safir.

Preface

How many times have you heard yourself or others say "But that's not the way I thought things would be. Why didn't someone tell me?" Even after we are "old enough to know better," we expect things to turn out the way movies and fairy tales tell us they should: the hero rides off into the sunset; the frog turns into a prince. We make choices and go on about our daily business, secure in the belief that we will live happily ever after.

Career choice, a major factor in shaping our lives, is one of the decisions most subject to this myth. Most of us grow up believing that we will choose an occupation and stay with that choice as long as we work. Many of us have parents who did exactly that. But things change. Along with rapidly growing technology has come the periodic creation and disappearance of groups of jobs as well as entire industries. With increasing affluence come greater mobility and higher expectations. More and more people are looking for meaningful jobs, not just paychecks.

So, growth and change must be built into any career decision: they are the heartbeat of the process of career planning. We are both producers and products of change. As our goals, interests, and needs change, we try to arrange our work or educational settings to accommodate new visions. We are constantly adapting to changing educational, environmental, and work demands. Sometimes we feel sad about what we must leave behind, but most of the time we look forward to new opportunities.

Focus of the Text

A number of social scientists have observed that the people who thrive in the midst of change are those who anticipate change, have the skills to deal with it, and, ideally, take advantage of it. *Discover the Career within You* will help you acquire the skills and attitudes to plan effectively for and manage the changes you will experience during your career. We believe that people who are effective in organizing and carrying out their career goals possess six important skills:

1. They are aware of and know how to use several decision-making strategies.
2. They have a clear understanding of their personal interests, values, and abilities and how those qualities develop and change over time.

3. They understand how the world of work is organized and see the information they gather about different occupations in the light of their own lifestyle needs and preferences.
4. They know how to integrate their knowledge of themselves, the beliefs and desires of others, and career information into realistic and satisfying career options.
5. They can use several strategies for locating and securing employment.
6. They understand the social demands of the workplace.

This text presents skills in an easy-to-follow sequence in which one skill builds on another, and theory is applied through practical activities.

Organization of the Text

Discover the Career within You starts with a broad view of how work meets our life needs and fits into the overall patterns of our lives, and it identifies important questions to consider and skills to develop for effective career planning. This is followed by a discussion and application of skills for planful and effective decision making. The focus then shifts to self-awareness, the lifelong process of career development, and the personal qualities that are applicable to the world of work. Inventories to help you clarify preferences, interests, abilities, and values are included.

After an overview of the structure and functions of occupations within the world of work today, techniques for gathering information about occupations are presented, as well as techniques for assessing this information in light of one's own individual needs and lifestyle preferences. In the next step in the career-planning process, personal and occupational exploration come together as self and career information are integrated to come up with career options. The importance of overcoming beliefs and differences with others that impede effective career planning is discussed. Ways to carry out career goals through effective strategies for locating and securing employment are followed by an overview of the hidden social requirements of the workplace and a discussion of how you can continue your self-development through work.

In this way, the text completes a circle that starts with self-awareness and ends with self-enrichment. That truly is our hope: to provide you with an increased sense of self-awareness and practical skills for building your future in a changing world.

New to This Edition

Readers who are familiar with earlier editions of this book will immediately notice that the title has been changed from *Career Planning: Skills to Build Your Future* to *Discover the Career within You*. We have made this change because the new title more adequately reflects our belief that the process of career development is an adventure in self-discovery, a kind of ongoing personal revelation that occurs as one engages in educational and occupational pursuits during the course of his or her career journey. When viewed in this light, the process of career planning—the mastering of the six skills identified in this book—may create a sense of self-empowerment. And that really is our objective, to help students recognize that they have the freedom and the responsibility to make career choices that are consistent with their inner visions of themselves and their personal capacities.

In addition to this change, several other changes have been made to strengthen the book. Chapter 1 has been expanded to show how career decision making is related to one's life tasks as well as one's life needs, lifestyle, and life stages. Chapter 3 now provides more complete coverage of the social/environmental factors that shape adolescent development, particularly in the area of sex-role socialization. Chapter 4 includes more complete coverage of the changes that women are experiencing in their attitudes toward work. Chapter 5 has new information about the historical origins of work values in our society, anticipated trends in the work force over the next decade, and questions to ask when interviewing someone for career information. Chapter 7 includes additional questions commonly asked by employers during the job interview. Chapter 8 now includes information about the importance of specific communication skills in the workplace, effective time management, managing stress on the job, and strategies for dealing with harassment in the work setting.

We believe these changes provide a clearer and more integrated flow for the reader, do a better job of demonstrating how career planning is an integral element in the process of life planning, and provide a more complete picture of the skills needed for career success and satisfaction. We welcome readers' comments on how effective we have been in strengthening the text in these ways. If you have specific suggestions for change, including new ideas and classroom activities, please contact the senior author in care of the Health and Counseling Center, Kenyon College, Gambier, OH 43022.

Acknowledgments

This book is the product of the energies of many people. Whenever possible, we have identified and acknowledged the creators and publishers of material used in this book, and we appreciate their willingness to allow us to adapt their material to our framework. Five individuals deserve special mention for their contributions. Don Streufert, a good friend and creative colleague, must be recognized first for the significant role he played as co-author of the first edition of the text. Many of his creative ideas and written contributions remain in this edition. Russ Sewell deserves recognition for contributing the first draft of "Finding a Job Is a Job!" (Chapter 7) and for his willingness to accept our revisions. Similar thanks are due Casey Green for "Work Adjustment and Career Expansion" (Chapter 8). Amy Reynolds added to this edition as a co-author of "When Others Challenge Your Career Choice" (in Appendix F). Mitchel D. Livingston also helped by writing resumés of his own work history for Chapter 7.

We would also like to acknowledge the support of our colleagues at The Ohio State University, especially Joe Quaranta, Carolyn Carder, Bob Kazin,

Jackie Vice, Alice J. Tenney, Dianne Greenler, Janice Sutera Wolfe, Karen Taylor, Connie Michele Ward, Lesley Jones, Louise Douce, and Barbara Benton.

We would like to thank the following reviewers for reading the manuscript and making helpful comments and suggestions on this edition: George Barnett of Richland College, Dennis L. Nord of the University of California at Santa Barbara, Joseph A. Petrick of the University of Cincinnati, and Charles Pulvino of the University of Wisconsin at Madison.

Our highest praise is given to those who in typing the manuscript over the years had to put up with our indecisiveness, last-minute brainstorms, and often illegible handwriting. Lillian Rice and Maryann Marsh did an outstanding job typing the first edition, often under considerable deadline pressure. The same praise is due Lisa Quinn and Jacquie Jones for typing the second edition. Marcella Haldeman takes sole praise for her typing and editorial comments on the third edition. She graciously held off her retirement until the book reached the editor's desk. Gail Lyall, who replaced Ms. Haldeman and quickly set about typing the revised *Instructor's Guide,* also deserves special mention for her fine effort. Harriet Serenkin shaped the first edition in its final form through her fine editing; the talents of Peggy Hoover and Pat Harris smoothed and refined the second and third, respectively. And our sincere thanks to Claire Verduin and the production staff at Brooks/Cole Publishing Company for seeing that this edition made it from manuscript to book form.

Finally, Vicki and Leland should receive a warm thanks for their encouragement and for recognizing when to step back as we struggled to fit the pieces together.

Clarke G. Carney
Cinda Field Wells

Contents

CHAPTER EIGHT

Work Adjustment and Career Expansion   166

APPENDIX A

Experiential Exercises   196

CHAPTER ONE

It All Has to Do with Life Needs, Styles, Tasks, and Skills

Living is—

Living is
    a thing you do
Now or never—
    which do you do?

—Piet Hein

The classroom fills slowly. Students come in one at a time, sometimes in twos, only occasionally in larger groups. Those who aren't sorting through books and papers or looking out the window at the sunny afternoon sky chat about their hometowns, how they spent their vacations, people they know in common, or courses they are taking. They avoid talking about their majors or their plans for after graduation. Instead, they concentrate on topics that don't remind them that they haven't yet made up their minds about what to major in or what they want to do with their lives.

Kathie sits with Camille, a high school acquaintance. Kathie entered college intending to become an engineer because she had heard about promising employment prospects in that field. She does well in math and science courses but finds something missing. She likes to help people and wonders if she should be a psychologist instead. Camille likes people, too, but has a difficult time with the science courses in her nursing curriculum. Her adviser has suggested that she choose another major, but Camille's not sure she can do that; she's always wanted to be a nurse like her favorite aunt.

Bonnie enters the room and finds a seat away from the others. Because she's the oldest member of the class, she feels isolated. She thinks they wouldn't understand what it's like to be a recently divorced mother of three starting college after being out of school for 15 years. Bonnie is not sure how she'll manage a full load of classes while raising her school-age children, but she knows it may be her only shot at finding a fulfilling career. She has done volunteer work at a community service agency but feels that she's starting over again because it wasn't "paid" employment. She wants to do something more than be a "homemaker," but she doesn't know what.

Tracy and George, who know each other from other classes, take seats together. Tracy has been taking courses for several years but doesn't seem to be heading anywhere. His parents have begun pressuring him to "do something" and not waste his time and their money being a "professional student." His adviser is also pressuring him to declare a major because he's accumulated too many hours as an "undecided" student. Tracy has considered several career fields, but none appeals to him. He likes being in a fraternity and spends a good part of his leisure time in sports activities with fraternity brothers.

George's story is different. He is financing his education through loans and part-time work. He likes biology and does well in it but realizes that when he graduates he may have to take a job that isn't exactly what he wants because he can't afford graduate school and does not want to go any deeper into debt. His tight finances have become even more of a concern this past week because his father was laid off from his job and doesn't know when he will be able to return to work.

Sue wants to be an art major but knows that her choice will disappoint her father, who wants her to become a partner in his firm when she graduates. It's difficult to argue with him when he points out how hard it is to make it as an artist and predicts that she will probably "wind up waiting on tables for the rest of her life." Vera, sitting behind Sue, feels lost. Unlike Sue, who was raised in the city and seems to know her way around the campus, Vera is away from home for the first time, and she is the first person in her family to attend college. Most of her friends stayed home to work in town or on family farms. Vera hasn't had the opportunity to make any important decisions before this and has no work experience. She wants to be successful but doesn't know what she wants to do. She'd like to make a quick decision to take the pressure off but realizes that she doesn't really know what kinds of things she likes to do or which occupations would meet her needs.

Other students enter the room. Pat, with many talents and interests, finds it difficult to focus on a specific major. Craig had hoped to use college as a springboard to a career as a baseball player but was forced to give up his dream because of a serious knee injury. Now he's not sure what he wants to do. Hoyte is thinking about becoming an attorney but doesn't know what major will best prepare him for law school. Jackie, the last to enter the room, is anxious to make the "right" career choice but can't find a career that suits her. Her lack of direction bothers her. She wants to find a counselor who will give her a test that will tell what career she should pursue. The students wait expectantly.

As she walks from her office to the classroom, Dr. Stranges, director of the campus counseling service, reflects on the past few days. It has been hectic preparing for this class and being involved in several important decisions at the same time. Two days ago, she had met with the college president to discuss career enrichment programs for faculty and staff. She has also been helping a teacher who had been an education major find an alternative career. And she began this day by helping a learning-disabled student explore career possibilities and learning resources relevant to his particular skills. Things have been going well, though, and she is enthusiastic about teaching this class on career and life planning. Entering the classroom, Dr. Stranges is reminded that she needs to think about her own retirement, only four years away.

Like the students in this imaginary class, career undecidedness has many faces, and it will affect most people at some time in their lives. Statistics show that changing one's mind about a major or an occupation is natural for students.

Some 30 to 40 percent of college freshmen will not graduate with their class. Of those who remain, 30 to 50 percent will have changed their majors two or more times. Students who are secure in their academic area when they enter college often lack detailed information about their major and the occupational specialties it may lead to when they graduate.

Some 25 percent of workers in the United States today are in occupations that did not exist 25 years ago. By the year 2000, some 75 percent will be in jobs that do not yet exist.

At one time, labor analysts predicted that the average 20-year-old American worker would change jobs six to seven times during his or her working life. Analysts now predict that people who enter the labor force today will change professions, not simply jobs, three to five times during their working lives.

In addition to these statistics, a number of surveys have consistently shown that career planning has recently been a major source of concern for college and university students. In an article written for *Change* magazine in 1973, educator J. Hitchcock observed that a "new student vocationalism" had emerged on American college campuses. He noted that many students were so invested in the pursuit of their career goals that they were neglecting opportunities to participate in the cultural, social, and recreational areas of college life. Surveys of students at Ohio State University, conducted by the senior author of this book and his colleagues from 1976 to 1987, have consistently found that career planning was the most highly rated concern of university students. More recently, in 1988, Alexander Astin and his colleagues at the University of California, Los Angeles, surveyed entering freshman students from across the nation for the American Council on Education. They noted: "Students today, more than ever before, seem preoccupied with developing their careers rather than using the college years as a time for learning and personal development" (p. 7). Thus, 15 years after Hitchcock's observation about the new student vocationalism, students continue to be preoccupied with the pursuit of their career goals.

Given the importance that work has assumed in our lives, and the increasing emphasis that work and individual initiative have been given in our society, it is not surprising that uncertainty or indecision about a college major or occupational direction may make many students feel anxious, guilty, or embarrassed.

While research indicates that the majority of students will change majors at least once during the college years and will do the same in work after they graduate, many students believe that there is one "right" job for them. For this reason, the choice of career may be scary and appear irreversible, because they are afraid of losing time and money or because they feel it is a sign of immaturity to change their minds. Perhaps this is what Robert Frost meant when he described his decision to become a poet:

The Road Not Taken

Two roads diverged in a yellow wood,
And sorry I could not travel both
And be one traveler, long I stood
And looked down one as far as I could
To where it bent in the undergrowth;

Then took the other, as just as fair,
And having perhaps the better claim,
Because it was grassy and wanted wear;
Though as for that, the passing there
Had worn them really about the same,

And both that morning equally lay
In leaves no step had trodden black.
Oh, I kept the first for another day!
Yet knowing how way leads on to way,
I doubted if I should ever come back.

I shall be telling this with a sigh
Somewhere ages and ages hence:
Two roads diverged in a wood, and I—
I took the one less traveled by,
And that has made all the difference.[1]

Some people will follow only one path, but for most of us, our careers will reflect a number of paths and choices. Because of this, it is likely we will be able to see clearly the paths we have followed only later in our lives. Regardless of the number of paths we take, our careers will share the common element of personal choice and development in our changing society.

During your lifetime, you will have many opportunities for exploration, growth, and change as you choose a major, take your first job after graduation, consider opportunities for advancement, change employers, and prepare for retirement. Over time, these choices will become linked into a pattern that reflects the unique shape of your career. This pattern may become clear to you only later in life as you reflect on the choices you have made and the paths you have taken in your educational and work pursuits. The career decisions you make will shape your life in several other important ways. Your work will provide you with resources for living, fill your time, challenge your abilities, support your leisure pursuits, and offer you a place to receive recognition and develop new relationships. It may also dictate where you live. Because your career choices will have such a major impact on your life, it is important that you understand how your work pursuits can fulfill your personal needs and fit into the total pattern of your life.

Why We Work

The career paths we follow greatly affect our views of ourselves and others. As writer Eugene Delacroix once said, through work "we seek not only to produce but to give value to time." The everyday process of getting acquainted also reflects the special value we give to our work in our society. When people first meet, their conversations often begin with references to work: "What's your job or major?" "What do you plan to do when you graduate?" When asked "Who are you?" most people respond "A teacher," "A student," or "A homemaker" rather than "An extrovert" or "A U.S. citizen."

---

[1]From *The Poetry of Robert Frost*, edited by Edward Connery Lathem. Copyright © 1916, 1969 by Holt, Rinehart and Winston. Copyright 1944 by Robert Frost. Reprinted by permission of Holt, Rinehart and Winston, Publishers.

Psychologist Abraham Maslow (1954) suggested that in addition to giving us an important form of social recognition, work helps us meet other important life needs as well. Maslow's theory of human motivation assumes that human needs are arranged like steps on a ladder. Once the needs of the first step are satisfied, the needs at the next step become more important and press for satisfaction. Our most primitive needs—the needs for food and water—lie at the base of the ladder. While these physiological needs are relatively simple and self-centered, they are also the most potent. We can't live without satisfying them. The second step on the ladder is associated with our need for safety. After we are assured of three meals a day, we work to secure warmth and comfort, protection from harm, and a stable future. The needs at the third step, which become our greatest concern after we have established the necessary security, have to do with belongingness. Working with others provides us with opportunities for friendship and associating with a group that has a common purpose. We need to know that our interests, beliefs, and problems are shared and accepted by people who are important to us, such as family and colleagues. Self-esteem emerges as the fourth level of need on the ladder. Through work we strive for a sense of competence, worth, and prestige. The fifth step—self-actualization—is more complex. It involves using work to express our creativity, to experience a sense of personal meaning and integrity, to know and understand the world around us, and to share wisdom and feel a part of something greater than ourselves.

Maslow's research suggests that we are likely to meet the needs at the upper steps of the ladder only after we have sifted through and successfully coped with our more basic needs, which seem more pressing during our youth and early adulthood. He also suggests that the way we feel depends on the degree to which our needs are satisfied. When the basic physiological and safety needs go unmet, we are apt to become angry and actively seek to satisfy those needs, sometimes even through force. When the needs that are higher on the ladder go unmet, we are likely to experience anxiety or feel lost because our goals were not met.

It is easy to see how the ladder of needs operates. For example, when you're really hungry, you're not apt to be thinking about your studies or what you will do when you graduate. And needs are also tied closely to values. If you've been hungry for a long time, you must decide how you will go about obtaining food. If you have the money, you can buy it, but if you're broke, you could borrow from others. If you value industriousness and honesty, you might drop out of school and look for a job to earn money for food. If these values aren't important to you, you might beg or steal from others to feed yourself. In the same way, what we do for a living has a lot to do with our views of why and how we live.

Variations on a Lifestyle Theme

From popular advertising, most of us are acquainted with the term *lifestyle*. We frequently hear, for example, about the California lifestyle, the singles lifestyle, the executive lifestyle, and the lifestyle of the retired community. These lifestyles may differ from our own, and because they are so different they can have a special appeal to us. The snowbound midwesterner may envy the free and sunny lifestyle of the southern Californian. The bored toll-booth operator may fantasize about becoming a jet-hopping executive. Our daily lives reflect our attempts to reconcile our fantasies and aspirations with the realities of what we are capable of achieving. How would you describe your own lifestyle? Sociologists P. J. Miller and G. Sjoberg (1973) suggest that you would most likely describe it in terms of how you spend your time. When we are not sleeping, most of us spend our time studying or working, engaging in leisure and recreational activities, or interacting with family and friends. Taken together, these three types of activities form a triangle that can be used to represent the pattern of our lifestyles (see Figure 1-1).

At different points in your life, you will play roles that are associated with each side of the lifestyle triangle. Donald Super (1980), a psychologist who has made the study of career development his life's work, has suggested that we will play a number of different roles during the course of our lives. We will touch briefly on some of these roles here and describe them in more detail later when we closely examine the different phases or stages of our lives.

The first kinship/friendship role we assume in our lives is that of son or daughter. Early in our lives we learn from family members how to give and receive affection and how to be part of an intimate social network. After a while, the roles associated with that side of the triangle reach beyond the family to early childhood friendships. Later, generally when we are in our 20s, these roles may extend to spouse or life partner, homemaker, and parent. Another important social role is that of citizen. It starts when we first become involved in school politics or in religious or civic groups whose goals are to contribute to the betterment of society. Thus, like all our life roles, kinship/friendship roles become more complex over time as they involve more people and assume greater levels of responsibility in the community.

The next important life role members of our society are expected to assume is that of student/worker. This role begins when we start formal schooling, usually around age 5, and continues throughout our lives even as we pursue advanced studies, attend professional conferences, or seek further education for personal enrichment. Our role as workers started when we took our first position as a paid employee—perhaps as a babysitter or newspaper carrier or performing odd jobs for a neighbor. Around age 20, students may become involved in more permanent full-time positions, which often start with some form of apprenticeship, progress to the role of an established professional colleague, and eventually lead to the role of mentor or supervisor.

Our involvement in the leisure/recreation side of the lifestyle triangle began in infancy with play used to express ourselves and explore the world around us. Leisure/recreational pursuits can include any number of activities that we enjoy. How we use our leisure time will be important later in our lives in relation to how we rejuvenate ourselves and how we spend our retirement years. Some people use it simply to escape the demands of work. This kind of leisure is often characterized by passivity, freedom from responsibility, avoidance of effort, and a wish to be entertained by someone or something. An example of

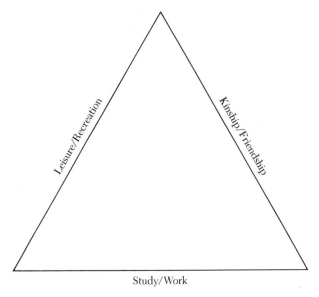

FIGURE 1-1 The lifestyle triangle. (Reprinted with permission from NTL Institute, "Urban Middle-Class Lifestyles in Transition," by Paula Jean Miller and Gideon Sjoberg, p. 149, *Journal of Applied Behavioral Science*, Vol. 9, Nos. 2/3, copyright 1973.)

someone engaged in this form of leisure would be the person who sits in front of the TV, soft drink in hand, too tired to move.

Leisure time can also be used in a more active, purposeful way—for recreation and rejuvenation. Unlike the first form of leisure—work avoidance or passivity—this use of leisure time supports the work effort by rekindling lost energies through active involvement in such spare-time activities as sports, clubs, exercise classes, or cultural groups.

For some people, leisure can have a third purpose, one that is not related to work. This is leisure pursued for the sake of or enjoyment of an activity itself. In this sense, leisure is concerned not with what is produced, accomplished, or avoided but with what is happening at the moment. This form of leisure can be experienced in any setting, including work. A celebration is an example of this type of leisure experience to the fullest.

The degree to which we emphasize the different activities and roles in the lifestyle triangle will vary during our lifetimes. It can also vary from day to day as we strive to meet our life needs. Young children have little interest in the work of adults and spend time and energy playing and interacting with family members. On the other hand, the student who has spent several days cramming for exams knows what it's like to be exhausted by too much work and dreams of free time to spend in leisure and recreational pursuits or with supportive family and friends.

The way we apportion the activities and roles on the sides of the lifestyle triangle thus has a great deal to do with how we view our lives. Too much or too little of any of the activities on the triangle can make our lives a struggle. There will always be brief periods of imbalance in our activities, but we can manage them by finding an appropriate balance. In fact, periods of imbalance serve to challenge us and keep us in touch with ourselves. Research on human motivation shows that when things have been in harmony for too long, people become bored and seek to upset the balance of things to create new challenges for themselves.

How comfortable we are with our lifestyles is determined in part by how effectively we match our energy levels with the requirements of our classes or jobs. Lee Hall (1980), president of the Rhode Island School of Design, vividly described his balancing act as a top-level executive when he jokingly said:

> According to my "bestiary" of Presidential qualities, I will need: the aloofness of a cat; the cunning of a fox; the eye of an eagle; the hide of an elephant; the slipperiness of an eel; the courage of a lion; the stubbornness of a mule; the tenaciousness of a terrier; and the wisdom of an owl, to which should be added: a heart of gold; nerves of steel; and a stomach of iron. (p. 48)

University presidents, like doctors and many executives, often find that their periods of leisure are in constant jeopardy from unanticipated crises. Unless they have a great deal of stamina or can get away frequently, they may be too tired or "burned out" to enjoy time with their families or to take part in leisure and recreational pursuits. Students may find themselves in the same position. Certain courses of study require a similar time commitment and energy level.

In recent years a growing number of researchers have become sensitive to the burnout syndrome that occurs when a person takes on responsibilities beyond the limits of his or her available energies. This syndrome is a frequent cause of educational or job dissatisfaction, decreased efficiency, and strained relationships. It is interesting to note that people who have been working under pressure for long periods of time are apt to develop minor illnesses, such as colds, when the pace of the job abruptly slows down. If a person works too long without a restful break, more severe ailments, such as chronic fatigue, sleeplessness, high blood pressure, ulcers, and depression, may develop.

All this suggests that for you to feel satisfied with your career choices, you will need to plan a lifestyle that balances your time, energies, abilities, and needs with the demands and rewards of your work. We will return to this theme throughout this book.

The Four Developmental Tasks of College Students

Another way of looking at how our career plans fit into the overall course of our lives is to think about the college years as involving the mastery of important developmental tasks. The idea of mastering developmental tasks was conceived in the 1940s. Robert Havighurst (1972), who was trained in chemistry and physics but later became interested in adolescent development, suggested that developmental tasks arise at or about a certain period in the life of the individual—for example, in late adolescence. According to Havighurst, successful mastery of a particular task leads to feelings of happiness and to success with later tasks, while failure leads to unhappiness in the individual, disapproval by society, and difficulty with later life tasks. Expectations about the importance of specific life tasks arise from the individual's physical maturation, social expectations, and personal aspirations and values.

Based on our experience in counseling college and university students over the past two decades, and on the work of theorists such as Arthur Chickering (1969), who first applied the concept of developmental tasks to college student development, we have come to believe that students who enter college directly after high school seem to be confronted with four developmental tasks during their college years. The four tasks are presented in Figure 1-2.

Like all of the developmental tasks shown in Figure 1-2, the task of learning how to learn starts at home, with the adoption of family attitudes toward reading and other school activities. Difficulties in mastering the task become evident during the college years among students who are not able to cope with rigorous academic requirements, cannot synthesize diverse ideas into a cogent whole, cannot clearly and effectively state their own views of a problem or topic in written or spoken form, are not motivated to study, or are not organized in study habits. The need to master the task of learning how to learn extends beyond college into the workplace, where one is expected to be motivated to work, set priorities, manage stress, complete work assignments, and have a commitment to lifelong learning for career enrichment and professional advancement.

The task of learning how to relate and communicate effectively with others links the personal and work spheres of our lives in a number of ways. It involves learning how to manage and express our feelings and developing a capacity for intimacy, support, openness, and fair play in our relationships with our families, friends, lovers, and spouses, and with children, if having a family is part of our lives. It also requires that we be able to relate effectively to a variety of people at school or work, some of whose tastes, beliefs, attitudes, and lifestyles may differ from ours. Our relationship and communication skills thus play a significant role in our professional socialization and development, both in securing a job through written and verbal communication and in profiting from cooperative relationships with others as we seek to advance in our careers.

The task of learning how to earn a living involves developing specific work skills based on our preferences, interests, abilities, and values. It also involves answering some important questions about ourselves and developing six skills for effective career planning. These questions and skills are summarized on the pages that follow. As you use this book to master the task of learning how to earn a living, we issue a challenge and a promise. The challenge is that a great deal of time, thought, and effort will be required for you to benefit fully from the ideas and guidance presented in this book. The promise is that if you take a professional attitude toward the readings and activities, you will gain

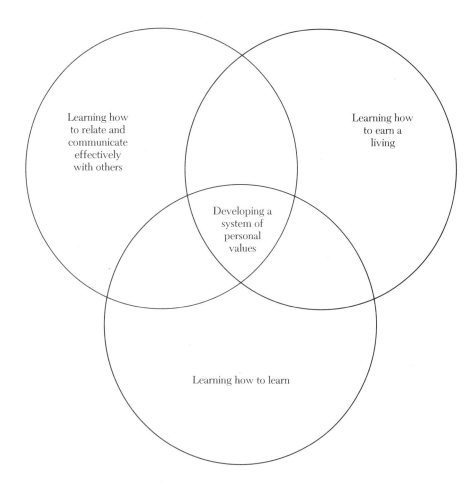

FIGURE 1-2   The four developmental tasks of college students. (From "Psychological Dimensions of Career Development: An Overview and Application" by C. Carney, 1975, paper presented at a training conference for the Ohio Department of Education, Columbus, OH.)

a clearer perspective of your future and develop a better sense of control over your career.

At the center of these three developmental tasks—learning, relating, and working—is the task of developing an integrated system of personal values. Our values, the things we cherish most in life, shape our attitudes and actions regarding how and what we choose to learn, the type and quality of our intimate and work relationships, and the direction we give to our career pursuits. When independently chosen and freely expressed, our values give purpose, coherence, and integrity to our philosophy of life and our actions as we work to create a satisfying lifestyle and endeavor to meet our important life needs.

Career-Planning Questions

In her book on career planning, Celia Denues (1972) points out: "To know where you want to go, you must know where you are and who you are." So the best place to start the career-planning process is with yourself—specifically with your wants and preferences. Let's begin with questions about *you*. You will need to answer five questions about yourself as you chart your current and future career path, but you don't have to be concerned with answering them yet. Here we're simply going to identify them and emphasize their importance. This will give you guidelines for understanding the process of career and life planning.

1. *Who are you?*
2. *How do you want to live?*
3. *Where do you want to live?*
4. *What will you do for a living?*
5. *Who will you spend your time with?*

By the time you have finished this book, you will have the skills and knowledge to answer most of these questions in detail. In addition to knowing who you are and where you are in the career-planning process, you will also know where you want to go. Now let's turn to the skills you will need to build your career effectively, now and in the future.

Six Skills for Effective Career and Life Planning

How can we plan for the future and still remain open to change as our needs and goals, and those of society, evolve over time? For effective career planning to occur, this question must be answered. We believe the answer is to develop now the skills that will prepare you for a lifetime of career decision making. By doing this, you will be able to anticipate and manage your growth effectively in a changing world.

Whether you are making a choice for now or new choices in the future, you will need to master six essential career-planning skills. This book is organized around these six skill areas. *The first skill you will need to understand and develop is that of effective decision making.* Our decisions form a bridge between our wants and needs and the world around us. We shape our lives through our decisions. Every day, each of us makes a great many decisions. Some of these decisions require little thought and planning; others require a great deal. Whether your decisions are large or small, if you have not developed the skills for effective decision making you may find yourself feeling powerless and directionless. Chapter 2 will help you focus on and refine your career decision making skills.

Effective career decision making begins and ends with ourselves, with the way we shape our worlds to accommodate our unique capabilities, interests, and values. *The second essential skill—self-assessment—involves the ability to pull together the bits and pieces of information you have about yourself to create a picture of who you are occupationally.* Because you are likely to change as you mature and gain work experience, the images you have of yourself are more like the frame in a motion picture than a snapshot. You will need to plan for an ongoing self-review process, which may occur in a number of ways, including observations about your skills and interests from others and feedback provided through self-assessment inventories. By providing you with the ability to organize information about yourself and an understanding of how your goals, dreams, and needs are likely to change over the course of your career, we hope to prepare you to manage your own career development. Chapters 3 and 4 explore in depth how personal and environmental influences can shape the course of a person's career.

The third essential skill is that of gathering and assessing career information. We probably are all familiar with a number of occupations, but only a few of us have a real sense of how seemingly unrelated occupations fit together to form unified industries and economic networks. Like pieces of a puzzle, each occupation shares characteristics with the pieces around it. As you acquire knowledge of the puzzle as a whole, you will begin to see how your particular talents and interests may be used in varied settings. By teaching you skills for gathering accurate occupational information, we hope to help you identify several occupational areas that suit your work and lifestyle preferences. Chapter 5 provides an overview of how the world of work is structured. In Chapter 6, you will learn *the fourth essential skill—how to integrate career information and the wishes and views of others with your knowledge of yourself in order to develop personally satisfying options.*

When you have polished your decision-making skills, clarified how your interests and talents can be used in a number of occupational settings, and chosen an educational or occupational direction to pursue, you will probably want to take action on a specific goal. We do not believe that everyone must make a career choice after using the materials in this book, but we encourage you to learn and practice the skills of implementing a career objective by undertaking a job campaign. This will allow you to implement a career objective when you are ready. Thus, *the fifth essential career planning skill is effectively communicating your skills, interests, values, and experiences to employers.* To do this, you must learn to identify potential sources of employment and to market yourself to employers through correspondence, prepared resumes, and person-to-person interviews. Finding a job requires hard work. Chapter 7 will help you develop skills to make it easier.

Our society exerts tremendous pressure on people to be flexible and to adapt to a variety of interpersonal situations. As mentioned earlier, Donald Super (1980) observed that at different times during our working lives we will be called on to fill the roles of family member, student, trainee, colleague, instructor, supervisor, and citizen. Each role requires that we be sensitive to our needs and the needs of others, that we recognize differences and commonalities with others and be able to communicate effectively with them, and that we take directions, act independently, or work interdependently as the need arises. Many people who find it difficult to master these requirements lose, or fail to get, jobs because they cannot get along with other people. So *the sixth career-planning skill is that of work adjustment and career expansion.* Chapter 8 is devoted to this subject and shows how you can promote the development of your career by managing the stress of the job; negotiating the culture of the work setting with integrity and professionalism, and taking advantage of new learning opportunities.

These six skills—decision making, self-assessment, occupational exploration, integration of information and development of options, job campaigning, and work adjustment and career expansion—form the core of this book. They build and spiral back on one another with each career decision you make. Essential to a self-directed lifestyle, they are skills that can be learned and refined with practice and used throughout your career as you make new choices and enter new situations. People who master these skills can meet a changing world with hope, optimism, and confidence in their own personal resources.

Some Questions to Consider

1. Turn back to pages 2–3, where the classroom situation was described. Reread the descriptions of the students and identify the one who is most like you.
   a. How are you similar to that person in terms of your background and the type of career decision you are making?
   b. How are you different from that person?
2. Find a family member or friend who has been working for a while and is willing to talk with you about his or her career. Ask that person the following questions:
   a. What influenced your decision to choose your field of work?
   b. Why do you work?
   c. What is most satisfying about your job? What do you like to do when you are not at work?

In addition, try to find out which needs are being met through family and friendships. What are the most important roles that the person is playing in his or her life? What are the challenges or developmental tasks that the person is presently attempting to master? Ask the same questions of yourself, and identify how you are similar to or different from the person you have interviewed.

3. Take a large sheet of paper and draw four lifestyle triangles. Use the first triangle to depict your lifestyle when you were 4 years old, the second triangle to depict your life now, the third triangle to predict your lifestyle after you have graduated and have been working for ten years, and the fourth triangle to predict your lifestyle after you have retired. Use the lengths of the sides of each triangle to indicate how you have spent, and will spend, your time. In a sentence or two, try to describe why you have drawn each triangle the way you have.

4. Which life roles are you playing now? List them in order of their importance to you—most important to least important. Starting with the least important role, pretend you have the opportunity to give it up. Would you exchange it for another role? If so, why? If not, why not? Repeat the sequence for each of your current roles. When you complete the process, ask yourself: What have I learned about myself through this activity? How would I change my life if I could right now? In five years? In ten years?

5. What does the term *career* mean to you personally? How does your definition differ from the way the word is used on page 3 of this book?

6. In your own words, describe the six important skills for career planning. Which skill(s) have you already developed? Which do you want to develop or refine by using this book?

7. What do you want from college? From this book? From your career?

8. Write down an important change you have made in your life and describe how that change occurred by answering the following questions:
   a. What changed?
   b. How did the change occur? Was it your choice to make the change? Was there a specific event that created the need to change?
   c. How did you cope with or manage the change?
   d. Who supported you in making the change? If anybody got in the way, how did you work with or around that person?
   e. As you look at it now, what would you do differently?
   f. How is this particular change affecting your life now?

References and Resources

Astin, A. W., Green, K. C., Korn, W. S., Schalit, M., & Berz, E. R. (1988). *The American freshman. National norms for fall 1988.* Los Angeles: University of California, Higher Education Research Institute, Cooperative Institutional Research Program.

Carney, C. G., & Barak, A. (1976). A survey of student needs and student personnel services. *Journal of College Student Personnel, 17,* 280–284.

Carney, C. G., Peterson, K., & Moberg, T. (1990). How stable are student and faculty perceptions of student needs and a university counseling center? *Journal of College Student Development, 31,* 423–428.

Carney, C. G., & Savitz, C. J. (1980). Student and faculty perceptions of student needs and the services of a university counseling center: Differences that make a difference. *Journal of Counseling Psychology, 27,* 597–604.

Carney, C. G., Savitz, C. J., & Weiskott, G. N. (1979). Students' evaluation of a university counseling center and their intentions to use its programs. *Journal of Counseling Psychology, 26,* 242–249.

Chickering, A. (1969). *Education and identity.* San Francisco: Jossey-Bass.

Denues, C. (1972). *Career perspective: Your choice of work.* Worthington, OH: Charles D. Jones.

Foote, B. F. (1980). Determined—and undetermined—major students: How different are they? *Journal of College Student Personnel, 21,* 29–34.

Goodson, W. D. (1981). Do career development needs exist for all students entering college or just the undecided major students? *Journal of College Student Personnel, 22,* 413–417.

Hall, L. (1980, July 21). *Chronicle of Higher Education.*

Havighurst, R. J. (1972). *Developmental tasks and education* (3rd ed.). New York: David McKay.

Hitchcock, J. (1973). The new vocationalism. *Change, 5,* 46–50.

Hopson, B., & Hough, P. (1973). *Exercises in personal and career development.* New York: APS Publications.

Kojaku, L. K. (1972). *Major field transfer: The self-matching of university undergraduates to student characteristics.* Los Angeles: University of California. (ERIC Document No. ED 062 933)

Maslow, A. (1954). *Motivation and personality.* New York: Harper.

Miller, P. J., & Sjoberg, G. (1973). Urban middle-class lifestyles in transition. *Journal of Applied Behavioral Science, 9*(2/3), 144–162.

Naisbitt, J., & Aburdene, P. (1990). *Megatrends 2000.* New York: William Morrow.

Noel, L. (1985). Increasing student retention: New challenges and potential. In L. Noel, R. Levitz, D. Saluri, and associates (Eds.), *Increasing student retention: Effective programs and practices for reducing the dropout rate* (pp. 1–27). San Francisco: Jossey-Bass.

Slaney, R. B. (1980). Expressed vocational choice and vocational indecision. *Journal of Counseling Psychology, 27,* 122–129.

Super, D. E. (1980). Life-span, life-space approach to career development. *Journal of Vocational Behavior, 16,* 282–298.

Tinto, V. (1985). Dropping out and other forms of withdrawal from college. In L. Noel, R. Levitz, D. Saluri, and associates (Eds.), *Increasing student retention: Effective programs and practices for reducing the dropout rate* (pp. 28–43). San Francisco: Jossey-Bass.

Titley, R. W., Titley, B., & Wolfe, W. M. (1976). The major changers: Continuity or discontinuity in the career decision process. *Journal of Vocational Behavior, 8,* 105–111.

CHAPTER TWO

Making Career Decisions: Self, Strategies, and Stages

A Psychological Tip

Whenever you're called on to make up your mind,
  and you're hampered by not having any,
the best way to solve the dilemma, you'll find
  is simply by spinning a penny.
No—not so that chance shall decide the affair
  while you're passively standing there moping,
but the moment the penny is up in the air,
  you suddenly know what you're hoping.

—Piet Hein

Paige tipped her head back, closed her eyes, and sighed. Lines of print danced inside her eyes. Only a few more weeks of writing and tests and she would have her M.B.A. Even this close to her goal, she still wondered if she knew what she wanted to be when she grew up. She had worked so hard to find the right career, and sometimes that scared her. If this was really "right," why hadn't it come easily? Her friend, Alison, who had wanted to be a doctor since kindergarten, was now in medical school. Her neighbor, Jon, who had always been a math whiz, had fallen easily into engineering and the family business. Yet she had had to struggle and search to match her interests and abilities with a career path, and she still wondered if it would really work.

She looked back, remembering her discomfort when high school and college friends had started choosing careers. Paige had tried to examine what she liked and was good at, taking into account feedback from others, feelings, experiences, and available information. Then she tried to match this "vocational self" to the working world. The B.S. in computer science and the M.B.A. in marketing seemed to open many doors while combining her technical and detail aptitudes with her interest in people and psychology. She could work for many different types of businesses and change locations if she wished. With an M.B.A., hard work could lead her to promotions and new challenges, or her interest in programming or market research might supply a part-time job when children came along. Her training had been good, and last year's summer internship at Digital Equipment Corporation had been exciting.

Paige took a drink of her Coke and turned back to her book with a sigh. She was committed, and her fears were natural. She would continue her interviews, find a place where she felt comfortable, and give it everything she had. She would learn, take advantage of opportunities, and reevaluate her choices. Later, if things didn't seem right, she could always seek different training or experience and start a second career, as her mom had done.

Our self-concepts—the images that come to mind when we ask ourselves "Who am I?"—provide the strands of continuity we experience as we grow and change. Our self-concepts are most evident in the decisions we make and the actions we take. They reflect the wisdom gained from our past experiences. Any marked change in our lives challenges our self-concepts and causes feelings of uncertainty. Graduating from college, changing majors, taking a new job, getting married, moving, being promoted, or going on vacation are all common changes that most of us experience during our lives. Each change requires us to make decisions that reflect our self-concepts.

Even though we may not be aware of it, our decisions are based on the beliefs, attitudes, and values that are woven into the fabric of our self-concepts. These beliefs, attitudes, and values are shaped by messages we receive from and behaviors we observe in our family and culture. Our *beliefs* represent our personal views about how the world operates. Our *attitudes,* on the other hand, predispose us to like some situations or people and not to like others. Because we cannot have direct experience in every area, many of our attitudes and beliefs are based on information we get from others, even though it may be distorted or inaccurate. Our *values* tell us what we should or should not do. What we define as right or proper is a reflection of our values. Our values are also shaped by the society in which we live and by parents, teachers, and friends.

All these influences affect our decisions indirectly through our beliefs, attitudes, and values. In order to be sure that our decisions reflect what we want for ourselves rather than what we have been told by others, we must learn to look at our feelings and experiences objectively and to separate our reality from the biases and distortions we absorbed during our growing-up years.

Because of the changing nature of society and of ourselves, each of us must frequently try to balance what we have now against what we think will exist in the future. We are torn between the security that comes with keeping things as they are and the insecurity involved in deciding to reshape our lives. In making decisions, each of us must be willing to say "This is what I value" by freely choosing to give up some options and by assuming responsibility for the consequences of our choices. We are free to choose and to take responsibility for our choices only when we have two or more options based on our independent assessment and are capable of acting on them. Lacking choices and the ability to act, we cannot make real decisions.

In all likelihood, most of our choices will not be permanent. Living involves growth and change, and the future holds twists and turns that cannot be predicted. While the decisions we make as we adjust to changing life events may be looked at separately, each is actually a link in a long chain of choices. Every decision builds on our previous decisions and in turn stimulates and influences future decisions.

In looking at an individual decision, it is important to distinguish between the *decision process* and the *decision outcome.* The decision-making process is irreversible in the sense that time cannot be reversed. It propels us forward through a series of decisions. The outcomes of our decisions—the actions we take and their consequences—can often be changed by making new decisions as alternatives become available.

The quality of our decisions is affected by the information we use to make them. If we lack the proper information, we can run into blind alleys. If we fail to consider carefully all available information, we limit the number of alternatives to consider or make a premature choice. In addition, the information we use may be distorted because it is outdated or misrepresented by its source.

We ourselves can even unwittingly distort information when we view it through our personal beliefs, attitudes, and values. Finally, new information may change our decisions. Suppose you are planning to spend your summer working at a camp, and your academic adviser tells you that you must take classes during the summer to graduate on schedule. Instead of facing the single decision of how to obtain a camp job, you would now need to decide between camp and graduation.

Learning How to Decide

The situations that require us to make decisions will vary greatly throughout our lives. The pressure to change or to decide may come from ourselves or from the environment—often both. According to psychologists David Tiedeman and Robert O'Hara (1963), how realistic or efficient we are at making a decision often depends on how well we know ourselves and our environment.

Figure 2-1 demonstrates graphically how information affects our decisions over our lifetimes. As infants, we had no real control over what happened—all we could do was vocalize our discomfort while our parents tried to guess its source. As children, we learned more about ourselves and the world and began to use two new strategies for decision making. If we didn't really know what we wanted to do but knew about our environment, we were probably inclined to make *dependent decisions*. ("I'll get spanked if I don't do what Mommy says. I'd better do it her way.") If we knew what we wanted to do but were less certain about the conditions in the environment, we probably made *intuitive decisions* ("I don't want spinach. I want ice cream.") As we grew older, we retained the ability to make these two types of decisions and added another strategy as well. That strategy, which we call a *planful decision*, takes into account our knowledge both of ourselves and of the environment. When we use this strategy, we weigh the internal and external demands of the situation and the pros and cons (or costs and benefits) of the various alternatives we see. If there is time, we may gather and consider additional information about alternatives and possible consequences for ourselves and our environment. The choices we make tend to fit our needs and our life situations better when we make planful decisions.

Choosing a Strategy

Since there are three alternative strategies for making a decision, each with its own advantages and disadvantages, the first task in making a decision is to decide which strategy to use.

Dependent Decision Strategy

The *dependent decision strategy* may appear to be the easiest—we've certainly had the most time to practice it! All we need to do is defer the choice to others; let someone else decide. In a situation where the outcome is of little personal

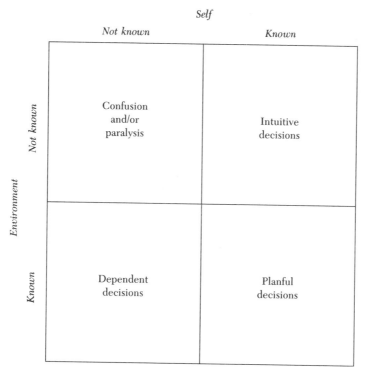

FIGURE 2-1   Learning decision strategies.

importance, this approach can save time and energy. If you're like most of us, many of your dependent decisions are made in the spirit of compromise, as in the case of participating in a group decision. There are also situations that may call for a more informed dependent choice. If your doctor recommends surgery, for example, you may wish to get a second opinion or have the reasons carefully explained. Knowing that you don't have enough information to make the final decision, you must depend partly on your doctor's judgment.

A dependent decision can be self-defeating and produce unhappy results if it is used out of fear of making a choice on your own or to avoid the work of exploring the options. Deferring a choice whose outcome is important out of fear or indecision does not help us to avoid the problem. It means only that the decision will be out of our control and will be made by others or by circumstances. The results will affect our lives just as if we had made the choice. Even if we have transferred the decision making elsewhere, we will still have to cope with the results.

Intuitive Decision Strategy

Decision makers who use the *intuitive decision strategy* rely on "gut-level" reactions. They check out their internal signals to see if something feels good. Because intuitive decisions are made spontaneously and below one's level of awareness, they take little time, data gathering, or conscious planning. They are useful in situations where time is at a premium, such as emergencies or unforeseen opportunities. Intuition often helps us in interpersonal relations, where factual data about the other person's reaction are not available. When used appropriately, intuition can help us retain both authority and responsibility in a difficult decision situation.

But an intuitive decision can have uncomfortable results if it is used as a substitute for or to avoid gathering needed information. In situations that are emotional or very important, intuitive hunches are sometimes hard to distinguish from wishful thinking or personal bias. If the information and time to review a decision are available, it is usually wise to take advantage of them. After exploring, however, intuition or feelings may still play a part in the final decision. Intuition enjoys a better reputation now than in the past, since we realize that hunches may really be perceptions based on information that is taken in over time but not consciously remembered. Nevertheless, it is probably wiser not to decide something on the basis of intuition alone if there is other information available.

Planful Decision Strategy

The *planful decision strategy* involves exploration of our needs and of the environment and a rational weighing of the various alternatives, costs, and benefits. The pace of this approach is slower than others but allows maximum time for data gathering, exploring, and experimenting. Attention can be paid to details, and questions can be raised and answered. These questions will help us anticipate possible problems and make implementation of the decision smoother and more efficient. This approach does not exclude consideration of personal feelings about the choices (intuition) or the opinions of experts and loved ones (dependence), nor does it intend to exclude personal and idiosyncratic decision strategies.

Because the planful approach to decisions can consume a great deal of time and energy, it is not always appropriate. Many decisions are not important enough to be worth this amount of effort, and sometimes needed information is not available. Another problem is that in any situation the data are never all in, and waiting for everything we need to know can be a way of delaying a decision. Finally, anyone who takes this decision style literally runs the risk of making a totally rational or totally independent decision, which may not reflect reality, since our feelings and the opinions of significant others are important.

Ideally, a balanced decision will include elements of all three decision styles. Such a choice would consider information available from internal and external sources, weigh the validity of that information, and invest time in further exploration if necessary. A productive decision will usually take into account whatever information one can marshal about self, others, and the environment.

Stages of a Planful Career Decision

There are a number of ways to describe a planful career decision process. The decision stages that we have found most useful are summarized by the decision cycle shown in Figure 2-2.

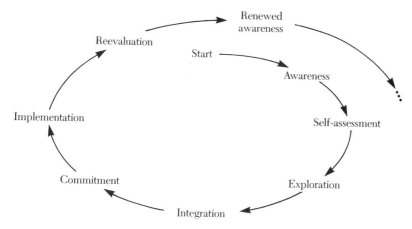

FIGURE 2-2   The decision cycle.

Awareness

The awareness stage is usually heralded by a feeling of increasing discomfort in some area of our lives—an awareness of pressure for change. Unless we are willing to let the circumstances control us, we feel the need to make a decision. Sometimes this need is a happy one, heralding an exciting leap into a new venture. Often, however, it is accompanied by doubts about the future and a desire to delay for fear of making a wrong choice, as well as a desire to act even if we are not ready. An important element of readiness lies in learning, examining, and refining our decision-making strategies. As we mentioned in Chapter 1, decision making is the first of six skills we must learn in order to plan our careers.

If the changes that awareness demands are frightening, we sometimes postpone the decision until it is almost upon us. This may contribute to the fear or even panic that sometimes accompanies awareness.

A major part of making the best decision in any situation is being sure that the problem is clearly defined before beginning the search for a solution. Sometimes we are so anxious to learn about alternatives that we fail to spend enough time sorting out the elements that comprise the problem. Examination of the things that are blocking a decision can provide clues about where to look for help and what to do first. Understanding the problem requires referring to our own beliefs, attitudes, and values as well as to those of our society. Time devoted to defining the problem may be well spent, particularly for those who feel confused by a multitude of options that they cannot organize or compare in any meaningful way. Confusion and anxiety can often be alleviated by pinpointing specific fears, irrational expectations, or skill and information deficits contributing to the problem.

Self-Assessment

As in defining the problem, the best source of information for identifying desirable alternatives is ourselves. At this stage, we begin to utilize the second of the six career-planning skills—self-assessment. Checking solutions against our beliefs, attitudes, and values can help us generate ways to deal with situations that are consistent with our self-concepts. At this stage, in order to determine what we want and what we are willing to give up, we must take the time to determine the most-valued outcomes of the decision. In short, the question to be answered is "What do *I* most want the outcome of this decision to be?" If we are not really sure which outcome we most value, problems may occur at this stage. People who have made past decisions largely on a dependent or intuitive basis may not be fully aware of their own preferences and resources or of what they are willing to sacrifice. This will also be true of people who have learned to put the wants and needs of others ahead of their own.

Exploration

The purpose of exploration is to make sure we have enough information about the situation and alternative ways of achieving the most-desired outcomes. The third career-planning skill involves learning needed strategies for gathering career information. Based on relationships and discoveries synthesized from various kinds of information, alternatives for dealing with decision situations can be generated. It may be helpful to spend some time on each alternative, trying to think through the possible outcomes and how we would feel about them. As appealing alternatives are discovered, risks can be weighed, as well as the probability and cost of possible negative outcomes. After a number of realistic alternatives have been collected, deciding among these possible courses of action can be approached in two ways. We may start by eliminating the least acceptable alternatives and examine what is left, or we can start with the attractive ones and weigh each of them to identify the most practical and attainable.

The process of exploring can be uncomfortable. It often creates confusion, conflict, and anxiety. The sheer amount of information available in many career areas increases the complexity of decision making and presents new considerations or options that cause us to think we have to start over. Awareness of requirements and commitments involved in many choices can awaken fears of risk and failure. Such awareness can also bring the unwelcome realization that favored dreams and solutions may be blocked or perhaps too difficult to be worthwhile. Although we can imagine ourselves as corporation presidents, we may discover that we do not have the personal resources to strive to the corporate world's top levels.

People who have very many—or very few—areas of interest often discover several alternatives that appear to be equally attractive, but they have difficulty prioritizing them. Greater in-depth exploration or volunteer or trial work experience may help differentiate interests, test abilities, and increase confidence. It may also help to review one's personal beliefs and goals.

Integration

Before a firm or even tentative commitment can be made, it is necessary to assess the ways of fitting together the various alternatives with what we know about ourselves. In assessing the likelihood of turning our hopes and options into realities, we must weigh the influence of other important factors, such as commitments to significant others (spouses, family members, employers), financial resources, and time constraints. We may also find ourselves reevaluating some of our own beliefs and attitudes as we explore career possibilities and the world outside our family structure.

The process of integration, which leads to readiness for commitment, is not smooth sailing for many of us. Many people encounter some conflicts when they attempt to fit their desires and options with these other realities. Some conflicts are with loved ones whose opinions we value—parents who feel we are taking the "wrong" path, a spouse who may suffer hardship because of our career choice. Other conflicts will be internal—difficult decisions over how best to spend time or money, discomfort because what we want is not what we believe we "should" want, inability to see our options clearly or to choose because of guilt, fear, or dependence on others. The stages, problems, and hoped-for resolutions of this process of integration will be discussed fully in Chapter 6.

Commitment

As we change, explore, and move ahead, we reach a point where we feel ready to try something. This does not mean we are guaranteed success or that we have no fears. It simply means that we have learned enough about ourselves, our options, and how they fit with the lives we envision, and are comfortable enough with the unavoidable risks, that we are willing to go forward on the basis of our hopes and preparation. Sometimes we are not sure we are ready, but we do know that we are tired of being undecided, that we have done the best planful decision making that we can, and that there is no way to find out whether a decision will work except to try it!

At some point we must choose one alternative to pursue, although others may be kept in reserve. Choosing one solution means eliminating others, at least temporarily and sometimes permanently. This is difficult to do. We are afraid we will be wrong, and we hate to close off other options. Unfortunately, no single course of action can be pursued to its most successful conclusion if we are emotionally divided or if we are spending energy trying to keep alternatives alive. The only way to discover whether something will really work for us is to make a wholehearted commitment to it. Although some choices may be irreversible in the sense of time and personal resources spent, almost any decision can be reevaluated, altered, or abandoned at a later stage if we have the courage to look at it honestly. The outcomes of a commitment made and pursued to the best of our abilities are generally very positive in terms of growth and learning, even if the commitment is later changed or abandoned.

Implementation

Once we have made a commitment, we implement the decision by initiating new courses of action or behaviors. We may gather information and start acquiring new skills or equipment. We many begin formal procedures for entering a training program or begin a job campaign. We may be able to change an old situation or create a new one using skills and opportunities that are already available. In all these situations, we will need the fourth career-planning skill: the ability to find available jobs and to market ourselves. As we implement our decisions, we need to be aware of the feedback we are getting about the choice we have made. Does it fit our values? Have we done enough exploring? Have any of the circumstances changed?

If self-assessment, exploration, and integration have been complete, any difficulties encountered in implementing a goal will not be a complete surprise. (However, things do happen that cannot be foreseen or controlled, such as financial reversals, illness, or sudden changes in the environment.) Of course, hurdles and setbacks on the road to any goal—especially if it is a long-term one—may appear bigger or more discouraging in reality than they did in imagination, but that can often be remedied with a little rest or moral support. But if the path to implementation seems full of unpleasant surprises, exploration may have been incomplete or the goals unrealistic.

Implementation of a chosen goal can still be blocked or delayed. An undergraduate aiming for graduate school may find that grades are not high enough or that needed funds will not be available. A person whose decision seems permanently blocked may spend some time coping with the disappointment before returning to the beginning of the decision cycle to search for attractive alternatives. In some cases, implementation of choices is simply delayed and can be successfully completed only at a later time. People in such situations must wait, investigate other alternatives, or alter dreams to fit their present circumstances.

Reevaluation

After a decision is implemented, new behaviors are put into practice and life patterns are altered. This stage of career development utilizes the final career-planning skill identified—work adjustment. Adjusting to a new work situation involves learning how to do tasks and how to take and give direction while working cooperatively with other people. Keeping in tune with the job means finding out how to get new information and learning new skills as they are needed.

After mastering the requirements of a new environment or role, an individual can begin to examine more closely whether it is fulfilling his or her expectations. If this course of action has not had the anticipated or desired results, the person may want to reevaluate goals and alternatives. For example:

1. Feelings, rewards, and goals may no longer seem appropriate or satisfying. They have changed or need to be changed.
2. Anticipated courses of action may no longer be practical, or perhaps things are going so well that they are not necessary.
3. Preferred alternatives that were previously unattainable may now be within reach.

New information and experiences should be examined regularly to see if they have brought about a change in one's perspectives or possibilities.

Even if the initial choice has good results, circumstances may change or the situation may become monotonous because new challenges do not arise over a period of time. If unforeseen changes occur or hoped-for changes fail to occur, awareness of the need to reevaluate leads us back to the beginning of the decision cycle to go through each stage again. Even if we feel we know our present situation well, taking shortcuts in the decision process may keep us from uncovering information that is essential to our next step. We may fail to reevaluate decisions, thinking that we have a right answer that will work indefinitely. As we will note later, fear of change can keep us from recognizing the need to reevaluate, even when we are in a position that is beyond our abilities.

The most important thing to remember about decision making and about what to look for in reviewing decisions is the inescapable nature of change. Everything changes. Our own beliefs, attitudes, and values will change. Our environment is changing with ever-increasing rapidity. In 25 or even 5 years, many of our goals and skills will be obsolete. Even when we are in control of the externals, growth goes on within us long after we think we are grown up. We can never be sure that any decision will be the right one at any time beyond the moment we make it. Our decisions and our world must grow and change with us.

Decision-Style Worksheet

Each box on page 28 focuses on a decision-making approach that you might use to make daily choices or important decisions. List three situations in each box that might prompt you to use the form of decision making represented in that box. Think of decisions you have made or discussed, or decisions made in such areas as family, friends, activities, classes, or jobs.

After you complete each box, review your answers. Do the situations in each box share anything in common? If they do, what is it?

How do the decisions you listed in each box differ from the decisions noted in each of the other three boxes?

Where Am I in the Career Decision-Making Process?

Each box on pages 29–36 contains a stage in the process of making a planful career decision. The goal or desired outcome of each stage is described and an example is provided. Review each of the stages and identify what stage in your own career decision making you are now in. Then write what you will have to do to move to the next stage. When you complete this exercise for your own plans, you may wish to use the vignettes in Appendix A to sharpen your decision-making skills. Each vignette presents a person who is attempting to make a career decision. Try to formulate a planful decision-making approach for that individual.

Three decisions that might cause me to become confused or paralyzed are:

1. _____

2. _____

3. _____

Three decisions that I might let others make for me are:

1. _____

2. _____

3. _____

Three decisions that I might make intuitively are:

1. _____

2. _____

3. _____

Three decisions that I would be planful about are:

1. _____

2. _____

3. _____

1. *Awareness*

GOAL   To define clearly the decision you need to make.

EXAMPLE   I need to decide on an academic major at the end of this term.

The decision I need to make is:

2. *Self-Assessment*

GOAL   To decide how important the decision is to you, what you want to accomplish by it, and what effort or sacrifice you are willing to make to achieve it.

EXAMPLE   My decision about an academic major is very important to me. I want to go to law school, and I need to major in an area that will most help me get into law school. I need to make this decision by the end of this term so I can graduate on schedule.

What I want to accomplish by this decision is:

_____

_____

_____

_____

_____

_____

_____

_____

_____

_____

_____

_____

_____

3. *Exploration*

GOAL   To identify and explore at least two possible courses of action.

EXAMPLE   I'll explore political science and psychology, since both are applicable to law. I'll take three weeks to explore both fields by reading about them in the *Occupational Outlook Handbook* and professional literature, talking to people in both fields, and talking to academic advisers in each area. Before I do, I'll make a checks-and-balances sheet about each field. This will allow me to compare them with each other in terms of things that I like and don't like about each.

Two areas that I want to explore are:

A. _____

_____

B. _____

_____

The ways that I will explore them are:

A. _____

_____

B. _____

_____

C. _____

_____

D. _____

_____

I will complete my exploration by _____ .
                                              (date)

4. Integration

GOALS

- To develop a prioritized list of career options that reflect your preferences, interests, values, and abilities and that are realistic for you to pursue.
- To consider the feelings of others who are important to you without being totally dependent on their wishes and needs.
- To examine and change any beliefs you may have about your social role or about occupations that may restrict your career options.

EXAMPLE   I'll review my information about psychology and political science and decide what about those courses of study appeals to me and what bothers me. I'll talk over my feelings with my family and a few friends and listen to their feedback. Then I'll go over everything carefully and try to weed out myths and prejudices so that my choice will be realistic and personally satisfying.

In order of priority, the most personally fulfilling and feasible career options for me to pursue are:

A. _____

B. _____

C. _____

D. _____

Whom do I want to inform about my plans?

A. _____

B. _____

C. _____

D. _____

4. *Integration* (continued)

What areas of disagreement or misunderstanding might we encounter?

A. _____

B. _____

C. _____

How might I or my family have a limited view of my choices or my actions because of prejudices or stereotypes?

A. _____

B. _____

C. _____

On what concerns of mine do I want feedback from others?

A. _____

B. _____

C. _____

I will talk with the people I have listed by _____ .
                                                (date)

5. *Commitment*

GOAL   To choose one alternative and inform others about your choice.

EXAMPLE   I've decided on political science. I'll tell my academic adviser about my decision. I'll inform my family as well, since they are interested in what I do. I'll let them know about my decision in four weeks.

I've decided to:

_____

_____

_____

_____

_____

_____

The people I want to inform about my decision are:

A. _____

_____

B. _____

_____

C. _____

_____

I will inform all of them by _____
                                         (date)

6. *Implementation*

GOAL   To act on your decision.

EXAMPLE   After I ask my adviser which political science courses I should take, I'll sign up for them at preregistration for next term.

The actions I need to take to implement my decision are:

A. _____

_____

_____

B. _____

_____

_____

C. _____

_____

_____

D. _____

_____

_____

E. _____

_____

_____

7. Reevaluation

GOAL   After you have lived with your choice for a reasonable length of time, you'll review it and if necessary identify new choices to be made.

EXAMPLE   At the end of the next term, I'll spend some time reviewing how I feel about political science. If I'm uncomfortable with it as a choice, I'll identify what makes me uncomfortable and look at other possible majors that may be more consistent with what I like to do.

I'll reevaluate my decision by _____ .

(date)

When I do this, I'll make my judgment using the following criteria:

A. _____

_____

B. _____

_____

C. _____

_____

If needed, repeat the cycle.

References and Resources

Dinklage, A. B. (1966). *Adolescent choice and decision-making: A review of models and issues in relation to some developmental tasks of adolescence.* Cambridge, MA: Harvard University Press. (ERIC Document No. ED 010 371)

GeLatt, H. B., Varenhorst, B., Carey, R., & Miller, G. P. (1973). *Decisions and outcomes.* New York: College Entrance Examination Board.

Gordon, V. N. (1984). *The career undecided college student.* Springfield, IL: Charles C Thomas.

Harren, V. A. (1979). A model of career decision-making for college students. *Journal of Vocational Behavior, 14,* 119–133.

O'Neill, N., & O'Neill, G. (1974). *Shifting gears: Finding security in a changing world.* New York: M. Evans.

Tiedeman, D. V., & O'Hara, R. P. (1963). *Career development: Choice and adjustment.* New York: College Entrance Examination Board.

CHAPTER THREE

The Emerging Self:
Birth to Adolescence

Sow an act and reap a habit;
Sow a habit and reap a character;
Sow a character and reap a destiny.

—Boardman

It is a special morning. Snow from the distant mountains has come down to blanket the houses and frost the trees. Inside, 9-year-old Sarah is helping with breakfast. John, age 10, is outside shoveling the walk with his dad. After breakfast Sarah opens the biggest present under the tree—a beautiful doll. Four-year-old Jimmy wails with envy and reaches for it. Mommy hands him a shiny new truck. Jimmy wonders why he can't have a doll.

Jerry sits in biology class, staring out the window. He is Uncle Harry's favorite nephew, and the family has always assumed he will become a doctor and share his uncle's practice. Jerry has tried to tell his dad he likes auto mechanics and shop better than science, but his father tells him he can do those things as hobbies—he will have plenty of time once the money starts rolling in from his medical practice. But Jerry is not even sure he wants to go to college right now. Several of his friends have joined the navy, and they look great in their uniforms. They are traveling around, meeting girls, and making their own decisions. Jerry thinks that if he did that for a while he could figure out some things about himself.

Every minute of every day, people of all ages and backgrounds are struggling with the timeless question "Who am I?" They are going through a time of change, discovering that they no longer fit comfortably in their skins or situations and that something must go—or grow. Old decisions and commitments once seen as permanent may need to be reviewed. When new situations occur in which old behaviors and solutions do not work anymore, new behaviors and solutions must be created.

Choices having to do with a career are among the most major and far-reaching decisions of our lives. They also present the greatest challenges and cause the strongest feelings of not being able to turn back again. Self-expression through work fills not only a large part of each day but many of our needs as well. Consequently, any major changes in who we are, how we see ourselves, and how we live significantly affect us vocationally.

You Are a Person Who . . .

Processes that define and redefine an individual's total self-concept—including the vocational part of it—begin at birth, although no one is certain exactly how these processes operate. From the start, an infant's physical appearance, abilities, limitations, and problems affect the way he or she copes with the environment and the feedback he or she receives from the outer world. Infants' attempts to influence their surroundings are instinctive, and their success—or lack of it—influences their sense of competence from life's first months. The responses they receive to their crying, laughter, and first tentative words determine their basic attitudes about themselves and their relationship to their environment.

The most critical influences on an individual's personal development are largely social and cultural. In infancy and early childhood, for example, children learn that they are acceptable when they smile, walk, talk, become toilet trained, and dress themselves. They imitate older siblings and adults (especially those of the same gender) and soon adopt family beliefs and ways of expressing attitudes about work, love, religion, and loved ones. Because these beliefs and values are learned at such an early age and in such subtle ways, adults often are not aware of having them or of how they were acquired. Nonetheless, by age 3 or 4, many of these expectations, especially those associated with gender, are firmly established in a child's mind.

In school, children rapidly learn that study is the order of the day and that recess is a treat to be earned through successful work. The work ethic thus begins to influence a person early in his or her life. And, whether or not mothers stay at home, an important prejudice gets passed on to many children—the idea that real work is associated with being away from home and with external reinforcements such as grades or money.

During childhood and into early adolescence, fantasy role tryouts also play an important part in an individual's vocational development. Many early vocational role models come from storybooks and TV. Children dress up and play at being parents, teachers, nurses, or sports heroes.

Robert Fulghum, a Unitarian minister, humorously and insightfully suggests that other important values and bits of wisdom are taught in elementary school to guide us in our adult personal or professional role:

> All I really need to know about how to live and what to do and how to be I learned in kindergarten. Wisdom was not at the top of the graduate school mountain, but there in the sandpile at Sunday School. These are the things I learned:
>
> Share everything.
> Play fair.
> Don't hit people.
> Put things back where you found them.
> Clean up your own mess.
> Don't take things that aren't yours.
> Say you're sorry when you hurt somebody.
> Wash your hands before you eat.
> Flush.
> Warm cookies and cold milk are good for you.
> Live a balanced life—learn some and think some and draw and paint and sing and dance and play and work every day some.
> Take a nap every afternoon.
> When you go out into the world, watch out for traffic, hold hands, and stick together.

Be aware of wonder. Remember the little seed in the Styrofoam cup: The roots go down and the plant goes up and nobody really knows how or why, but we are all like that.

Goldfish and hamsters and white mice and even the little seed in the Styrofoam cup—they all die. So do we.

And then remember the Dick-and-Jane books and the first word you learned—the biggest word of all—LOOK.

Everything you need to know is in there somewhere. The Golden Rule and love and basic sanitation. Ecology and politics and equality and sane living.

Take any one of those items and extrapolate it into sophisticated adult terms and apply it to your family life or your work or your government or your world and it holds true and clear and firm. Think what a better world it would be if we all—the whole world—had cookies and milk about three o'clock every afternoon and then lay down with our blankies for a nap. Or if all governments had as a basic policy to always put things back where they found them and to clean up their own mess.

And it is still true, no matter how old you are—when you go out into the world, it is best to hold hands and stick together.[1]

Who Am I?

An adolescent is expected to start looking ahead and think about how he or she will choose to live and achieve financial independence after high school or college. Sometimes the decision is predetermined. Some adolescents pursue one outstanding talent or interest with dedication. Others have a family business or parental occupation that they are expected to, and want to, train for. For others, adolescence heralds the beginning of a struggle to be free from family directives and to "do their own thing," or do what their peers are doing. A mass of choices lie ahead, offering new opportunities for self-discovery.

At the same time that they see their horizons expanding and encounter new risks, most adolescents are met with the demand that they declare a career choice, or at least an educational objective. Fantasy gives way to confusion and exploration. Even if they do not know what they want to do, many feel pressed to make a decision and want it to be the right one. So they struggle to establish new external and internal guidelines for their thoughts, feelings, and actions. They begin to explore their interests and test themselves to discover their abilities. They may become intensely involved with one activity or friend, then, when that no longer fits, move on. They try out various clubs, hobbies, jobs, classes, attitudes, roles, and relationships. Gradually they develop a relatively stable pattern of interests and values and begin to base their decisions on them. Thus, through work and other forms of self-discovery, the process of role socialization advances and the adolescent's vocational and personal identity becomes more defined.

According to David Hamberg and Ruby Takinashi (1989) of the Carnegie Corporation, adolescents today are facing greater challenges than ever before as they attempt to shape the course of their lives. These challenges arise from four sources. First, because of advances in health care, the reproductive capacity of today's teenage women develops around age 12½, whereas several generations ago first menses occurred around age 16. Coupled with the tendency of teenagers to engage in unprotected sex earlier in life, this change places young women at great risk for unwanted pregnancy or infection by a sexually transmitted disease.

Second, today's adolescents are liable to be more confused about adult roles, and have greater difficulty than their predecessors in seeing the future, because they mature physically much more rapidly than they do socially, intellectually, and vocationally. Where previous generations of teens gradually learned about adult roles through instruction and observation prior to puberty, today's adolescent reaches puberty prior to being socialized into adult ways of thinking and acting.

Confusion in the sex-role socialization process may have painful consequences for some adolescents. Unlike some societies that expect men to set limits on sexual involvement, our society has traditionally placed this responsibility on its women. Consequently, many American males who are struggling to define themselves socially and sexually feel they must push the limits of sexual involvement with women to prove their masculinity. In their way of thinking, "no" means "maybe," or even "yes" if they push long enough. A survey (cited in the *Columbus Dispatch,* May 3, 1988) of 1,200 ninth-graders who attended the Rhode Island Rape Crisis Center's assault awareness program at schools across the state vividly demonstrates how this attitude may be ingrained in a person's value system at an early age: One-fourth of the surveyed students believed that a man has the right to force a woman to have sexual intercourse if he has spent money on her. Sixty-five percent of the boys and 47 percent of the girls in seventh through ninth grade believed it was acceptable for a man to force a woman to have sex if they have been dating for six months to a year. Fifty percent of the students indicated that a woman who dresses seductively and walks alone at night is asking to be raped. Fifty-one percent of the boys and 41 percent of the girls in sixth through ninth grade said a man has the right to force a woman to kiss him if he has spent "a lot of money" ($10 to $15) on her. And it seems that the same attitude gets carried over into early adulthood. More than 4 percent of college males surveyed by one investigator admitted to the use of violence to obtain sex, while an additional 27 percent had used lesser degrees of physical and emotional force when a woman was unwilling to have sex with them. Studies of college women have shown that more than half of the women surveyed reported experiences of sexual aggression in the form of verbal threats, physical coercion, or violence at some time from someone they knew. Although they did not specifically use the term "rape," one in eight of the students reported an experience of assault that met the legal definition of rape. It has also been reported that women aged 16 to 24—the age span of most college students— are at greatest risk for victimization by a rapist. Seventy-five percent of college freshman women said they had experienced an act of sexual aggression, most often during their senior year of high school or freshman year of college.

Third, as will be discussed more fully in Chapter 5, our society changed dramatically when it moved from a farm-based economy to an industrial-based economy. Adolescents who grew up in farming communities usually had a stable base of support in their families and family friends from which they could receive cultural guidance, support for coping with the stresses of life, and vocational wisdom. With industrialization, our society has become more mobile, extended families have fragmented, and single-parent families have increased, leaving fewer adults accessible for teens to turn to for support, comfort, and advice.

Fourth, and finally, today's adolescents have greater access to alcohol and drugs, smoking, cars, and weapons. Consequently, they are at greater risk for illness, accidents, suicide, and lethal conflict.

Many adolescents probably carry some stereotypic beliefs and attitudes into adulthood without understanding how these may limit and disrupt their personal relationships and career pursuits. The result is that they may have blind spots or prejudices. They see their own abilities and vocational opportunities—or those of others—as restricted by factors that may not be relevant, such as sex, race, or age. Sometimes, because of such childhood learning, they may believe they cannot do, or are not interested in, things they have never tried. And males who cling to the image of the strong-willed, sexually privileged man may carry this attitude into the work setting, where it may be displayed in more subtle forms, such as sexual harassment. This is a new era, however, and in many communities and schools, support groups and resources are now available to encourage personal and work-role experimentation. Women can take classes in shop or auto mechanics or get help with anxiety over math. Boys find that they can enjoy being expressive and supportive, and girls find leadership roles available and assertiveness rewarding.

Recent legislation and increased awareness of these stereotypes are changing attitudes and opportunities both in the schools and in the job market, and you as an individual may challenge these old rules. Equal employment opportunity legislation is aimed at encouraging the hiring of people who want to work at jobs not traditionally available to them. We now see increasing numbers of male nurses and homemakers, female engineers and doctors, and African American lawyers and business executives. And employers have developed policies, procedures, and educational programs to reduce incidents of sexual harassment on the college campus and in the office.

Examining stereotypes that you hold about yourself and others can thus open up new perspectives about relationships, careers, lifestyles, and yourself. You may choose to keep some of your old beliefs or to change them. The important thing is to be aware that you have the freedom and responsibility to examine your values and make your own decisions.

I Am a Person Who . . .

In young adulthood, the pressure is on to make decisions and carry them out. The playful question "What are you going to be when you grow up?" is no longer amusing. It is imperative. Young adults are expected to make choices for themselves but may not feel ready. People at this age have many ways of coping with this threatening freedom. Some are challenged and excited by it, some try to avoid it, and some keep their options open, perhaps making tentative commitments.

Separating oneself from the family, physically and emotionally, is the primary goal of this age span. A balance must be achieved between one's desires for autonomy and dependence on others. Driving means freedom, but often only with permission to use the family car. College often means living away from home and the pleasure of self-direction, but these freedoms may conflict with continued dependence on family money. Emerging adults spend their energies on gaining control over their own lives and learning to make decisions. The emotional isolation and responsibility that come with young adulthood can be lonely and confusing. Young adults may socialize and "party" in an effort to learn what emotional and sexual options are available, how these fit their values and attitudes, and how to implement their choices. The family no longer meets all their emotional needs, yet they may lack the skills and courage to start building an emotional support system of their own. This gap may be filled by school friends or roommates, fraternities and clubs, a premarriage or marriage commitment, or an organization such as a religious group or the military.

The choices young adults make about how to meet their personal needs help to shape their lifestyles. They consider whether they want to be married or single, parents or not, conservatives or swingers. They begin to form ideas about where they might want to work, during which hours, and with what kind of people. Such decisions about lifestyle can be joyous and exciting, but if these commitments are made in the fear of freedom, they can be ways of handing over the making of one's life decisions to someone else.

It is especially important at this time to strive to sort out one's own feelings and dreams from social and familial pressures. Rebelling when a career might be right, or conforming because it is safe or comfortable, is often easy and sometimes is a "knee-jerk reaction." Young adults who see these tendencies in themselves should examine their view of the future carefully. People tend to gravitate toward a career for which they are stereotyped (for example, a son into Dad's business, women into teaching or nursing). Young adults need to explore their motives and enthusiasms to see if they are shying away from an unexpected career choice due to outside pressures. For some, occupational or life decisions come easy; others may remain confused or choose goals hastily to escape uncertainty. It takes courage to choose to remain confused, but if those who have not decided can keep their minds open to new information about the world and themselves, they will eventually begin to identify avocational and vocational activities that represent a comfortable combination of what they want and what they perceive as possible and acceptable. The building blocks of dealing with the tasks of adulthood can be shaped and fit together to form one's vocational self-concept. The balance of all the pieces will never be ideal and will require periodic adjustment as each person develops and continues to perceive new opportunities.

These pieces of our vocational selves are identified in Table 3-1 in terms of when we most likely acquired them, what they are, and how they influence our careers. The table also indicates where in this text the various parts of our vocational selves are discussed.

As shown in Table 3-1, the hallmark of childhood was that we accepted what others told us to believe about ourselves and the world around us. We used fantasy to project our ideal vocational self-images and developed an emerging awareness of how best to balance our time and energies. Adolescence is marked by questioning, exploring, and sometimes challenging old standards in order to assess ourselves realistically. With experience, preferences about work give way to a more realistic assessment of our interests and skills. In young adulthood, the urge to become one's own person, to become autonomous, leads us to clarify what we value and want and how we will work to get it.

As we begin to know and understand ourselves, we need a way to organize our self-knowledge and to determine how our personal qualities fit into the world of work. Based on its surveys of worker characteristics and work tasks, the U.S. Department of Labor suggests that our personal and vocational characteristics tend to pull together and seek expression in three interacting spheres of activity (see Figure 3-1).

The overlapping of the spheres in Figure 3-1 acknowledges that individual variations on the data/people/things dimensions are really best understood in "more than/less than" terms. Because we have the basic endowment and life opportunities to develop a variety of abilities, we may have skills in all three areas but tend to prefer work activities in only one or two. Avocational activities may balance these three areas or provide outlets for interests and skills not tapped in the work setting.

Generally speaking, an individual who is oriented toward and skilled at working with people enjoys involvement with others and prefers interpersonal situations that allow opportunities to lead, persuade, teach, or counsel. The individual with interests and competencies that are more strongly focused on the "data" dimension tends to enjoy working with numbers and abstract concepts expressed through words and symbols. As the name implies, an individual with a "things" orientation likes working with machinery, tools, and instruments and enjoys problem solving in "real," physical situations.

The functional skills associated with the data/people/things dimensions of work are summarized in Tables 3-2 and 3-3. Note that the skills in each area are arranged in a hierarchy: those at the top of the list are more complex and require more education and training.

TABLE 3-1   Factors Affecting Vocational Self-Concepts

What	*Influence on your career*

Childhood

Your *energy level* is the amount of physical and mental energy you have. It influences the amount of energy you wish to invest in each of your daily pursuits, including your work and leisure activities.

Your energy level is affected by heredity, diet, patterns of activity and rest, age, and health. Since your energy level influences the amount and intensity of your activities, it will shape the level and types of responsibilities you pursue at work, the amount of stress you can handle, and the amount of physical and mental exertion you can invest in work and leisure tasks (your lifestyle).

Your *attitudes and beliefs* are your subjective views of the world around you—the way you expect things to be and believe they "should" be, the way you perceive and form opinions about things.

Your attitudes and beliefs can have a positive or negative effect on the way you view yourself and your work. Decisions based on unrealistic, incomplete, or outdated career-planning myths and beliefs may cause you to restrict your options or undertake too much and can result in disappointment with your career (see Chapter 6).

Your *aspirations* are the things you fantasize or dream about doing soon or "someday."

During childhood most of us saw work in idealized ways. We dreamed of being somebody special and often played at being people of high status or prominence, largely because of their uniforms, their work, their ability to influence others, or the excitement of their jobs. Whether you fulfill your childhood dreams depends largely on your talents, the opportunities to develop them, and the time and energy you invest in developing them. The chapters that follow show how the balance between your dreams and what you can actually achieve may affect how you see yourself as an adult and the levels and kinds of work at which you can be most successful.

Your *preferences* are what you would like to do if reality would permit.

As we gain in life experience and are exposed to more information about the world of work, fantasies give way to

(continued)

TABLE 3-1   Factors Affecting Vocational Self-Concepts *(continued)*

What	*Influence on your career*

Childhood *(continued)*

preferences, and mental self-portraits become clearer. We can identify occupations that appeal to us, but we can also recognize that we may not have the skills to be successful at all of them. The self-assessment activities in Appendix B and the information in Chapter 5 show that understanding what your most preferred occupations have in common can help you identify the skill and interest areas you would like to develop and related majors and occupations to explore.

Adolescence

Your interests are more realistic than your preferences. They reflect the experiences or ideas you have had about work-related activities that you like or dislike.

Because our interests reflect the direct experiences we have had with different occupationally related activities, they tend to become more stable as we get older. Occupational interest surveys can be used to compare your interests with those of people who are successful and satisfied in a variety of occupations. Such comparisons can help you identify occupational areas that employ people who have interests that are similar to yours. They can also give you an idea of how you would have to reshape your interests in order to enter and enjoy occupations that employ people whose interests are not like yours. Appendix B contains one such survey.

Your *skills* or abilities are the things you can do. They help you define the level on which you could operate within various areas of interest.

Like interests, our skills reflect the experiences we have had with work-related activities, especially those that require particular ways of thinking, moving, or relating to others to achieve a goal or to produce a product. Like interests, your skills can be measured and compared with the skill requirements of different professions and academic areas. Your *functional skills* can be transferred to and implemented

(continued)

TABLE 3-1   Factors Affecting Vocational Self-Concepts *(continued)*

What	*Influence on your career*
	Adolescence (continued)
	in many different interest areas. Your *adaptive skills* reflect your ability to get along smoothly with others in the work setting and to manage the different stressors on the job. Your *technical skills* reflect your ability to perform the tasks associated with a specific occupation or profession. It is important to identify your skills in each of these three areas and to separate them in your mind from interests. The survey in Appendix B will allow you to compare your skills with those of people in different areas. Chapter 5 explores how your preferences, skills, and interests can be tied into different occupations.
	Adulthood
Your values are what you are for or against, what is important to you, and in what order. They determine what you want from your life.	Because our values reflect the things that we cherish or prize, they help us judge the appropriateness of specific work activities for us and the importance we place on work in comparison with home life and leisure pursuits. An inventory that will help you identify and explore how your values have emerged and changed over time and what you currently value is provided at the end of Chapter 4.

When looking at the list of functional skills in Tables 3-2 and 3-3, it is important to recognize that these skills can be transferred from one occupation to another. For example, the "instructing" skill, listed under "People," can be applied across a variety of jobs, including teaching in the classroom, training others on a specific task in an industry, or childraising. Knowing which skills may be transferred from one situation to another may be useful in selecting a new area of study, looking for a job at graduation, or changing jobs.

Other types of skill areas that have been identified by the Department of Labor are adaptive skills and technical skills. *Adaptive skills* are primarily related to specific work settings and to the people in those settings. The ability to manage a complex and demanding work routine is an example of an adaptive skill, as

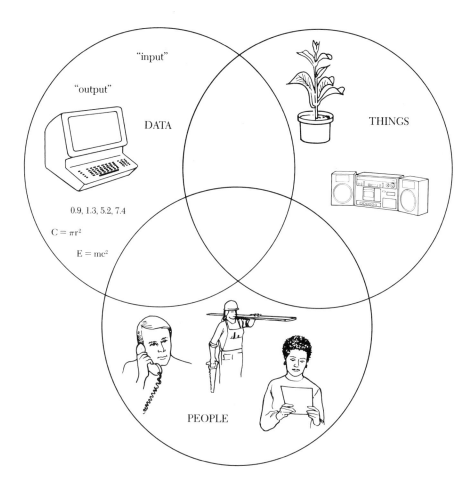

FIGURE 3-1   Spheres of work activity.

TABLE 3-2   Hierarchy of Functional Skills Associated with Working with Data, People, and Things

Data	People	Things
Synthesizing	Mentoring	Setting up
Coordinating	Negotiating	Precision working
Analyzing	Instructing	Operating/Controlling
Compiling	Supervising	Driving/Controlling
Computing	Diverting	Manipulating
Copying	Persuading	Tending
Comparing	Speaking/Signaling	Feeding/Offbearing
	Serving	Handling
	Taking instructions/Helping	

TABLE 3-3 Functional or Transferable Skills, U.S. Department of Labor

Data

Information, knowledge, and conceptions, related to data, people, or things, obtained by observation, investigation, interpretation, visualization, and mental creation. Data are intangible and include numbers, words, symbols, ideas, concepts, and oral verbalization.

Synthesizing: Integrating analyses of data to discover facts and/or develop knowledge concepts or interpretations

Coordinating: Determining time, place, and sequence of operations or action to be taken on the basis of analysis of data; executing determination and/or reporting on events

Analyzing: Examining and evaluating data; presenting alternative actions in relation to the evaluation is frequently involved

Compiling: Gathering, collating, or classifying information about data, people, or things; reporting and/or carrying out a prescribed action in relation to the information is frequently involved

Computing: Performing arithmetic operations and reporting on and/or carrying out a prescribed action in relation to them; does not include counting

Copying: Transcribing, entering, or posting data

Comparing: Judging the readily observable functional, structural, or compositional characteristics (whether similar to or divergent from obvious standards) of data, people, or things

People

Human beings; also animals dealt with on an individual basis as if they were human

Mentoring: Dealing with individuals in terms of their total personality in order to advise, counsel, and/or guide them with regard to problems that may be resolved by legal, scientific, clinical, spiritual, and/or other professional principles

Negotiating: Exchanging ideas, information, and opinions with others to formulate policies and programs and/or arrive jointly at decisions, conclusions, or solutions

Instructing: Teaching subject matter to others, or training others (including animals) through explanation, demonstration, and supervised practice, or making recommendations on the basis of technical disciplines

Supervising: Determining or interpreting work procedures for a group of workers, assigning specific duties to them, maintaining harmonious relations among them, and promoting efficiency; a variety of responsibilities is involved in this function

Diverting: Amusing others (usually accomplished through the medium of stage, screen, television, or radio)

Persuading: Influencing others in favor of a product, service, or point of view

Speaking-Signaling: Talking with and/or signaling people to convey or exchange information; includes giving assignments and/or directions to helpers or assistants

(continued)

TABLE 3-3 Functional or Transferable Skills *(continued)*

People (continued)

Serving: Attending to the needs or requests of people or animals or the expressed or implicit wishes of people; immediate response is involved

Taking instructions–Helping: Helping applies to "nonlearning" helpers; no variety of responsibility is involved in this function

Things

Inanimate objects as distinguished from human beings, substances, or materials; machines, tools, equipment and products. A thing is tangible and has shape, form, and other physical characteristics.

Setting up: Adjusting machines or equipment by replacing or altering tools, jigs, fixtures, and attachments to prepare them to perform their functions, change their performance, or restore their proper functioning if they break down; workers who set up one or a number of machines for other workers or who set up and personally operate a variety of machines are included here

Precision working: Using body members and/or tools or work aids to work, move, guide, or place objects or materials in situations where ultimate responsibility for the attainment of standards occurs and selection of appropriate tools, objects, or materials and the adjustment of the tool to the task require exercise of considerable judgment

Operating-Controlling: Starting, stopping, controlling, and adjusting the progress of machines or equipment; operating machines involves setting up and adjusting the machine or material(s) as the work progresses; controlling involves observing gauges, dials, etc., and turning valves and other devices to regulate factors such as temperature, pressure, flow of liquids, speed of pumps, and reaction of materials

Driving-Operating: Starting, stopping, and controlling the actions of machines or equipment for which a course must be steered, or which must be guided, in order to fabricate, process, and/or move things or people; involves such activities as observing gauges and dials, estimating distances and determining speed and direction of other objects, turning cranks and wheels, pushing or pulling gear lifts or levers; includes such machines as cranes, conveyor systems, tractors, furnace charging machines, paving machines, and hoisting machines; excludes manually powered machines, such as handtrucks and dollies, and power assisted machines, such as electric wheelbarrows and handtrucks

Manipulating: Using body members, tools, or special devices to work, move, guide, or place objects or materials; involves some latitude for judgment with regard to precision attained and selecting appropriate tool, object, or material, although this is readily manifest

Tending: Starting, stopping, and observing the functioning of machines and equipment; involves adjusting materials or controls of the machine, such as changing guides, adjusting timers and temperature gauges, turning valves to allow flow of materials, and flipping switches in response to light; little judgment is involved in making these adjustments

(continued)

TABLE 3-3   Functional or Transferable Skills *(continued)*

Things (continued)

Feeding-Offbearing: Inserting, throwing, dumping, or placing materials in or removing them from machines or equipment which are automatic or tended or operated by other workers

Handling: Using body members, hand tools, and/or special devices to work, move or carry objects or materials; involves little or no latitude for judgment with regard to attainment of standards or in selecting appropriate tools, objects, or material

Source: Dictionary of Occupational Titles (4th ed.), Vol. 2: *Occupational Classifications* (Appendix A), U.S. Department of Labor, 1977, Washington, DC: U.S. Government Printing Office.

are such personal qualities as courteousness, dependability, cooperativeness, initiative, creativity, leadership, tolerance, and persistence. *Technical skills* are essential in the performance of a particular task for a specific occupation, such as a pharmacist creating a prescription remedy. Because technical skills are so narrowly focused, they are more easily transferred to identical jobs than they are from one occupation to another.

Psychologist Dale Prediger (1976) and his colleagues at the American College Testing (ACT) program have separated the "data" dimension in Figure 3-1 into two categories: data and ideas. These four dimensions—data, ideas, people, and things—form the basis of the ACT career-planning program that is used in many high schools to guide graduating seniors and in colleges to place students in different academic majors.

According to Prediger, the tasks associated with working with data involve impersonal processes such as recording, verifying, and organizing facts and data related to a specific product or service. The tasks associated with ideas involve intrapersonal processes and include the creation, discovery, interpretation, and integration of abstractions, theories, knowledge, and insights and expressing that information through writing, equations, and music. People-oriented tasks involve interpersonal processes that generally help modify human behavior in some way through helping, educating, serving, entertaining, motivating, and directing others.

Prediger describes the "things" dimension of work activities as utilizing nonpersonal processes. This set of tasks usually involves tools, machines, materials, and physical and biological processes that are built, produced, transported, serviced, or repaired. Prediger also suggests that these four categories can be divided further to form the six different job clusters shown in Figure 3-2.

John Holland (1973), a psychologist who has also been associated with the ACT program, has developed a different classification system based on the Department of Labor's worker trait groups. Like Prediger, he suggests that there are six ways to classify occupations, but instead of referring to work tasks he has attempted to classify work and worker personality types. These personaltiy types are summarized in Figure 3-3, along with the activities associated with each type. The labels in parentheses under each personality type are taken from

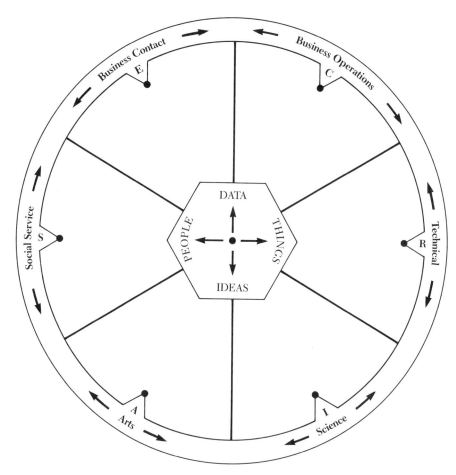

FIGURE 3-2   ACT World-of-Work Map for classifying occupations and job tasks. (©
1985 by the American College Testing Program. All rights reserved. Adapted and
reprinted with permission.)

Prediger's classification system to show the similarities between the two theorists.
According to Holland, a person's work personality type is clearly set in early
adulthood. Changes in a person's choice of job over time may reflect choices
that are more *congruent* with a person's work personality, a forced change such
as loss of employment, or an inability to make wise career decisions, but not
a change in the person's work personality associated with aging.

Types that are on adjacent corners of the hexagon are said to be *consistent*.
That is, the closer two types are on the hexagon, the more psychologically similar
they are. Thus, if you have "realistic" characteristics, you are more likely to
exhibit a personality pattern that shares "conventional" and "investigative" interests, skills, and values. If your orientation is more "social," you may have
some "artistic" and "enterprising" qualities. Since types can compete within
one person, you may have difficulty determining a preferred occupational direc-

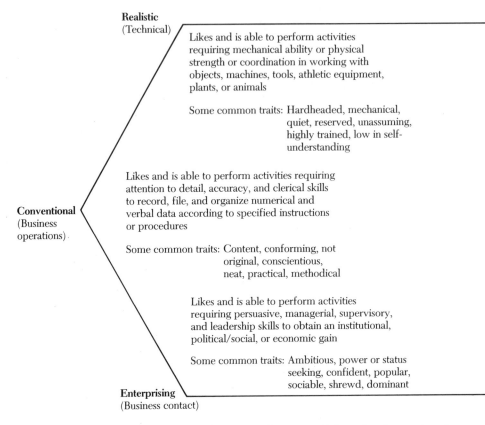

Realistic
(Technical)

Likes and is able to perform activities requiring mechanical ability or physical strength or coordination in working with objects, machines, tools, athletic equipment, plants, or animals

Some common traits: Hardheaded, mechanical, quiet, reserved, unassuming, highly trained, low in self-understanding

Likes and is able to perform activities requiring attention to detail, accuracy, and clerical skills to record, file, and organize numerical and verbal data according to specified instructions or procedures

Some common traits: Content, conforming, not original, conscientious, neat, practical, methodical

Conventional
(Business operations)

Likes and is able to perform activities requiring persuasive, managerial, supervisory, and leadership skills to obtain an institutional, political/social, or economic gain

Some common traits: Ambitious, power or status seeking, confident, popular, sociable, shrewd, dominant

Enterprising
(Business contact)

FIGURE 3-3   Holland's work and worker personality types. (Adapted and reproduced by permission of Psychological Assessment Resources, Inc., Odessa, Florida 33556, from the *Self-Directed Search Professional Manual* and *Self-Directed Search Manual Supplement* by John L. Holland, Ph.D. Copyright 1985 and 1987.)

tion if you relate to several types with equal intensity or are oriented toward types located at opposite points of the hexagon.

After examining the six personality types, most people agree that they possess characteristics associated with all corners of the hexagon. However, specific corners are probably more representative than others. By rank ordering the six types, you may begin to explore the kinds of work activities that interest you. The three that you rank highest may provide clues about work activities that you like and help you determine which occupational directions you should explore.

Predicting Your Holland Personality Type

Carefully read the descriptions that follow. Then rank order the six personality types, starting with the one that is most like you and ending with the one that

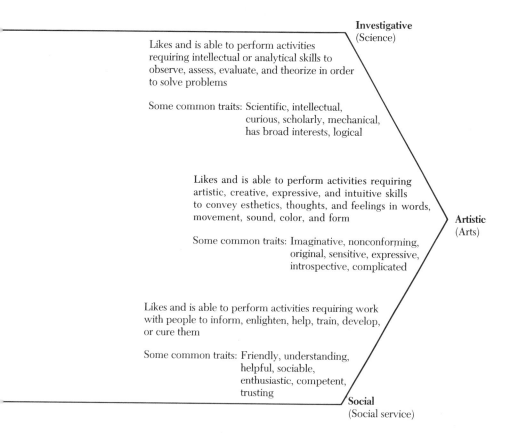

Investigative
(Science)

Likes and is able to perform activities requiring intellectual or analytical skills to observe, assess, evaluate, and theorize in order to solve problems

Some common traits: Scientific, intellectual, curious, scholarly, mechanical, has broad interests, logical

Likes and is able to perform activities requiring artistic, creative, expressive, and intuitive skills to convey esthetics, thoughts, and feelings in words, movement, sound, color, and form

Some common traits: Imaginative, nonconforming, original, sensitive, expressive, introspective, complicated

Artistic
(Arts)

Likes and is able to perform activities requiring work with people to inform, enlighten, help, train, develop, or cure them

Some common traits: Friendly, understanding, helpful, sociable, enthusiastic, competent, trusting

Social
(Social service)

is least like you. Write "1" on the line beside the type that is most like you, "2" beside the type that is next most like you, and so on, until you have put a number beside each of the six types.

Ranking   Personality Type Description

_____ *Realistic:* I am interested in and skilled at activities requiring mechanical ability, physical strength, or coordination in working with objects, machines, tools, athletic equipment, plants, or animals. I also see myself as hardheaded, mechanical, quiet, reserved, unassuming, highly trained, and low in self-understanding.

_____ *Investigative:* I am interested in and skilled at activities requiring intellectual or analytical skills to observe, assess, evaluate, and theorize in order to solve problems. I also see myself as scientific, intellectual, curious, scholarly, mechanical, broadly interested, and logical.

_____ *Artistic:*   I am interested in and skilled at activities requiring artistic, creative, expressive, and intuitive skills to convey esthetics, thoughts, and feelings in words, movement, sound, color, and form. I also see myself as imaginative, nonconforming, original, sensitive, expressive, introspective, and complicated.

_____ *Social:*   I am interested in and skilled at activities requiring work with people to instruct, educate, train, or counsel them or to treat their ailments. I also see myself as friendly, understanding, helpful, sociable, enthusiastic, competent, and trusting.

_____ *Enterprising:*   I am interested in and skilled at activities requiring persuasive, managerial, supervisory, and leadership skills to obtain an institutional, political/social, or economic gain. I also see myself as ambitious, power or status seeking, confident, popular, sociable, shrewd, and dominant.

_____ *Conventional:*   I am interested in and skilled at activities requiring attention to detail, accuracy, and clerical skills to record, file, and organize numerical and verbal data according to specified instructions or procedures. I also see myself as content, conforming, not original, conscientious, neat, practical, and methodical.

In ranking the types of activity just listed, you have, in a way, predicted the outcome of any interest or abilities inventory you might take that uses Holland's personality types as its format. One inventory that uses Holland's approach is provided in Appendix B. To get a sense of how well your predictions about yourself compare with your inventoried preferences, interests, and abilities, turn to Appendix B and complete the inventory there, or contact the counseling service on your campus to take other interest and ability tests to survey your work personality. Professor Holland suggests that another way to get feedback about your work personality type is to give the descriptions provided above to a close friend or family member and have that person rank the types according to how he or she sees you. You can then compare your self-assessment with the assessments of others to see if your day-to-day involvements with others are consistent with the way you see (or would like to see) yourself.

Functional Skills Survey

The following list includes the functional skills described in Tables 3-2 and 3-3. Place a check mark to the left of each skill that you currently possess. In the space provided, describe the setting(s) where you acquired that skill. Be as specific as you can about the setting—for example, "a class in accounting," "working as a lifeguard during the summer," "serving as president of my class." This information can be useful to you later as you think about settings in which you want to work, new skills you would like to develop, or a job at graduation.

1. Data Skills

———— A. The skill I possess is *synthesizing*. I acquired this skill through

———————————————————————

———————————————————————

———— B. The skill I possess is *coordinating*. I acquired this skill through

———————————————————————

———————————————————————

———— C. The skill I possess is *analyzing*. I acquired this skill through

———————————————————————

———————————————————————

———— D. The skill I possess is *compiling*. I acquired this skill through

———————————————————————

———————————————————————

———— E. The skill I possess is *computing*. I acquired this skill through

———————————————————————

———————————————————————

———— F. The skill I possess is *copying*. I acquired this skill through

———————————————————————

———————————————————————

———— G. The skill I possess is *comparing*. I acquired this skill through

———————————————————————

———————————————————————

2. People Skills

_____ A. The skill I possess is *mentoring*. I acquired this skill through

_____

_____

_____ B. The skill I possess is *negotiating*. I acquired this skill through

_____

_____

_____ C. The skill I possess is *instructing*. I acquired this skill through

_____

_____

_____ D. The skill I possess is *supervising*. I acquired this skill through

_____

_____

_____ E. The skill I possess is *diverting*. I acquired this skill through

_____

_____

_____ F. The skill I possess is *persuading*. I acquired this skill through

_____

_____

_____ G. The skill I possess is *speaking/signaling*. I acquired this skill

through _____

_____

_____ H. The skill I possess is *serving*. I acquired this skill through

_____

_____

3. Things Skills

_____ A. The skill I possess is *setting up*. I acquired this skill through

_____

_____

_____ B. The skill I possess is *precision working*. I acquired this skill

through _____

_____

_____ C. The skill I possess is *operating/controlling*. I acquired this skill

through _____

_____

_____ D. The skill I possess is *driving/controlling*. I acquired this skill

through _____

_____

_____ E. The skill I possess is *manipulating*. I acquired this skill through

_____

_____

_____ F. The skill I possess is *tending*. I acquired this skill through

_____

_____

_____ G. The skill I possess is *feeding/offbearing*. I acquired this skill

through _____

_____

_____ H. The skill I possess is *handling*. I acquired this skill through

_____

_____

References and Resources

Brooks-Gunn, J., & Furstenberg, F. F., Jr. (1989). Adolescent sexual behavior. *American Psychologist, 44*, 249–257.

Crites, J. O. (1969). *Vocational psychology*. New York: McGraw-Hill.

Fulghum, R. (1988). *All I really need to know I learned in kindergarten*. New York: Random House.

Hamberg, D. D., & Takinashi, R. (1989). Preparing for life: The critical transition of adolescence. *American Psychologist, 44*, 825–827.

Holland, J. L. (1973). *Making vocational choices: A theory of careers*. Englewood Cliffs, NJ: Prentice-Hall.

Holland, J. L. (1985). *The self-directed search professional manual—1985 edition*. Odessa, FL: Psychological Assessment Resources.

Holland, J. L. (1987). *1987 manual supplement for the self-directed search*. Odessa, FL: Psychological Assessment Resources.

Koss, M. P., Gidyez, V. S., & Wisniewski, N. (1987). The scope of rape: Incidence and prevalence of sexual aggression and victimization in a national sample of higher education students. *Journal of Consulting and Clinical Psychology, 55*, 162–170.

Matteson, D. R. (1975). *Adolescence today: Sex roles and the search for identity*. Homewood, IL: Dorsey Press.

Prediger, D. J. (1976). A world of work map for career exploration. *Vocational Guidance Quarterly, 24*, 198–208.

U.S. Department of Labor (1977). *Dictionary of occupational titles* (4th ed.). Washington, DC: U.S. Government Printing Office.

CHAPTER FOUR

The Emerging Self: Beyond Adolescence

In the last week of May, when they got home from college, I was traveling in another country. By the start of June, when I came back, their time already was spoken for. They had summer jobs to go to, and old friends to occupy the evenings.

Never mind, we said. There were still the weekends.

But for a month it rained on weekends, and June was gone. That left July and part of August. But now the usual spell of brutal midlands heat has settled in. The days are breathless, the nights unfit for sleeping.

And the place where, more than any other, we'd looked forward to spending days together—a rough cabin in a clearing of the Ozark woods—can be a misery in this time of year.

That leaves only half of August. By then, though, even if by some miracle the weather breaks, thoughts will have started running ahead to autumn and the mechanics of separation.

There will be plane tickets to reserve, boxes to ship, suitcases to start filling, a new round of goodbyes to be begun.

And in a rush, the house will empty out.

It surprises and saddens me every time—this brevity of summer. The season used to arrive so expansively, and be able to contain so much: a week or two in the far North, with chilly starshine reflected in the night waters; some time spent in a mountain place, hiking the steep trails by day and afterward, warming in front of slow fires. Great adventures, and several smaller ones between.

Why, summer was an easy eternity! That's how we foolishly expected it would always be.

So what I find myself saying now—making myself a bore—to people whose children are younger, and whose lives together still are in the adventure years, is: "Hold those times carefully, tenderly. Because it's funny about change. By the time you know anything about it, the knowing's of no use."

I can't help trying to convince them, but I think they only pretend to listen. You live in the moment, and the moment's fine. Then time, unexpected as a mugger on a familiar street, comes at you from the blind side.

—*C. W. Gusewelle*

It's two o'clock on an autumn afternoon. Bill sits at the window and watches a squirrel gather nuts for a bitter east coast winter. He has been retired since June. The first few months of retirement were full of freedom and fun, like a vacation. Now free time, so precious during the working years, is becoming a burden to Bill. There's nothing to plan for or rest up for, no tasks whose value can be measured by a paycheck. Friends that Bill planned to lunch or fish with during these years have moved to warmer climates or passed on. He's not really a parent anymore—his children are parents themselves. For the first time in many years, Bill is uncertain about what he wants from the rest of his life.

Sondra sits on her front step watching her children play. She concentrates on how lucky she is, mentally listing her nice home, healthy children, and adoring husband, Joe. She has a part-time job as receptionist at a mental health center—a lucky break for someone with an associate degree in psychology and no experience. The people Sondra works with have encouraged her to go back to school. She and Joe have talked about rearranging child-rearing and household responsibilities so she can do that. Sondra knows it will take a lot of time and energy, but she has decided to give it a try.

In this society the pressure is on very early to grow up, to become mature, to be an adult. We are supposed to sort out our values, choose a vocation and a lifestyle, and then settle down. The implication is that if we make the right choices we will be safe—home free for the rest of our lives. Children are expected to grow, change, make mistakes, and modify themselves. But once we reach adulthood we are supposed to be serene, sure, and stable. Adults don't get confused, act foolish, evade reality, or feel dependent. Or do they?

The myth of adulthood is that if we do what we are supposed to, regardless of what we *want* to do, certain things will happen. This is what George and Nina O'Neill (1974) call "the maturity myth." We are tacitly promised by our culture that if we follow the rules,

1. We will be home safe when we reach our 40s.
2. We will be stable and not restless.
3. We will have emotional security.
4. The future will be manageable.

The major problem with these guarantees is that they might come true. However, this is not very likely, since no one can foresee or guarantee the future, let alone its quality. But if these predictions should come true, each has its negative corollary:

1. When you are living safely there will be no new directions, nothing to anticipate but old age.
2. When you are less restless, you will be less curious and your life will be repetitive.
3. The more you expect emotional security, the more threatening change will be—and change is unavoidable.
4. If it is totally manageable, your future will be without challenge or excitement.

Adult Life Stages

To the extent that these promises come true, we will stop growing and changing, and that only happens when we are dead. As Germaine Greer put it: "Security is when everything is settled, when nothing can happen to you. Security is a denial of life."

Researchers on adult development are finding more and more evidence of an orderly series of adult stages and transitions through which we will change and grow as long as we live. As scary as this may seem, it takes the pressure off. We no longer have to have it all together or to make all our decisions by a certain age. We no longer have to pretend to others, ourselves, or our children that we are faultless. We can take our confusions and problems out from under wraps.

Maturity is not a goal but a growth process. However, it is difficult for us to win permission from ourselves and from society to grow, experiment, and change. Psychiatrist Roger Gould (1978) attributes this to the magical expectations of adulthood and adults that we learn as children—the maturity myth. He believes that we are in for minimal growth and maximal misery as adults unless we confront the realities of adulthood and stop expecting that we should be perfect and have all the answers.

Growth circles back on itself. Change is both the impetus for growth and its product. Change is where career decisions—as all major decisions—begin and end. It is both exciting and frightening, and it is unavoidable. Change often travels with crisis; in part, this has to do with timing. Sometimes change comes when we are not ready for it, such as a personal loss or a job that is phased out. Or we may be ready for a change that does not come—a promotion, a raise, or some new friends. Even when a change is well timed, it involves an act of faith, a letting go of the familiar to embrace the unknown. Part of learning to cope with change is learning to believe in growth, to put aside fear and frustration long enough to realize that change is a catalyst for transition. Everything around us is growing. If we try to stand still we will not avoid change; we will simply be giving up our option to choose and to help direct the change. A crisis is often the chance for a ride to the next stage of our development—not a free ride, but often a real bargain in terms of experience.

Adult life stages appear to be ordered: each one must be completed before the next one can be genuinely undertaken. There is great temptation and sometimes pressure to jump ahead. Time and competition are important to Americans. Sometimes we are so anxious to go forward that stopping to sort out and tie up loose ends seems like wasted time, but there are no shortcuts. Like infants, we must crawl before we can walk. People who try to circumvent growth phases by leaping forward to keep up with the expectations of a parent, employer, or spouse are setting the stage for serious trouble for themselves and for their relationships.

Each person's existence is guided by internal beliefs and external demands. It is much easier to see and understand the external elements. Our social, family, and job roles are filled with things we perceive to be controlling us—I should do this, I have to do that, I can't do something else. We often define our lives in terms of external success and the opinions of others, and we may be tempted to blame failures and distress on spouses, jobs, and society's problems. We may try to define the appropriateness of our attitudes and values according to external events and expectations, and when or if the two do not mesh, we blame ourselves.

Inward is the first place we need to look to find our own direction, not the last. Which of these things is right for me? How do I feel about each of them? Although crises and growth experiences may be altered by and attuned to our environment, they frequently begin and end inside us.

Life-stage theory is further complicated by differences in the subgroups and their roles and goals. These differences are just beginning to be understood. Most early studies were done with white males, so this research may have limitations in its application to women and minorities. It is becoming apparent with the increasing research that, although the ultimate goals of human development may be the same for all human beings, the paths by which women, African Americans, Hispanics, or Asians arrive at them may be different. Some of these differences will be pointed out in this chapter. Keep in mind that many basic similarities remain.

Each life stage has its own implications for all the decisions we make—for our work, our personal selves, and our lifestyles. In general, the discoveries made about adult development have triggered the realization that a career choice is usually a series of choices. As the environment changes, our internal landscape is changing as well. As we gain new life experiences, our values, interests, feelings, and even our capacities may shift. If it is to be fulfilling, a career choice may need to be reevaluated too.

Early Adulthood (Ages 20 to 30)

In our early 20s (or sooner) we face a conflict between the desire for stability and the desire to explore. At this age we are expected to start making commitments to a life system of our own and to detach ourselves from our parents. For many postadolescents, this push to commitment comes when there are still too many loose ends. Young adults respond to this confusion in many ways. Some continue to explore different sets of values and attitudes by experimenting with various kinds of living arrangements and temporary jobs. But many appear to turn their backs on unexplored horizons and begin working to establish themselves. Some may have sorted out what they want and feel ready to settle down. For others, a career choice and/or marriage may seem to be the right path to adulthood and security. For them the misfortune is not in the doing but in the fact that many people believe that deciding simply in order to decide will guarantee happiness—again, the maturity myth.

Society has traditionally given us the message that our 20s are years in which we should start a family and establish a career direction. Recently, however, national surveys have shown that social change is accelerating and different options are becoming available, especially for women:

1. Women have been entering the labor force and college in increasingly greater numbers. Census figures reveal that the number of working women has tripled since just before World War II. The 1985 Virginia Slims American Women's Opinion Poll, published in *USA Today* (October 21, 1985), found that 52 percent of women work, up from 29 percent in 1970. According to John Naisbitt and Patricia Aburdene (1990), authors of *Megatrends 2000,* 79 percent of women with no children under age 18 presently work outside the home. More than half of all full-time freshmen entering college are women. This increasing ability of women to put personal development first represents a slow but signif-

icant change, and it has created problems as well as opportunities. Women's sex-role confusion and ambivalence regarding autonomy was first spotlighted by Horner's research on the "fear of success" (Horner, 1972). Briefly, she found that women fear that achievement or autonomy will mean the loss of femininity, relationships, or social acceptance. More recent researchers (Belenky et al., 1986) have found that advantaged college women may still fall back into the "good girl" mentality when faced with diversity of opportunity. These women prefer to observe, listen, and try to find identity in their relationships with others. These researchers conclude that neither the families nor society seems to support risk taking in women. Although women are trying many new things and shifting priorities, they are having difficulty reconciling these changes with the traditional roles of wife, mother, and homemaker, which they still fill.

2. Our attitudes about marriage and work are changing. According to census figures, the median age at first marriage has gone up for both sexes as increasing numbers of men and women postpone marriage for college and career. In 1951, the median age for men to marry for the first time was 22.8 years; in 1987, it was 25.8 years. For women, the increase was from age 20.3 to age 23.6. In the Virginia Slims survey, 72 percent of the women said that marriage is not a prerequisite for happiness, and only 48 percent ranked a loving husband as more important than self-fulfillment (compared with 64 percent a decade ago). Given a choice between homemaking and working outside the home, 51 percent of the women said they would choose the job (up from 35 percent a decade earlier), and 85 percent of working women said they received "great" or "moderate" satisfaction from their work.

3. There are more dual-career couples in the labor force. The 1985 Virginia Slims survey mentioned earlier reported that 63 percent of women wanted to combine career and marriage and/or family. According to the early 1989 census, one-half of all married couples in the United States have both spouses employed outside of the home.

4. Our attitudes toward work and childbearing have been changing. The number of working mothers has increased dramatically over the past four decades. Census figures reveal that the number of working mothers has inceased twofold since World War II. Census data also show that the number of women in the labor force following the birth of a child increased from 31 percent in 1976 to 51 percent in 1987. Sixty-three percent of the working mothers in 1987 had four or more years of college.

Increasingly, couples have been postponing having children until they are in their 30s so that the wife can get a head start on her career. According to census figures, one-third of the children born in 1988 had mothers aged 30 and older. And many couples no longer see having children as vital to a happy marriage. Data from the 1985 Virginia Slims survey revealed that 80 percent of the women and 76 percent of the men did not feel that they needed children to have a happy marriage, another view that was thought to be "unhealthy" or "selfish" in the past.

Another interesting research finding regarding social change and the personal development of women (Stewart & Healy, 1989) suggests that a major social event (for example, the women's movement) causes differing changes depending on a person's life stage. For women who were in the late-adolescent transition to adulthood during the 1960s, the women's movement had tremendous power to shape their identity. They developed a strong vocational identity, as evidenced by the high number of employed women in this age group. These young women reported that they did not see family and career as mutually exclusive or in conflict. Women in mature adulthood, however, who had embarked on their adult lives before the 1960s, were affected differently. If they went to work, they viewed this as "for the family" rather than as self-fulfillment. They viewed motherhood and a career as strongly conflicting. Although many of them worked, their basic belief system and identity still centered on family and motherhood; only their behavior was changed.

Thus, the same behavior may have very different meanings and may create a real "generation gap" between mothers and daughters. Emerging adult women will experience internal (and possibly external) conflict if a change in their role definition or in the environment puts them at odds with their upbringing and their role model (Mom). So, parental models apparently exert less influence during an adolescent's identity formation if there are major social changes occurring.

5. Work has a positive effect on a woman's self-esteem and family life. A 1978 national survey of adults conducted by the Target Group Index (published in *Working Women* in March 1979) found that women who work described themselves in more positive terms than did nonworking women. Women employed outside the home tended to rate themselves higher than homemakers rated themselves in terms of their self-assurance, intellect, humor, and ability to get along with and support others. A survey of goals of readers of *Working Women* found that being financially well off, having a good family life, and having a job or career were all endorsed by 50 percent of the female readers. More recently, in 1989, psychologist Lois W. Hoffman published a survey in *American Psychologist* that summarized the result of a number of studies comparing working mothers and homemakers. She concluded that compared with nonemployed mothers, working mothers had fewer psychosomatic and stress-related ailments and experienced less depression. She also observed that children, especially daughters, of working mothers had fewer stereotyped attitudes about sex roles and that husbands of working mothers were more involved in family life if they also worked. Finally, Hoffman reported that the quality of interactions between working mothers and their daughters is more positive, while their relationships with their male children change very little, when mother works.

6. Finally, it appears that numerous homemakers and workers of both sexes are returning to school or to work after their 20s to launch new careers. It is predicted that by 1992 (Clinton, 1987), half of all college students will be older than 25 and one in every four will be older than 35. Interestingly, from the results of a study by Etaugh and Spiller (1989) it seems that older returning students, especially women, tend to be more liberal than their younger classmates in their attitudes toward women's roles.

In effect, as social change occurs, many people are changing their attitudes and lifestyles. Some are forced to change because of loss of a job or spouse. Others are choosing change in order to take advantage of new opportunities. Thus, a commitment during the 20s that later turns out to be uncomfortable need not be a devastating mistake. In fact, research seems to indicate that those who commit themselves wholeheartedly to something in this stage—even if they outgrow it—are better equipped for much of the growth that occurs later in life.

One implication of these changes and options is that growth and development tasks become more complex. For men in their 20s, priorities must be realigned to include attention to home, family, and a wife's job, as opposed to more traditional times, when almost all a man's energy went into career building in those early years. Women in their 20s have, in addition, new priorities and some difficult choices. Women who want both a career and a family must develop themselves simultaneously as nurturers and achievers, because statistics suggest that, despite slowly changing attitudes, most nurturing and homemaking tasks still fall to women. If women choose to postpone or give up one of these options, they must deal with guilt, risk, and loss. Even with a career, women in their 20s are likely to continue to work at developmental tasks revolving around relationships and commitment to others—something that men are more likely to postpone.

One kind of relationship that is important to both sexes in their 20s and 30s is unique to the task of developing a career and a professional identity. This is a relationship with a mentor.

A *mentor* is someone who is far enough along in his or her own emotional and career development to guide and help younger workers. The mentor has more experience than younger colleagues have and is usually at a higher occupational level. He or she can provide an informal source of information, influence, and support. Most unexperienced workers who have a mentor are able to refine their skills and learn shortcuts, informal (often unspoken) rules, and processes in a particular business environment or career area.

The mentor can be a boss or a co-worker, or someone outside the immediate work environment, even in a different career area. Although mentors are most often of the same sex as the "mentee," cross-gender relationships are becoming increasingly common. This is especially significant for women, who may need the informal tutoring and sponsorship of a mentor but have had difficulty finding one because of a lack of females at the higher levels of many work environments and the hesitation of many males to mentor a female (due to kidding from other males or sexual overtones). The situation is now changing, and during the years when their careers and skills are developing most people will have several mentors as they change jobs or advance within a field.

Reexamination (Ages 30 to 40)

No matter how settled the 20s may have seemed, the pathway into the 30s often involves a reappearance of some of the confusion and self-doubt that we put aside or thought we had solved in adolescence. In this stage, there may be conflict between obligations we have taken on and unfulfilled personal desires. We begin to understand that some of our "shoulds" were accepted from our families and society, and we ask "Why *should* I?" We begin to realize that the rewards we expected for doing what we were told may not be forthcoming. We may think about rearranging our obligations in order to realize our hopes and dreams. At age 35, according to U.S. life expectancy tables, we have lived half our lives.

It is around this age that many of us also begin to feel pressed for time. These feelings of lost opportunity, combined with the prospect of middle age and old age ahead, create a feeling of urgency that Gail Sheehy (1976) has called the "last chance" syndrome. We feel that if we miss the opportunity to do what we really want to do now, it will be too late. This feeling often impels people at this stage to reexamine and reevaluate personal values and attitudes, as well as their career progress and goals. In doing this, we may find that some of our beliefs and goals are no longer attainable or appropriate.

Many people in their mid-30s today find that values and attitudes about basic things like work, sex and marriage, family structure, and sex roles are now radically different from the traditions that they grew up with. A study done by Daniel Yankelovich in 1978 indicates that the old motivations—money, security, and status—no longer have meaning for many of today's workers. The majority of the workers Yankelovich interviewed said that leisure, not work, was their major source of satisfaction. Workers today seem to feel that they have a right to a secure living and that the most important rewards of their jobs are increased independence and self-fulfillment. Many workers, especially women, value a paycheck as recognition of their contributions as an individual.

If we are to be comfortable in our culture, our attitudes and expectations must change in relation to the changing demands of reality and of changing attitudes. One result of the American worker's increased affluence, mobility, and quest for self-fulfillment is a new attitude toward job change. Many of us have a parent or grandparent who was a loyal employee of one firm for 30 or 40 years and retired with a ceremony and a gold watch. Today the average worker is likely to change jobs several times during his or her career and may retrain at some point to enter a partly or entirely different area. Additional changes we face include growing competition for jobs, changes that come about from changing social attitudes and legislation, and a growing number of jobs that are becoming overcrowded or obsolete. Although we often cannot foresee these changes when we are training ourselves for a first career, we can stay alert for change by keeping our learning and decision-making skills sharp and by observing our surroundings and maintaining our flexibility.

Over our working lives many kinds of changes can occur. In addition to a job shift—being fired, laid off, quitting, taking a new job, or even starting a whole new career—changes are common within one company or enterprise, or even within a job. These include promotion, demotion, shifts in job duties, a leave of absence, a transfer to a new location, a change of income, additional school or on-the-job retraining, the loss of employees, bosses, or colleagues, or even something as subtle as a change in feelings about one's job. The late 30s is the time when many workers leave their last mentor relationship, strike out to form their own power base, and perhaps prepare to become a mentor for someone else.

Whether we view these changes as good or bad, they will require adjustments and decisions on our part and will affect our present and future feelings and behaviors. Single workers may find that such changes affect friends, roommates, dates, or parents. Career-related events in the lives of married workers will affect the spouse (and any other family members). Dual-career marriages present special problems, including that of finding a location where both spouses may pursue their career interests. The feelings and the household routines of husbands and children can present problems for a wife who wants to begin working or a woman who wants to have a family while continuing to work.

These effects on other people who may be in our lives—spouses, children, parents, or friends—will be important considerations for most of us. A man who gets a job offer in a new city may want to involve his family in the decision, especially if his children are involved in the community or if his wife has a career outside the home. If either spouse wishes to invest time and money in school or retraining, this may involve asking others to cut back on their standard of living or to assume new responsibilities.

Women in their 30s today are being affected by inflation, by divorce or widowhood, by social attitudes, and by the realization that the job of motherhood fills only 10 to 20 of their 40 (or more) working years. Women in their 30s who have chosen the more traditional career paths or who have had their children while young may have developed themselves in the context of commitment to others. According to Maggie Scarf (1980), these women reach a point at which they prepare to let go of these roles in order to develop a more independent identity. Other women, whose principal investment during the 20s was often in a nontraditional career, may feel a need to develop their nurturing side as they enter their 30s and turn to marriage or childbearing.

Although they are not receiving as much publicity, men also face some confusing new options. Job changes and even second careers are much more acceptable now than in the past, and a man who has a working wife may have more freedom to make changes than he anticipated. Of course, these new options and pressures provide sources of imbalance and conflict in marriage, parenthood, and other types of relationships.

A job shift—whether it is small or major, whether it affects just ourselves or others close to us—will always be scary, even if it is exciting. The best thing we can do for ourselves throughout our working lives is to try to be prepared emotionally, financially, and vocationally to make change work *for* us when it comes our way.

Mid-Life Shift (Ages 40 to 50)

The age-40 transition is the eye of the storm—the warm front of all the dreams pursued since childhood bumping into the cold front of reality. Limitations of time, ability, and opportunity collide. This can be a sad time for workers who have fallen short of a dream.

The big culprit in this rude awakening at the 40-year mark is the maturity myth that most of us bought into during our teens and 20s. If we did what we were "supposed" to do, instead of exploring our own inclinations, we are expecting a reward at this stage of life. If the promises have not come true and we are not safe, secure, and stable, we feel cheated and outraged. If the promises have come true, our lives may be boring, repetitive, and unexciting, and we feel cheated and outraged. The maturity myth is a developmental catch-22—it gets us either way.

People who are unhappy with their personal or vocational lives at this time may again reexamine their values and beliefs. Those who feel that doing what they were supposed to do did not reward them may decide that there is something else they *want* to do. People who do not discover a happy ending in their present job may decide to take more risks. Many people leave jobs to start over, go back to school, become self-employed, or do something they have always wanted to do. Women whose changing attitudes and values have caused them to outgrow old roles may start school and/or work.

For more and more people, a series of different vocations is beginning to make sense, because we grow and change and because our productive and energetic years are being prolonged. It does not make sense to be stagnant in one job all your life or dead-ended in one at age 40. This is especially true because in the current economy the promised security is often not forthcoming anyway. Companies are bought and merged; jobs or whole departments are phased out by changes in policy or management; highly paid executives are let go to save money on salaries or to avoid paying retirement benefits.

More people are taking risks, retraining in their 30s, 40s, or 50s, changing jobs if the old one is a compromise, and starting new businesses at 50 or second careers after retirement. When life expectancies were shorter, facing disappointments and unfinished dreams at 40 might have been an invitation to depression. Now it can be the beginning of a new reality, based on the opportunity to be the new you. People who value highly something about their present job (for example, security, salary, or location) may not want to leave it. Instead, they may shift their search for personal fulfillment or recognition to hobbies, community involvement, or family activities. They may find new challenge and fulfillment in taking new roles. Reevaluation of jobs, roles, or values by one or both partners in a relationship may create a need for change in the balance of the family.

There are often major differences between men and women during this reevaluation period. Men may be changing careers or adjusting to loss or disappointment, but more often they will be consolidating career decisions and actions already taken—pushing for a promotion or cutting back on work time to enjoy more leisure. On the other hand, women who have had children, particularly if they did not have a full-time job outside the home, are really being forced into a "retirement" of sorts. As their children grow up and leave home, they must adjust to the loss of a major life role. At this point, women may be eager to try making their way competitively in a career (a developmental task that most men started in their 20s), or they may be unwilling to give up the role of full-time wife and homemaker.

During this period of reevaluation and change, many men become more nurturing. They may seek increased involvement with their spouse and growing children, or they may become a mentor to a younger co-worker. This is the stage Erik Erikson calls generativity. Women who have been primary caregivers for children or others have probably already completed this stage. Many women, in turn, are now discovering a more aggressive side of themselves, which the men may have developed earlier in their careers. This gives rise to a disturbance in the balance and harmony of some relationships.

A husband and wife whose activities and needs can be balanced at this stage may find they have more time than ever to spend relating to each other and developing leisure activities. For ourselves and significant others, these are tasks that developmental theorist Robert J. Havighurst (1950) has identified as those that most Americans do not accomplish until middle age. The fact that these essential things remain undone until this age clearly spotlights the pressures that the first two decades of adulthood put on us. The awareness of limitations and lost dreams that often comes at this stage can be painful. The important thing to remember vocationally is that at 40 we still have at least 25 working years ahead. Although it is sometimes more difficult to get a job at 40 than at 25, there are many ways and many enterprises in which age and experience offer real advantages.

Refocusing (Ages 50 to 60)

If we are to live constructively and positively from age 50 on, we must possess integrity in many senses of the word. We need the kind of integrity that stems from internal motivation, from self-determination and self-reward, because many of the life activities that generated external approval, such as work and child-raising, are drawing to a close. And we need the kind of integrity that comes from the root of the word *integrate* to face and accept as a part of ourselves the inevitable aging, lost dreams, and mistakes that we cannot undo. For those who have dealt with these realities and determined to move on, the 50s can indeed be a time of redirection. Even as we become concerned about dwindling time and health, these same limitations sharpen our sense of the preciousness of our remaining years. The work that society designated as ours is largely done, and there is an unhurried feeling, a redefinition of values, where other human beings become more important than money and power.

Many people at this age develop new activities and goals to implement this new outlook on life. With ever-increasing affluence and spectacular strides in health care, many in this age group are extending and enjoying their years prior to retirement. They may start businesses, begin new full-time and part-time work, give time to community action, or develop leisure pursuits such as hobbies and travel. These ways of branching out are also great beginnings for a necessary learning process: that of structuring one's own time, something many people never have to do until retirement. It is interesting to note that the research on social change and development mentioned earlier (Stewart & Healy, 1989) suggests that, like those in late adolescence, older adults are once again vulnerable to reconstruction of their views and values if a major social event affects them.

Redirection (Ages 65 and On)

To those of us wrapped up in colleges, jobs, or families, the idea of waking up one morning with permission to do nothing sounds like a dream. Retirement is something most of us look forward to and dream about in our busiest years. But the approach or arrival of that moment causes anxiety or depression in many people. Work, a source of social contacts, recognition, and structure, has been removed from our lives. In addition to income, the paycheck provided reassurance that we were needed and appreciated. Replacing these activities and learning to provide those feelings for oneself takes time and, often, help and support.

An additional problem of retirement is the psychological impact of the concept itself. There is prejudice against older people. We often picture them in cartoons as incompetent drivers, jealously guarding their fixed incomes and shaking their grey heads at the younger generation. We isolate the elderly, in part because they remind us that old age and death wait for each of us. Consequently, our attitudes cannot help but convey the idea that this is all we have to look forward to. Many older people do have real reasons to worry about dependence, ill health, financial problems, and loneliness. But for as many others, nothing but that fear itself is standing in the way of another 15 or 20 years of active enjoyment of life and continued growth. They can try new activities and pursue long-delayed leisure interests. They can feel satisfied with the contributions they have made and can continue to share their wisdom, memories, perspectives, and knowledge in part-time jobs, in volunteer capacities, or with younger friends and relatives.

The work of growth is seldom easy and is never completed. The realization that maturity is a process and not a condition gives us hope. It gives us permission to be unfinished, to make mistakes, to ask for help. We can continually recreate ourselves and our lives. We can change our minds, alter our lifestyles, experiment with new ideas, acquire new skills, accept new challenges, and start over. New learning and new beginnings are always available. We can now be comfortable with the knowledge that we will never be finished growing.

Exploring Your Personal Values

We have already seen that our values, attitudes, and beliefs govern our decisions and behaviors, both small and large. Our values reflect what is most important to each of us. An incomplete awareness of our values can interfere with effective decision making and lead us to make conflicting choices or to act in ways that we may later regret.

For these reasons, examining our own values is one of the critical steps in the decision-making cycle. It is an essential basis for self-assessment and self-understanding. If our decisions are to lead us where we want to go, we must first have a clear idea of where that is.

Following is a list of 13 values that psychologist Milton Rokeach suggests we may exercise through our daily choices and activities.[1] To help you gain a clearer picture of your values and of how they have emerged and changed over time, and to help you determine whether your current actions match your values, this activity requires that you rate each value on three dimensions:

1. A value that I held when I was younger.
2. A value that I have held but am questioning now.
3. A value that I hold now.

After each value listed below, there are lines for you to rate the value on these three dimensions. Place a check mark beneath the word "Younger" if you held that value in the past. If you are questioning that value, place a check mark beneath "Questioning." If you hold the value now and are not questioning it, place a check mark beneath "Now." Once you have completed this review, go back over the values you checked "Now" and place a number (1 through 5) in the box at the end of the appropriate line to indicate how strongly you hold that value now. A "5" would indicate a very important value, a "1" would be for a least important value.

Personal Values

Achievement/Recognition/Status   Feeling satisfaction for a job well done or a challenge well met. Receiving approval or attention from those whose opinions you respect. Achieving status in line with your talents and achievements.

Esthetic Considerations   Having the opportunity and time to appreciate the beauty in people, art, nature, surroundings, or whatever else you consider lovely and important.

Challenging Opportunities   Having opportunities to use your creativity, your training, your intelligence, and your other talents. Facing a variety of challenges rather than the routine. Having the freedom to try new ideas or creative approaches.

[1]From *The Nature of Human Values*, by Milton Rokeach (Free Press, 1973). Copyright © 1967, 1973 by Milton Rokeach. Reproduced by permission of Consulting Psychologists Press, Inc., 3803 East Bayshore Road, Palo Alto, CA 94303.

Health—Physical and Mental Feeling good in a physical sense. Being relatively free of anxieties, hang-ups, and feelings of being harried that can hinder your peace of mind.

Income/Wealth Significantly improving your financial position. Obtaining those things that money can buy.

Independence Having the freedom to do your own thing either on or off the job. Having time flexibility. Having control over your own actions.

Love/Personal Relationships/Family Caring for, sharing with, and giving to those who are close to you, such as family and peers. Being generous, sympathetic, loyal, and helpful to those you love. Having the time to devote to personal relationships.

Morality Maintaining without conflict your moral, ethical, and/or religious standards whatever their source. Being able to accept the goals, values, and standards of your organization.

Pleasure/Fun Having a good time. Enjoying the company of others. Having the time to play. Making new friends.

Power The ability to influence or control others. Getting others to follow the course of action you prefer.

Security Feeling safe. Feeling free of continual concern about the dangers of unexpected and/or unpleasant changes. Having the essentials you need.

Self-Development Increasing your wisdom, maturity, learning, and understanding of life for their own sake. Becoming a more rounded person. Having the time to pursue intellectual interests.

Service to Others Being a useful member of the groups with which you identify. Knowing you have accomplished things that will benefit others.

Younger   Questioning   Now

To get the maximum benefit from this form of self-analysis, try to use the information you have generated to answer the following questions for each value category:

1. Where did I first encounter this value? Have my feelings about it changed over time? If they have, what led to the change?
2. Is this a value I am questioning now? Why? What effect would giving it up or altering it have on my lifestyle?
3. If I hold this value now, do I exercise it frequently? How? If not, why not? What might I do to minimize any discrepancy?
4. Where does this value rank on my list? What does that tell me about myself? What does this value contribute to my picture of the ideal job?

The goal of this exercise has been to help you gain a better understanding of your values—which will help you choose vocational goals that reflect the ideal you. Having knowledge of your values will help you decide how you wish to spend your time and what rewards you desire. Such self-awareness will also help you maintain a sense of who you are during the personal and professional changes and events that will come with the various life stages just discussed.

As we go on to examine other aspects of the career decision process, your values will combine with your skills, interests, aptitudes, and experiences to help you identify a preferred lifestyle, the type and level of job that suits you, and the kinds of enterprises you might wish to work in. Later these elements of self-awareness will affect how you implement your job campaign and do your job.

Decisions and Values

You have already explored both the decision-making process and your own values. In the following exercise, several vignettes give you a chance to examine decision making and values in action.[2] After reading the description of each situation, think about what values are involved, what alternatives the people in the situation might have, what course of action you would choose in that particular case, and what your reasoning was.

> Jim has to declare a major soon, and he can't decide what to do. He has always wanted to be a doctor like his dad and has taken mostly pre-med courses. Jim's counselor says that he is not really sure whether Jim will be able to get into medical school. His grades have been good, but not spectacular. The way Jim sees it, he can take two more years of pre-med and risk "wasting" that time, or he can decide right now to switch to a related major, such as something in the field of biochemistry or an allied medical profession.

[2]Adapted from an exercise created by Cinda Field Wells, Ph.D., Dale Alexander, A.C.S.W., and Pat Jonas, M.D., Ohio State University, March 1980.

1. What values are involved here?

_____

_____

_____

2. What alternatives does Jim have?

_____

_____

_____

3. What course of action would be best for him?

_____

_____

_____

4. Which of your own values are you displaying in suggesting this course of action?

_____

_____

_____

Peggy is in business school. Her father has a large accounting firm and has always planned on having Peggy become his partner after college since she is the best mathematician in the family. Peggy likes accounting, but since starting college she has been longing to explore some of the other careers she has heard about, especially teaching. Her friends envy her because she has a secure, high-paying job waiting for her in accounting. They tell her she'd be crazy to change to education. Her father would be terribly disappointed, and she'd be out there competing for a limited number of jobs.

1. What values are involved here?

_____

_____

_____

2. What alternatives does Peggy have?

_____

_____

_____

3. What course of action would be best for her?

_____

_____

_____

4. Which of your own values are you displaying in suggesting this course of action?

_____

_____

_____

Jesse likes people and has always been good at handling their personalities and problems. He feels he'd be successful in a business setting, such as sales or public relations. He also likes the idea of helping people and has been interested in counseling the handicapped, which he did one summer as a volunteer. Even though he's not sure he'd like working with some of the business executives he knows, he's leaning toward business. He thinks the business world would probably be more exciting, and he is sure it will be more financially rewarding than counseling. He likes children and wants to be able to support a large family and to afford a big house, vacations, and maybe a boat.

1. What values are involved here?

_____

_____

_____

2. What alternatives does Jesse have?

_____

_____

_____

3. What course of action would be best for him?

_____

_____

_____

4. Which of your own values are you displaying in suggesting this course of action?

_____

_____

_____

Marianne is 31 and has been in school for a few months. She quit college in her senior year when she and her husband had their first baby. Their children are 10 and 7 now, and Marianne wants to finish school and get a job working with computers. Tonight, though, she's asking herself if it's worth it. She has two tests coming up, she wants to clean the house for company, and one of the children is sick. Her husband isn't crazy about the idea of her working, and she's beginning to wonder if he's right.

1. What values are involved here?

_____

_____

_____

2. What alternatives does Marianne have?

_____

_____

_____

3. What course of action would be best for her?

_____

_____

_____

4. Which of your own values are you displaying in suggesting this course of action?

_____

_____

_____

References and Resources

Astin, A. W., Green, K. C., & Korn, W. J. (1987). *The American freshman: Twenty-year trends.* Los Angeles: University of California, Higher Education Research Institute.

Belenky, M. F., Clinchy, B. M., Goldberger, N. R., & Tarule, J. M. (1986). *Women's ways of knowing: The development of self, voice and mind.* New York: Basic Books.

Boyce, M. (1985). Female psychological development: A model and implications for counselors and educators. *Counseling and Human Development, 17,* 1–12.

Clinton, B. (1987). Undergraduate education in an increasingly complex world. *National Forum, 67,* 43–44.

Etaugh, C., & Spiller, B. (1989). Attitudes towards women: Comparisons of traditional aged and older college students. *Journal of College Student Development, 30,* 41–43.

Gould, R. L. (1978). *Transformations: Growth and change in adult life.* New York: Simon & Schuster.

Havighurst, R. J. (1950). *Developmental tasks and education.* New York: Longmans Green.

Hoffman, L. W. (1989). Effects of maternal employment in the two-part family. *American Psychologist, 44,* 283–292.

Horner, M. S. (1972). Toward an understanding of achievement-related conflicts in women. *Journal of Social Issues, 28,* 157–176.

Levinson, D. (1974). *The psychological development of men in early adulthood and the mid-life transition.* Minneapolis: University of Minnesota press.

Naisbitt, J., & Aburdene, P. (1990). *Megatrends 2000.* New York: William Morrow.

O'Neill, N., & O'Neill, G. (1974). *Shifting gears.* New York: M. Evans.

Scarf, M. (1980). *Unfinished business: Pressure points in the lives of women.* New York: Doubleday.

Sheehy, G. (1976). *Passages: Predictable crises of adult life.* New York: Dutton.

Stewart, A. J., & Healy, J. M., Jr. (1989). Linking individual development and social changes. *American Psychologist, 44,* 30–42.

Super, D. E. (1957). *Vocational development: A framework for research.* New York: Teachers College, Columbia University Bureau of Publications.

Yankelovich, D. (1978). The new psychological contracts at work. *Psychology Today, 11,* 46–50.

CHAPTER FIVE

Paths in the Workplace

In a world so shrunken that certain people refer to "the global village," the term "explorer" has little meaning. But exploration is nothing more than a foray into the unknown, and a four-year-old child, wandering about alone in a department store, fits the definition as well as the snow-blind man wandering across the Khyber Pass. The explorer is the person who is lost.

When you've managed to stumble directly into the heart of the unknown—either through the misdirection of others or, better yet, through your own creative ineptitude—there is no one there to hold your hand or tell you what to do. In those bad moments, in the times when we are advised not to panic, we own the unknown, and the world belongs to us. The child within has full reign. Few of us are ever so free.

—Tim Cahill

Mary sits alone in her darkened room looking out her window at the moonlight and the fresh snow. A slight wind blows the snow toward the streetlight, creating a sparkling dance among the snowflakes. The city is quiet. Only a few people can be seen hurrying home from work or forays into the city's nightlife.

Mary's roommate, like most of the in-state students on campus, has gone home for the brief midterm break. Mary can't afford to go home. She needs the time to catch up on her studies and doesn't think it would be wise to spend two days on a bus for a short visit with her family. She also worries about her finances because she is surviving at the university on summer earnings and study grants.

In the middle of her random thoughts, Mary is struck with the contrasts and changes in her life. A Native American, raised on a small, remote reservation in the Midwest, it doesn't seem real to her that she is in her first year as an undergraduate at a prestigious private university, living in a major eastern city.

She recalls conversations with friends at home who don't understand her academic goals and her decision to experience city life, if only for a brief period as a student. She is also reminded of the distress that her adjustment to the social aspects of college life is causing her. She deeply values her cultural heritage but often feels alone because she is the only Native American on campus. She has grown tired of being called on in class to voice her opinion from the "Native American point of view." She also feels that her privacy is being invaded by the students' asking about her home life and innermost thoughts and by their lingering eye contact. And she is not comfortable with the strong emphasis they seem to place on their social life and careers. Being identified by her heritage is both special and lonely for Mary; it makes her stand out, yet feel isolated, in many ways.

Mary's thoughts drift back to the last gathering of her family two months ago at the bus stop near her home. She remembers the sense of pride and apprehension they shared as they sent their only child off to college. Although they openly assured themselves that she would return to the reservation when she completed her studies, they shared an unspoken understanding that the promise would be hard to keep because jobs are scarce at home, and most members of the tribe subsidize their earnings by farming, fishing, and hunting. There seems to be little need for someone with a liberal arts degree and no technical skills in such a place.

She promises herself that she will write home tomorrow to ease some of the uncertainty and loneliness.

Although she is native to the country, Mary shares a dilemma with many students whose families have recently immigrated to America from Africa, Asia, the Middle East, and South America. They stand at a cultural crossroad that reaches far back into history yet affects all of us presently in our work and personal lives.

A World of Change

Technology is a major force in the evolution of human cultures. Technological advances have made possible new and broader visions of ourselves and the universe. They have provided us with an ever-expanding means of acquiring food and comfort, of moving about, and of communicating. As technology has extended the realm of the practical, it has expanded our vision of what is possible. The science fiction writer has become the prophet of our time. Star Trek journeys into space are no longer farfetched exercises in imagination. In the past two decades, we have walked on the moon and lived for extended periods in space.

As technology pulls us into the future, it forces us to reconsider the meaning and purpose we give to our lives. New technological advances confront us with ethical dilemmas that require that we stretch our traditional notions of what is right and wrong. Now, as never before, we must grapple with the sometimes painful and complex issues of determining who shall live, how we shall live, and how long we shall live. These are questions of life purpose as well as personal survival. Thus, the history of our culture is a story of values in transition, reflecting an endless dance of belief and technology.

Although relatively little is known about our early ancestors, we may still find clues to the dilemmas with which students such as Mary struggle hidden in the flow of the past. In understanding the realities of the past, we will gain a clearer perspective of possibilities for the future and perhaps understand a bit better why our society, like its individual members, sometimes seems lost and confused. Table 5-1 charts the history of work and social beliefs from ancient times to the present.

TABLE 5-1 Work and Social Beliefs in Three Different Ages and Societies

	Time Line		
	200,000 years ago	*10,000 years ago*	*200 years ago*
Type of society	Hunting and gathering	Agricultural and pastoral caste system	Industrial class system meritocracy
Type of work	Nomads: hunting, gathering	Squatters: tilling, herding	Property owning, industrial product creating
Inventions	Early stone implements, gathering devices, snares, weapons, cooking of food; human power sources	Instruments for animal herding and tending, gardening tools, cloth processing, food processing for storage, craft specialties; animal power sources	Simple motors, computers, and space technology; transportation and communication by space technology; machine power sources
Dwellings	Natural and portable shelters	Villages and towns	Cities
Social values	Living in harmony with nature	Intervening in nature	Mastering nature
	Present-time or cyclical view of time		Future time orientation
	Explanation of natural phenomena through myths		Scientific explanation for everything
	Follow old ways		Climb the ladder of success
	Cooperation		Competition
	Collective responsibility		Individual rights
	Anonymity		Individuality
	Submissiveness		Aggression
	Work for present needs		Work to get ahead
	Share wealth		Save for the future
	Time is always with us		Clock watching/time lost cannot be regained
	Humility		Win first prize if at all possible
	Win once, but let others win also		Win all the time
	Status ascribed by age, intellect, or physical ability		Status achieved by what you do

Source: The content of this table was drawn from a variety of sources, including *Ancient Society* by L. H. Morgan, 1887, Chicago: Charles H. Kerr; "Psychological Research and the Black Self-Concept: A Critical Review" by W. W. Nobles, 1973, *Journal of Social Issues*, 29, pp. 11–31; *Crossing Cultures in Therapy: Pluralistic Counseling for the Hispanic* (pp. 30–44) by E. S. Levine and A. M. Padilla, 1980, Pacific Grove, CA: Brooks/Cole; *Counseling and Development in a Multicultural Society* (pp. 27–115) by J. D. Axelson, 1985, Pacific Grove, CA: Brooks/Cole; and *Sex and Power in History* (pp. 3–66) by A. de Riencourt, 1974, New York: David McKay.

Hunting and Gathering Societies

Hunting and gathering activities extend back at least 20,000 years, probably to our earliest origins, and still exist today in some parts of the world. The natural environment is the primary influence on social and work organization in these societies. Group membership and tribal roles change regularly to adapt to changing needs and environments. Tribes may split or combine membership, depending on available resources. In a few tribes, leadership and hunting roles are assumed by females, while males take on family-care tasks. Unlike our society, which places a high value on individuality and independence, hunting and gathering groups believe that an individual's worth is determined by what he or she contributes to the tribe. One conforms to the natural order of things; one does not attempt to alter them.

Technology plays a very minor role in these societies. Tools are crude, although their creation and ownership is a source of pride. Most dwellings are natural or very simply constructed. Human muscle is the primary source of transportation and power; social organization and cooperation are required to achieve most goals. Some anthropologists believe that societies like these have not changed over time because they must spend their time gathering food. The status quo, however, may also be maintained in part by strong belief in traditions and by putting group welfare above individual achievement and innovation. This illustrates that, even in these early communities, social beliefs and technology complement each other.

Agricultural Societies

A second style of living emerged some 10,000 years ago in the Middle East and Asia and about 5,000 years ago among the Incas in Peru. Agricultural and pastoral societies began with the domestication of sheep and goats and the cultivation of crops. This made it possible for tribes to settle in one place, grow larger, and establish villages. The unpredictable environment came under greater control as technology expanded. Land and livestock were harnessed and made to serve more people more conveniently. From this shift in the balance between environment and technology, new divisions of labor and new social values evolved.

The distinction between physical and nonphysical work roles, which still exists today, sprang up in these early communities. Manual labor included tending crops and animals as well as the handcrafting of household items such as fabric and pottery. Nonphysical roles, which carried greater prestige, revolved around an increased need for protection from the violence of nature and other people and communities. Astronomers predicted weather conditions; priests prayed over them. Carpenters and craftsmen made more durable shelters and implements. Community and judicial officials arbitrated disputes and encouraged community harmony.

Between 800 and 200 B.C., social values in parts of the Middle East, Greece, and China swung gradually away from a focus on group survival toward an emphasis on closeness and prosperity for each family unit. Living by nature's dictates gave way to a greater ability and desire to intervene in nature for human ends. The use of myths to explain natural phenomena gave way to logic and rationality; thus, the image of "Mother Nature" gave way to a more masculine, scientific form of reasoning. The equation of prosperity with hard work and integrity became central to the Western European agrarian society's religious and social traditions; thus, the "Protestant work ethic" was born. This lifestyle, based on hard work, family loyalty, and intervention in nature, is still a cultural basis for many nations of the world, including many areas of the United States.

Industrial Societies

Occurring only 200 years ago, with the harnessing of water power and automation, the industrial revolution dramatically changed American society. Jobs in urban centers took many workers away from their families and the land. The unprecedented rate of technological and scientific change summarized in Table 5-2 brought numerous unforeseen options and often confusing consequences. Technology became the primary influence on the lives of most Americans. Time came to be measured by the clock; it was no longer gauged by changes in the seasons or by social events. Families that had lived in the same community for generations began to split apart as a new emphasis was placed on mobility and personal gain. Old values were soon called into question.

As technology continued to conquer environmental limitations, it also challenged and altered the existing social organization, including the work setting, in complex and far-reaching ways. Prior to the industrial revolution, trade skills were passed on from generation to generation within families. When the work setting moved from the home and farm to the factory and office building, it became possible for greater numbers of people to enter occupations that were new or that previously had been closed to them. And where earlier generations of Americans had expected that their choice of job would last a lifetime, members of modern American society are aware that change is not only possible but very likely and sometimes unavoidable:

1. We are no longer a farming-based society. According to the U.S. Bureau of the Census (cited in the 1989 *Information Please Almanac*), 70.5 percent of the American labor force was employed in farming occupations in 1830. In 1980, 97.8 percent of the labor force was employed in nonfarming occupations (p. 59).

2. The knowledge explosion continues. Nearly two decades ago, British authors B. Hopson and P. Hough (1973) noted that at the rate knowledge is accumulating, by the time children born in 1973 completed their education, the amount of knowledge in the world would be 4 times greater than in 1973. By the time those individuals turn 50, in the year 2023, the amount of knowledge will be 32 times greater—and 97 percent of the knowledge in the world will have been acquired within their lifetimes.

3. Birth rates in the United States are on the decline. Data from the National Center for Health Statistics (quoted in the 1989 *Information Please Almanac*,

TABLE 5-2   A History of Inventions and Discoveries in Their Time and Place

When	What	Where
3600 B.C.	Wheel	Mesopotamia
1400 B.C.	Abacus	China
500 B.C.	Atomic theory	Greece
400 B.C.	Cast iron	China
300 B.C.	Geometry	Egypt
300 B.C.	Decimal system	China
200 B.C.	Negative numbers	China
200 B.C.	Paper	China
200 B.C.	Seismograph	China
200 B.C.	Steel manufacturing	China
700	Printing	Japan
1543	Sun-centered solar system	Poland
1590	Microscope	Netherlands
1630	Steam engine	England
1801	Electric lamp	England
1804	Locomotive	England
1835	Electric motor	England
1839	Ozone	Germany
1855	Plastics	England
1865	Laws of heredity	Austria
1885	Automobile	Germany
1886	Wireless radio	Germany
1895	Radioactivity	Germany
1904	Radar	Germany
1926	Television	England/United States
1930	Jet-propulsion aircraft	England
1938	Nuclear fission	Germany
1938	Xerography	United States
1944	Digital computer	United States
1948	Transistor	United States
1958	Laser	United States/USSR

Source: Information Please Almanac, Atlas and Yearbook, 1989 (42nd ed., pp. 531–533), Boston: Houghton Mifflin; and The Genius of China: 3000 Years of Science, Discovery and Invention by J. Temple, 1989, New York: Simon & Schuster.

p. 787) show that in 1910 the rate of births per 1,000 was 30:1. In 1950, the figure was 24:1; in 1987, the rate dropped to 15:7. If these trends continue, it is predicted that we will reach zero population growth by the year 2050 (p. 783).

4. Our population is getting older. According to census data presented in the 1989 *Information Please Almanac*, (pp. 768, 783), at the beginning of the 20th century, only 4 percent of Americans were over 65 years of age; that figure is now more than 11 percent. The group that includes people aged 85 and older is growing faster than any segment of the population. The median age of Americans during the past decade increased from 26.0 to 29.4, and, according to the Census Bureau, it will reach 36.3 by the year 2000. Many retired workers

are reentering the labor force to replace the declining number of teenagers available to fill lower-level positions in the service industries.

5. Our population is on the move. Census data cited in the 1989 *Information Please Almanac* (p. 771) show that in recent years the northeastern quadrant of the United States has had a significant loss of population, while the West has shown a substantial increase in population. Midwesterners and Southerners have been less inclined to move recently. Metropolitan areas have continued to grow, while central cities and rural areas have declined.

6. Our society is becoming more ethnically varied. Current rates of birth cited in the Fall 1989 *Occupational Outlook Quarterly* (pp. 6–11) suggest that in the future, Asians, African Americans, and Hispanics will be entering the American labor force in greater numbers than they are now; white birth rates are not showing a similar increase. It is anticipated that this change, coupled with higher numbers of women entering the labor force, will create a large number of female and minority workers who will enter at lower-level positions and eventually compete with white males for upper-level positions in the workplace.

7. A free trade movement is afoot throughout the world. According to John Naisbitt and Patricia Aburdene, authors of *Megatrends 2000,* trade barriers are falling between North American, European, and Pacific Rim countries as economic considerations transcend political ideologies. As described by Naisbitt and Aburdene (1990), "economic forces of the world are surging across national borders resulting in more democracy, more freedom, more trade, more opportunity, and greater prosperity" (p. 20). Consequently, a growing number of nations have been entering into joint ventures with American companies overseas or by establishing plants in the United States. This change will place many American workers in the position of working in more international settings under supervision of foreign managers and will require that they be more sensitive to intercultural differences and become more fluent in foreign languages.

8. We are becoming a high-tech and service-oriented society. Futurists such as Naisbitt and Aburdene have observed that our society is rapidly moving away from a manufacturing and industrial base toward a service-oriented economy involving high technology, rapid communication of information, rapid advancement in biotechnology for use in agriculture and medicine, increased utilization of health care services, and a rising volume of wholesale and retail sales. The U.S. Department of Labor's predictions of the fastest-growing occupations, shown in Table 5-3, mirror these observations. It has also been suggested that because of the ease of transmission of information through computer and phone linkages, more people will be working and shopping from their homes or in other decentralized locations, reducing the need for central-city corporate towers and retail malls.

9. We are becoming more conscious of the need to protect our environment. Social scientists and environmentalists (Easterbrook, 1989; Kohn, 1986; Sampson, 1989) are making us more aware of the need to restore the social value of living in harmony with nature and the importance of taking a "globalistic" social view, in which cooperation and interdependence prevail over

TABLE 5-3   Fast-Growing Occupations and Large Occupations Provide the Best Opportunities for Employment

Twenty occupations that are growing faster than average	Percent change in employment, 1988–2000
Paralegals	75
Medical assistants	70
Home health aides	68
Radiologic technologists & technicians	66
Data processing equipment repairers	61
Medical record technicians	60
Medical secretaries	58
Physical therapists	57
Surgical technologists	56
Operations research analysts	55
Securities & financial services sales representatives	55
Travel agents	54
Computer systems analysts	53
Physical & corrective therapy assistants	53
Social welfare service aides	52
Occupational therapists	49
Computer programmers	48
Human services workers	45
Respiratory therapists	41
Correction officers and jailers	41

Source: "Occupational Employment," in *Occupational Outlook Quarterly* (p. 30), U.S. Department of Labor, Bureau of Labor Statistics, Fall 1989, Washington, DC: U.S. Government Printing Office.

rugged individualism, competition, and the abuse of our natural resources. As part of this more environmentally and socially sensitive view, some corporations are hiring professional ethicists to help them examine potential social and environmental effects of their corporate actions. This pattern is also reflected in the tendency of some companies to hire liberal arts graduates, whose educational backgrounds frequently involve training in social, ethical, and moral issues.

10. The labor force has become more gender balanced and, as was mentioned in Chapter 4, women are postponing marriage and childbearing for college and career. More dual-career couples are in the work force, and increasing numbers of homemakers are returning to college courses to advance their careers.

Because change is so constant in American society, lifelong learning through continuing education has become a necessity, and people of diverse ages and backgrounds are going back to the classroom. Some, largely women, are new to the work force; some are changing jobs; some are upwardly mobile within a field or are required to accumulate additional education in order to keep their jobs. All these phenomena continue to send the educational level of the population spiraling upward.

As increasing numbers of women and minority-group members seek a place in the labor force, they continue to run into old beliefs about who should benefit from the gains of industrialization. Although the industrial revolution served to democratize the world of work for a great number of males, it did not do so for women until recently. Prior to the industrial revolution, a form of coequality existed between male and female family members. Each sex contributed to the goods and services that the family exchanged with other members of the community to meet their needs. With the industrial revolution, males began to work outside the home for pay, and as they did they took on the familiar breadwinner role and began to measure their success in terms of their accomplishments at work. Being privy to more information about what was happening in the society, the male had more direct influence over social issues. The female, on the other hand, was assigned the task of managing the home and could affect the socioeconomic issues of the day only by influencing the opinions of male relatives. Because of family background, racism, and other social barriers, certain racial and ethnic minority groups were also excluded from full participation in the society.

As Mary's situation, described at the beginning of this chapter, demonstrates, these historical events continue to haunt us today. Although our social institutions have—with some recent success—attempted to break down old barriers that prohibited the full economic participation of women and minorities, old cultural attitudes and beliefs still serve as a source of constant social tension during this time of change.

Until recently, participation in the American economy was restricted for women and minorities, who had access to only a limited number of occupations. Because of this, a disproportionate number of women and minority-group members are still in occupations that involve providing services to others, such as teaching, nursing, and social services. Those who have reached management-level positions tend to receive less pay for their efforts because they have only recently been hired.

Long-standing isolation from the professional and managerial ranks is the reason many women and minority-group members flounder and become frustrated, even though affirmative action laws have opened new doors for them. They have traditionally been in service roles and jobs, serving others. But now we are asking them to be comfortable in and to compete in situations that require individual achievement, managing others, and controlling the environment. Such a complete and dramatic shift cannot be made overnight. Old beliefs about one's roles and the roles of others change gradually, and new skills to meet the requirements of new opportunities take time to develop.

As you chart the course of your career, consider how your beliefs about the types of position you assume in society, and your ability to get along with others who differ from you in sex, age, and ethnic heritage, will affect your own career. It will also be helpful to know how the world of work is organized so you can identify new possibilities and make choices that coincide with your interests, abilities, and level of aspiration. As we shall see, the overall structure of the world of work remains essentially the same, despite shifts in the economy and new technology.

Where Am I Going? The World of Work

As you begin to explore the career path you might travel, keep three questions in mind: What types of work do I wish to pursue? What levels of work am I most suited for? What types of enterprises appeal to me? According to Canadian educator Gerald Cosgrave (1973), these questions will help you find your way through the world of work.

What Types of Work Do I Wish to Pursue?

Earlier we explored how Holland's worker personality types can be used to explain why people gravitate toward particular activities. Holland's system can also be used to describe work settings and occupations. Like Holland, Cosgrave believes that *people create their work environments.* Although a particular work setting is organized around common tasks, it is more than that. It is a social fabric woven around common tastes, problems, interests, and ideals. The unifying element in each environment is its personality type. Figure 5-1 illustrates how particular personality types are more likely to cluster in certain occupations. The same guidelines that we used to describe personality types (Figure 3-3, pages 54–55) apply to the occupation types in Figure 5-1. That is, people who work in occupations that are adjacent to each other in the hexagon have more in common than they have with people working in occupations that are across the hexagon.

When it is used flexibly, Holland's system can be a useful tool for describing people in different work situations. Although a particular occupation or profession may be characterized as a particular personality type, people are not so easily stereotyped. For example, professional accountants working under the job title "Accountant" in the same firm may work in different positions within that firm. The accountant with a "CES" (conventional/enterprising/social) personality pattern will tend to like enterprising and social activities and to perform the persuasive and supervisory aspects of an accounting position. The person with the "CIE" (conventional/investigative/enterprising) personality pattern might enjoy an accounting position involving analytical and theoretical tasks. Thus, individuals in the same occupation or profession may work under the same job title but be successful in different positions within the same organization. If the CES accountant is asked to perform more investigative tasks, he or she might become dissatisfied with the job. To resolve this situation, the accountant would be faced with the choice of changing preferences, renegotiating responsibilities, or moving to another position that agrees more with his or her personality.

What Levels of Work Am I Most Suited For?

Four decades ago, in the city of Cincinnati, 1,658 public school students were asked to state their choice of occupation. The results were summarized by Rebbecca Van Namm Dale (1948, p. 419):

What would Cincinnati be like if these students became the sole inhabitants of the city in the jobs of their choices ten years from now? . . . Health services would be very high, with every eighteen people supporting one doctor. . . . It may be, however, that they would be needed in a city that had no garbage disposal workers, no laundry workers, and no water supply, since no one chose to do that kind of work. . . . The two bus drivers . . . will find that their customers get tired of waiting and use the services of the sixty-seven airline pilots. It may be difficult getting to Crosley Field to see the forty baseball players.

Like Dale's study, other studies of the occupational plans and expectations of students point to the widely held belief that everyone should strive for the highest rung on the occupational ladder.

Society needs people working in all fields and at all levels. Cosgrave (1973) observed that there are six general levels of work in our society. People at the higher levels have more responsibility for making decisions and supervising others than people who work at the lowest levels. Starting at the lowest rung on the ladder, the six levels are as follows:

1. *Unskilled work* is simple and routine and requires little independent decision making or creativity.
2. *Semiskilled jobs* demand some minimal skill and knowledge or a high degree of manipulative skill in a limited range of tasks.
3. *Skilled occupations* require expert skills and specialized knowledge and judgment in carrying out assigned duties.
4. *Semiprofessional and lower managerial jobs* involve mental tasks demanding specialized knowledge or judgment.
5. *Regular professional and middle managerial jobs* require considerable knowledge and judgment.
6. *Higher professional and upper managerial jobs* require a high level of knowledge, mental ability, and autonomy.

Levels 5 and 6 require college or even graduate school training. Levels 3 and 4 demand high school, college, or other specialized training. Levels 1 and 2 require on-the-job training, or perhaps none at all.

The medical professions offer an example of how a common set of investigative skills may be redefined by attending two-year or four-year programs to enter different levels of work within the same professional area. Many people are interested in medicine, but they differ in their interests, abilities, personality, level of aspiration, finances, and the amount of authority and responsibility they want to assume at work. Those who aspire to and have the capacity for high levels of achievement might attend a professional college and wind up as surgeons, dentists, medical researchers, or head nurses. Other students might attend two-year programs to be trained as medical technologists, physicians' assistants, paramedics, or practical nurses. Those who do not elect to get training beyond high school might find on-the-job training opportunities and become aides or orderlies.

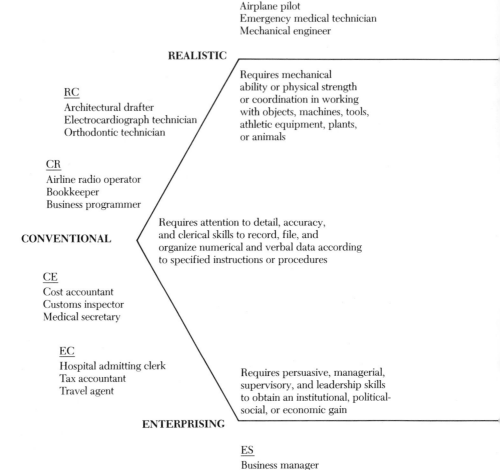

RI
Airplane pilot
Emergency medical technician
Mechanical engineer

REALISTIC

RC
Architectural drafter
Electrocardiograph technician
Orthodontic technician

Requires mechanical
ability or physical strength
or coordination in working
with objects, machines, tools,
athletic equipment, plants,
or animals

CR
Airline radio operator
Bookkeeper
Business programmer

CONVENTIONAL

Requires attention to detail, accuracy,
and clerical skills to record, file, and
organize numerical and verbal data according
to specified instructions or procedures

CE
Cost accountant
Customs inspector
Medical secretary

EC
Hospital admitting clerk
Tax accountant
Travel agent

Requires persuasive, managerial,
supervisory, and leadership skills
to obtain an institutional, political-
social, or economic gain

ENTERPRISING

ES
Business manager
Chief detective
Placement director

FIGURE 5-1 How occupations may be defined in terms of their Holland types, and the skills they require. Note how skills from different types (for example, R and I) may be combined in a single occupation (airline pilot). (Adapted and updated from *If You Don't Know Where You're Going, You'll Probably End Up Somewhere Else* by David Campbell. © 1974 Tabor Publishing, a division of DLM, Inc., Allen, TX 75002.)

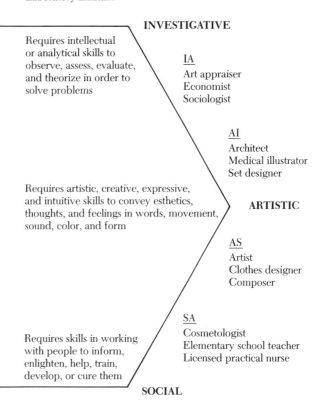

IR
Aeronautical engineer
Anthropologist
Laboratory assistant

INVESTIGATIVE

Requires intellectual
or analytical skills to
observe, assess, evaluate,
and theorize in order to
solve problems

IA
Art appraiser
Economist
Sociologist

AI
Architect
Medical illustrator
Set designer

Requires artistic, creative, expressive,
and intuitive skills to convey esthetics,
thoughts, and feelings in words, movement,
sound, color, and form

ARTISTIC

AS
Artist
Clothes designer
Composer

SA
Cosmetologist
Elementary school teacher
Licensed practical nurse

Requires skills in working
with people to inform,
enlighten, help, train,
develop, or cure them

SOCIAL

SE
Hospital administrator
Recreation leader
Social worker

Starting at a lower level does not mean that you must stay there. For example, a person trained in a medically related specialty at the two-year level may decide to advance by seeking a four-year college degree in a related area and perhaps later a graduate or professional medical specialty degree. Similarly, a photographer who has artistic skills may move up the ladder from a two-year technical training course to a higher professional level by pursuing an advanced degree. We may also find that the shop supervisor may take night courses and move toward a managerial position that became vacant when the manager moved up to company president.

The same basic functional skills can be used across a variety of occupations and settings. This is good to keep in mind when it comes to job hunting after graduation. For example, teachers who face a tight job market or who are considering entering a new field may use their teaching skills in business as salespersons, staff development specialists, public relations specialists, and managerial trainees.

Once you have an idea of the fields or types of work that appeal to you, you need to explore your values, abilities, and desires further and to decide at what level in your present or new field you want to start and what level you might ultimately want to reach. You should also be aware of how the same set of skills can be transferred to different work settings.

What Types of Enterprises Appeal to Me?

Cosgrave has identified 11 broad occupational clusters, each comprising a certain type of enterprise. Although you may prefer certain enterprises because of their purposes, surroundings, or personnel, it is important to remember that the same types and levels of work can be performed across a variety of enterprises. Clerical, teaching, or numerical skills are needed in many occupational settings, not just the most obvious ones. Keeping this in mind will help you to see a broader range of opportunities in today's job market.

As you read the descriptions of the types of enterprises below, try to identify several areas that appeal to you and what you like about them. Imagine how some of your skills and interests might be used in each area.

Agriculture   Agriculture, which takes in fishing and forestry, includes many occupations that would fit the label "realistic." Unskilled work in this area might involve physical labor or maintenance on a farm, at a park, or at a resort. Other jobs in agriculture require more education, such as breeding dairy cattle, managing a fish hatchery, or reforesting a lumber site. Professional-level jobs could range from heading an oceanography expedition to managing or teaching in the parks and recreation program of a large city or running a landscaping or agricultural business.

Mining   Mining industries need unskilled labor, trained workers such as mine inspectors, and even more highly educated workers, such as geologists, mining engineers, and researchers who deal with the extraction and use of minerals.

Construction   The construction industry requires unskilled laborers as well as numerous skilled tradespeople—carpenters, electricians, masons, welders, and other "realistic" types. Higher-level professionals whose work is related to construction include architects and engineers, who may be "investigative" or "conventional" as well as "realistic."

Manufacturing   Manufacturing is a vast network of industries that includes jobs in almost any area of interest. Common jobs at levels 1 and 2 are assembly line worker and supervisor. Level 3 and 4 workers might be managers or technicians who design and run equipment and plants. The upper levels in these enterprises can include product testers, researchers, or engineers. Although many of these jobs are "realistic" or "investigative," "social" people are also needed in personnel and public relations, as well as "enterprising" talents in sales and advertising.

Utilities   Our utilities require a large number of employees for function and upkeep. Lower levels in this area require "realistic" and "conventional" interests. Examples are repair persons, switchboard operators, and clerks. Level 3 and 4 jobs may include managing levels 1 and 2 or may be more "social" or "enterprising," such as sales managers and public relations specialists. People with the highest level of education in these industries might be the engineers, who solve problems and develop new products, or top-level managers with financial specialties.

Transportation   Transportation includes many semiskilled jobs, such as loading and delivery and dispatcher, trucker, or flight attendant. The next level includes such jobs as fleet manager, vehicle repair person, or highway inspector. Highest levels of training would include airline pilot, urban planner, or highway designer.

Communication   Communication fields expand to include almost all of Holland's six categories, although there are fewer semiskilled jobs here than in many areas. One example might be an apprentice technician with radio or TV equipment. Many entry-level jobs require an intermediate level of skill or education, such as newspaper reporter, copy editor for a publisher, TV camera operator, or photographer. Professional-level jobs may require substantial experience and/or skill. These might include news manager for a TV station, newspaper editor, publicity or public relations and advertising executives, or more glamorous jobs such as TV commentator, foreign correspondent, or novelist.

Trade   Trade and related enterprises offer many areas where a relatively untrained worker can start. Some are "realistic," such as loading trucks or stocking retail stores. Others require "conventional" interests, such as inventory ordering or cashiering. Still others require "social" and "enterprising" persons such as salespeople or product demonstrators. Jobs with more training or experience include buyer, department manager, or regional sales representative. Advertising employs people with "artistic" interests for copywriting, photography, or layout and design. The highest-level jobs often involve "enterprising" and "social" skills for managing employees or buying for whole areas or chains. Also employed at this level may be personnel or labor relations experts, industrial and consulting psychologists, educators, and public relations people. Many large companies have programs that permit an entry-level worker to work up to or train for middle- or higher-level jobs with the firm.

Finance   Finance often attracts people with "conventional" and "enterprising" characteristics. One may begin in this area as a bank teller or as a clerk for an insurance or loan company. Jobs with more responsibilities are auditor or loan officer. Higher-level jobs might be as an accountant or financial manager for a business.

Service   The service industries include jobs where something is being done for someone, and for this reason they attract many "social" and "enterprising" types. Persons at levels 1 and 2 could be a hospital orderly, a hotel or restaurant employee, or a volunteer in a helping profession. Jobs in service areas requiring some training include beautician or barber, lab technician, or probation officer. Higher-level professionals include doctors and nurses, psychologists, teachers, and museum curators.

Government   City, county, and federal governments hire people for varied kinds of work at all levels. Many jobs available in private industries are also available as government jobs. Admission and advancement in most government jobs are regulated by civil service tests, which must be passed to qualify for a certain job or level. Exams for beginning-level jobs test literacy and common sense as well as specific skills. Such jobs include clerk/typist or mail carrier. Middle-level jobs include office management, law enforcement, and the inspection of government-supported institutions such as schools and hospitals. High-level jobs include such varied positions as judge, environmental specialist, or economist. Many government jobs—from dogcatcher to U.S. President—are not under the civil service and are elected or appointed. These may require credentials or assets beyond one's ability or training, such as money for campaigns, political influence, and a willingness to take risks.

Your comfort, satisfaction, and competence with a job rests on the interaction of the three elements we have discussed: type, level, and kind of job. You will need to investigate and evaluate your personality and skills and various work environments. Which combination of realistic, investigative, artistic, social, enterprising, and conventional qualities best describes you? Look at the levels— higher professional to unskilled—that lie within each of those types and within your areas of interest. Pinpoint the various enterprises and areas of interests that appeal to you, and investigate the types of jobs they offer. Begin to evaluate how these match up with your aspirations and abilities. Job satisfaction is determined not by any single factor but by the relationship among what we aspire to do, what we can do, and the rewards and demands at a specific level of work.

Five Career-Planning Questions Revisited

The best place to start the occupation exploration process is with yourself—
your needs and your preferences. So, we'll begin with questions about you, and
then move on to see how your career goals can be matched with the rewards
and demands of particular majors or careers. We will use the five questions identified in Chapter 1 to guide you as you chart your current and future career paths.

Who Are You?

Our actions reflect how we see ourselves. If you had your way, what kinds of
things would you do on a daily basis in your studies or work to reflect your ideal
image of yourself? Do you like working most with things, ideas, data, or people?
What do you believe are the most important things you can do during your life,
at work, with others, or through leisure pursuits? In which activities do you
excel? Are your skills matched with what you like to do and with what is most
important to you? Your answers to these questions will reflect who you are as
a person and suggest ways in which you can best express yourself through your
career pursuits.

In previous chapters, we answered some of these questions by identifying
your occupational interests, abilities, and values and applying Holland's worker
personality schema to college majors and careers, so you already have information about occupations to consider. Let's take your self-knowledge a bit further
and explore a broader question.

How Do You Want to Live?

Assuming that you had at least 14 hours a day, 7 days a week to live the kind
of life you would consider ideal, how much of your time would you invest on
the three different sides of the lifestyle triangle? Even though the amount of
time would vary from day to day, it is important that you try to answer this question about time preferences early in the career-search process to help you
evaluate the educational and occupational possibilities you will be exploring.

Where Do You Want to Live?

How you live is influenced by where you live. Because some occupations are
concentrated in specific geographical areas of the nation, your preferences may
limit the occupations you consider. Other factors to consider are the type of
climate you prefer, the size of community you would like to live in, and the
cultural and recreational features of that community.

What Will You Do for a Living?

Once you have pulled together some of your lifestyle preferences, you can begin
to identify the more specific rewards and demands that will help make a major

or career suit your goal plans. It will be helpful to come up with a description of the duties and rewards of any major or career you consider, including entry requirements, time commitments, the amount of flexibility it provides, and the level of responsibility it requires. On the rewards side, it is important to know what the major or career provides in terms of potential job security, opportunities for entry and advancement, and physical surroundings.

Finally, you will need to know the types of educational and training experience required in order to enter and advance successfully in an occupation. In relation to this, you will need to consider carefully your skills, resources, and opportunities, as well as how willing you are to invest your time, energy, and money in meeting these requirements.

Who Will You Spend Your Time With?

Since few of us work alone, the people you will be associating with will be an important ingredient in your daily life as a student or worker. As you explore a major or a career, ask yourself: What are the people who choose this field like? Do I share many interests and values with them? If I do not, how will I deal with the differences? How will my choice of this field affect the people I am close to now? Will they support my choice, or will they challenge it? If they disagree with my decision, how will I deal with them?

By the time you have finished the process of gathering career information, you should be able to answer most of these questions in considerable detail. If you can, the odds are that, in addition to knowing who you are and where you are in the career planning process, you will also know where you want to go.

Finding the Facts

In exploring the world of work, you will need to answer the five career-planning questions just identified. Using these questions as guidelines, identify resources for obtaining *career information*—information about educational and occupational opportunities. You will need to know what to read, where to visit, and with whom to talk. How thorough you can be in the career exploration process will depend on how much time you have to invest in the process and on the kinds of resources available in your community.

Written Resources

The easiest place to start is with written materials. Most libraries and high school or college counseling offices contain books and pamphlets about different fields. The most frequently used resource is probably the *Occupational Outlook Handbook*. Published yearly by the U.S. Department of Labor, the *Handbook* contains general occupational projections for the United States as a whole and information about some 300 occupations, arranged by their common characteristics. Each occupation is described in terms of the nature of the work, place of employment, training and qualifications for advancement, employment outlook, earnings, and working conditions. Addresses are also provided for trade associations and state employment agencies that you can visit or correspond with to obtain additional information. Addresses of organizations are also provided for people with special interests and needs, such as women, the physically challenged, youths, and older workers.

The *Occupational Outlook Handbook in Brief* is a shortened version of the *Occupational Outlook Handbook* and provides a capsule summary of labor trends across the country and in specific occupations. Other helpful general sourcebooks include *What Can I Be? A Guide to 525 Liberal Arts and Business Careers, Encyclopedia of Careers, Occupational Briefs, A Guide to Careers Through College Majors, Your College Degree, College Placement Annual, Career Guide to Professional Associations,* and *National Trade and Professional Associations of the United States and Canada and Labor Unions.* Periodicals that you may find useful include *Changing Times, Glamour* magazine, *MS,* the *Journal of College Placement, Career World, Mademoiselle,* and two government publications: the *Monthly Labor Review* and *Occupational Outlook Quarterly.*

Human Resources

The information you obtain from written materials will come to life when you take the time to talk with people about their jobs, observe them at work, or read autobiographical sketches of people in different professions. Studs Terkel's book *Working* and the *Vocational Biographies* series (published by Vocational Biographies, Inc., Sauk Center, MN 56378), provide excellent sketches of people in different occupations.

Some people express dismay at the suggestion that they talk with people about their work. They say they do not know anyone in the field they are considering and that if they found such a person he or she wouldn't want to talk to them. A bit of detective work will solve the first problem, and a bit of self-confidence will solve the other.

Let's start with the detective work. Suppose you were interested in talking to an automobile insurance claims adjuster who happens to be a woman. (We've specified the person's sex because gender may be important to a female student who believes that the field provides limited opportunities for women.) If you know a female claims adjuster, you're in luck. All you need to do is call her to set up a visit. But let's make the problem more complex and assume you don't know such a person. One simple way of locating a female claims adjuster would be to look through the telephone yellow pages section under "insurance companies." Each insurance company will list its claims adjustment centers, so all you do is call several companies and ask if they have a female auto claims adjuster that you can talk to. If a company doesn't have one, you might ask the person on the other end if they know of a company that does. Your school or college placement officer may also be able to help you by providing the names of graduates in your area who could help you in your search.

Another way of approaching the problem would be to develop your own informational network. Social psychologist Stanley Milgram (1967) believes that we can contact anybody in the world with five to eight phone calls, even if we don't know the person. All we need to do is come up with a list of qualities the person must possess, including such characteristics as sex, place of residence, and occupation, and then plan a strategy for contacting that person. For example, if I wanted to contact a female claims adjuster in Boise, Idaho, I might start calling relatives or friends who live in or have visited Boise to get their ideas about whom I could contact in Boise. Or I might call my family's insurance agent about whom to contact. I would then call the persons that my local resources suggest, tell them what I was looking for, and, using their advice, whittle my search down a bit further. Milgram suggests that by the time you have made five such phone calls you should be in touch with the female claims adjuster from Boise. Needless to say, your task will be easier if you are looking for a person in the community where you live. But in either case, the basic method of investigation remains the same.

The second problem, that of overcoming reservations about talking to people about their professions, also has several solutions. Although many students believe that professional people are too busy to bother with students, our experience proves otherwise. Most people love to talk about what they do. Sure, there will be some who can't be bothered with talking about themselves, but if you are persistent and use your network of friends and relatives effectively, the odds are that you will be able to locate several people who are willing to spend some time discussing their work with you. We've also found that many graduates are willing to have students spend a day observing them at work. Thus, locating willing persons may not be a problem at all.

Students often stumble in this process because they don't have a clear set of questions they want answered. It is important that you clarify your lifestyle needs and use them as a framework for asking others about their lifestyles. If you are anxious about what to ask and how to ask it, you could develop a list of specific questions and find a friend or relative to help you through a practice interview. In that way you can refine your questions, overcome some of your fears, and sharpen your interviewing skills.

Here are some questions you might ask of the person you are interviewing:

1. Tell me a bit about your work history, the subjects you studied in high school or college, and the work experiences you have had that led you to your present position.
2. How long have you been in your present occupation and position?
3. What attracted you to your position?
4. Describe a typical day on your job.
5. What does it take to be a success in your field?
6. What do you enjoy most about your position?
7. What do you dislike about your position?
8. Are there specific skills that your position requires? What other fields require the same skills?

9. Are the demands of your position offset by the rewards it provides?
10. How does your job affect your home and leisure life? Does your work take you away from your nonwork pursuits more than you would like?
11. What does the future look like for someone in your professional specialty? Are there new or emerging areas in the field I should know about?
12. Do you have any specific advice for someone like me who is considering entering your profession? What courses should I take? What types of internship or work experience should I pursue? Are there professional journals in the field I should read or a local professional organization I might join to stay current in my knowledge of your field?

One final point: if you decide to use the interview-for-information approach, remember to send each person you interview a thank-you note.

Visiting, Volunteering, Working

Reading about an occupation and talking with people about it are two important ways of gathering career information. If you really want to explore an occupation, however, we encourage you to try to get some hands-on opportunities. Some corporations provide tours for the public to explain how they produce their products. You may be able to arrange a tour in a setting that employs people in the field you are interested in.

If you have the time and the motivation, you may be able to persuade an employer to allow you to work as a volunteer apprentice for one or more days as a way of finding out about an occupation and your reactions to it. It may also be possible to find part-time or summer work in the field or in related fields. Finally, you can take advantage of the cooperative education, internship, and externship opportunities that may be available on your campus. Through such programs, you will be able to work part-time in settings that relate to your degree program. An advantage of this, as well as of other hands-on opportunities you can participate in, is that in addition to being able to gather career information you will be building skills for securing a full-time job at graduation. In fact, many employers use volunteer and internship programs to evaluate and groom potential employees.

Evaluating Career Information

"Caution! Occupational information may be hazardous to your career." As far-fetched as this statement may seem, there is some truth to it. Hidden biases may be conveyed in occupational information. Labor projections are based on two premises—no war and no depression. Optimistic projections from some sources may represent an attempt to sell a field that is unstable. Be sure that your enthusiasm for a field with "opportunities for well-qualified applicants" does not blind you to its disadvantages (every field has some).

We noted earlier that until recently, participation in the American labor force was restricted for women and minorities, who traditionally have had access only to a limited number of service-oriented occupations. Recent surveys indicate that this picture is changing. According to a survey published in January 1985 in *Working Women* magazine and a 1988 U.S. Department of Labor survey, one-half to two thirds of women who are presently entering the labor force are choosing jobs that have traditionally been dominated by men. And, according to John Naisbitt and Patricia Aburdene (1990), authors of *Megatrends 2000,* the 1990s may witness more rapid changes than previous decades have. They observe that "women may have missed out on the industrial age, but they have established themselves in industries of the future" (p. 225). More specifically, women have taken two-thirds of the new jobs created by the information era and are reaching a "critical mass" (20 to 30 percent) in some administrative and management areas, where their ability to bring out the best in people and to facilitate rapid change through demonstrative and supportive leadership, rather than controlling and dominance, is an asset to their career success. Furthermore, in such fields as law, medical science, economics, university physical education teaching, petroleum engineering, and agricultural and food sciences, some women earn considerably more than men. However, social scientists Ann Morrison and Mary Ann Von Glinow (1990) have observed that despite these gains, many women and minorities still face an invisible and inpenetrable "glass ceiling" created by discriminatory hiring, training, and salary structures in the workplace that impede their career advancement. Available statistics from the U.S. Department of Labor (cited in *USA Today,* December 3, 1985, p. 6A) reveal that despite their increased entry into male-dominated positions, and the recent pattern of wives outgaining their husbands in salaries by about 12 percent, most women still lag behind men in their salaries, health insurance, and retirement benefits. These discrepancies are apparently caused by the high concentration of women in nonunion and service-related fields, which are traditionally weaker in fringe benefits, and by the lower wages and shorter job tenure of women.

In addition, a Virginia Slims survey of 4,000 adults (reported in *USA Today,* December 3, 1985) revealed that women are liable to feel discriminated against in a variety of jobs, including top government jobs, executive jobs, top professional jobs, and skilled labor jobs. More than 50 percent of the women surveyed indicated that they believed discrimination exists in these types of jobs. Thus, even though a growing number of women have been able to move out of traditional women's jobs, they continue to face subtle barriers in the work setting. According to the National Research Council (*USA Today,* December 3, 1985), these barriers for women include a tendency for employers to recruit employees from a male-dominated "old boy network," to require nonessential training and credentials, and to enforce departmental rather than company-wide seniority systems. Additional barriers noted in the *Working Women* survey mentioned earlier include the need for women to take time off to raise children (the major salary deflator for women) coupled with the tendency of women to take nontechnical subjects in school and to avoid careers that require many years of training.

One consequence of these barriers to career fulfillment for women and minorities has been a high number of discrimination complaints filed with the

U.S. Equal Employment Opportunity Commission. In 1988, the commission received close to 59,000 complaints. Data from the 1985 commission report indicated that, in descending order, the primary sources of complaints related to race, sex, and age. Most of these charges focused on the discharge of employees and on terms and conditions of employment, promotion, hiring, and wages. Another consequence of these discriminatory practices has been a flight of women and minorities from traditional corporate settings. Morrison and Von Glinow (1990) cite statistics that show that a growing number of women and African Americans are fleeing from corporate America to businesses that they have started on their own or to engage in other pursuits. Because of these discouraging patterns, the number of available role models for female and/or minority students interested in fields that have been traditionally open to white males are very few in number and may actually be declining in some work areas.

The sexual, ethnic, and racial biases associated with economic discrimination are subtly conveyed in many sources of career information. Pictures that show a person of a particular group working at a given profession tend to project the image that the field is for them only, thus confirming widespread and inaccurate beliefs about who should work where. This does not imply that the people who create informational materials want to exclude some groups from certain occupations, but it does demonstrate how the cultural stereotyping process has restricted the availability of potential role models for people wishing to explore certain fields. This can be discouraging, if you let it.

Be thorough. Use a wide variety of informational resources. Explore groups of related occupations and their different levels. Make sure the information you obtain is *current.* Check the date of each publication you read and compare the information it contains with the information from the most recent edition of the *Occupational Outlook Handbook.* And be sure that the information is *accurate* (and reasonably objective) by noting how the information was gathered, how many people were surveyed to obtain it, and who published it. Also, compare national trends with local trends. You may find that a field that is tight locally may be more open in other geographical areas.

Finally, use the activities in Appendix D to evaluate the information you have gathered in light of your lifestyle needs and preferences.

Some Questions to Consider

1. Spend some time with a family member who is knowledgeable about your ancestry. Have that person review your genealogy and the history of your family in the United States. Discuss family myths and stories and see if a pattern emerges that reflects some core cultural and family values. How do these values affect you and your family in the present? Where do these values fit along the historical continuum described in this chapter? How do they limit you? How do they support you?

2. a. What social stereotypes might be applied to you because of your
   (1) Age?
   (2) Race or ethnic background?
   (3) Gender?
   (4) Religious preference?
   (5) Sexual orientation?
   (6) Physical or intellectual capacities?

   b. How might these stereotypes limit your career? How might they enhance your chances of success?
   c. How do you feel about stereotypes that might be applied to you?
   d. How might your own attitudes and stereotypes about yourself help or hinder your chances of success?

3. What are your own views about "equal employment opportunity" and "affirmative action"? Should colleges and employers set aside positions or work contracts for groups of people who have been discriminated against in the past? If not, how would you address the problem if you were in an administrative or legislative position? Do you think the notions behind equal employment opportunity and affirmative action will help you or hinder you in your own career?

4. What level of work suits you the most right now? At what level do you plan to be in five years? In ten years?

5. Circle the three types of enterprises that most appeal to you as possible work settings when you graduate.

   a. Agriculture   g. Communication
   b. Mining   h. Trade
   c. Construction   i. Finance
   d. Manufacturing   j. Service
   e. Utilities   k. Government
   f. Transportation

6. In the spaces below, list the enterprises you have circled, tell why you selected them, and list the functional skills you have that may be used in that setting. (Use the Functional Skills Survey you completed in Chapter 3 to help you with your responses.)

   a. Kind of enterprise: _____

   (1) My reasons for selecting this enterprise are:

   _____

   _____

   (2) The functional skills I may use in this enterprise are:

   _____

   _____

b. Kind of enterprise: _____

   (1) My reasons for selecting this enterprise are:

   _____

   _____

   (2) The functional skills I may use in this enterprise are:

   _____

   _____

c. Kind of enterprise _____

   (1) My reasons for selecting this enterprise are:

   _____

   _____

   (2) The functional skills I may use in this enterprise are:

   _____

   _____

References and Resources

Axelson, J. D. (1985). *Counseling and development in a multicultural society.* Pacific Grove, CA: Brooks/Cole.

Bronowski, J. (1973). *The ascent of man.* Boston: Little, Brown.

Cahill, T. (1986). Getting lost: The case for creative ineptitude. *Outside, 11,* 25–28.

Campbell, D. (1974). *If you don't know where you're going, you'll probably end up somewhere else.* Niles, IL: Argus Communications.

Clinton, B. (1987). Undergraduate education in an increasingly complex world. *National Forum, 67,* 43–44.

Cosgrave, G. P. (1973). *Career planning: Search for a future.* Toronto: University of Toronto Press.

Dale, R. V. N. (1948, April). To youth who choose blindly. *Occupations,* p. 419.

Denues, C. (1972). *Career perspective: Your choice of work.* Worthington, OH: Charles D. Jones.

de Riencourt, A. (1974). *Sex and power in history.* New York: David McKay.

Downs, J. F. (1971). *Cultures in crisis.* Beverly Hills: Glencoe Press.

Easterbrook, C. (1989, July 24). The environment: Cleaning up our mess. *Newsweek,* pp. 26–42.

Holland, J. L. (1973). *Making vocational choices: A theory of careers.* Englewood Cliffs, NJ: Prentice-Hall.

Hopson, B., & Hough, P. (1973). *Exercises in personal and career development.* New York: APS Publications.

Information Please Almanac, Atlas and Yearbook, 1989 (42nd ed.). Boston: Houghton Mifflin.

Kohn, A. (1986). *No contest: The case against competition.* Boston: Houghton Mifflin.

Krannich, R. L. (1989). *Careering and recareering for the 1990s: The complete guide for planning your future.* Manassas, VA: Impact Publications.

Levine, E.S., & Padilla, A. M. (1980). *Crossing cultures in therapy: Pluralistic counseling for the Hispanic.* Pacific Grove, CA: Brooks/Cole.

Milgram, S. (1967). The small world problem. *Psychology Today, 1,* 62–67.

Morgan, L. H. (1887). *Ancient society.* Chicago: Charles H. Kerr.

Morrison, A. M., & Von Glinow, M. A. (1990). Women and minorities in management. *American Psychologist, 45,* 200–208.

Naisbitt, J., & Aburdene, P. (1990). *Megatrends 2000.* New York: William Morrow.

Neff, W. F. (1968). *Work and human behavior.* New York: Atherton Press.

Nobles, W. W. (1973). Psychological research and the Black self-concept: A critical review. *Journal of Social Issues, 29,* 11–31.

Rokeach, M., & Ball-Rokeach, S. J. (1989). Stability and change in American value priorities: 1968–1981. *American Psychologist, 44,* 775–784.

Sampson, E. E. (1989). The challenge of social change for psychology, globalization and psychology's theory of the person. *American Psychologist, 44,* 915–921.

Stewart, E. C. (1972). *American cultural patterns: A cross-cultural perspective.* LaGrange Park, IL: International Network.

Temple, J. (1989). *The genius of China: 3000 years of science, discoveries and invention.* New York: Simon & Schuster.

U.S. Department of Labor, Bureau of Labor Statistics (1988, September 7). *Labor force participation unchanged for mothers with young children* (USDL Publication No. 88–431). Washington, DC: U.S. Government Printing Office.

U.S. Department of Labor, Bureau of Labor Statistics (1989). *Employment and earnings 1989: 1988 annual averages* (no report number given). Washington, DC: U.S. Government Printing Office.

U.S. Department of Labor, Bureau of Labor Statistics (1989, April 28). *Employment and earnings characteristics of families* (USDL Publication No. 89–209). Washington, DC: U.S. Government Printing Office.

U.S. Department of Labor, Bureau of Labor Statistics (1989, first quarter). *Employment in perspective: Women in the labor force* (Report No. 767). Washington, DC: U.S. Government Printing Office.

U.S. Department of Labor, Bureau of Labor Statistics (1989, fourth quarter). *Employment in perspective: Minority workers* (Report No. 764). Washington, DC: U.S. Government Printing Office.

U.S. Department of Labor, Bureau of Labor Statistics (1989, Fall). *Occupational outlook quarterly.* Washington, DC: U.S. Government Printing Office.

U.S. Equal Employment Opportunity Commission (1985). *20th annual report.* Washington, DC: U.S. Government Printing Office.

CHAPTER SIX

Putting the Pieces Together

The future is not some place we are going to, but one
we are creating. The paths are not to be found,
but made, and the activity of making them
changes both the maker and the destination.

—John Schaar

It's the end of Career Day at Edgewood High School. The students had prepared,
with reports and research, to get the most out of meeting the adults who have
come from the community and a nearby college to speak and answer questions
as representatives of various careers and professions. The students have lots of
fears and conclusions and often disagree among themselves. Bret has his mind
made up. As the son of a professor, and coming from a family of educators, he
feels that teaching is the only road. He dismisses information about sales, small
business ownership, and vocational training with a slightly superior air, but inside he feels defensive. Gino tells Bret rather heatedly that there is more than
one career. Gino's father founded a successful construction company. Gino could
enter the family business right away, but his father would really be proud if
he went to college and maybe to law school. Gino is glad to have choices, but
he feels pulled in two directions. Gino talks about his older brother, Tony, who
has "stopped out" of college to work in a construction company owned by one
of their father's rivals. His dad is angry, and Gino thinks Tony is courageous
but maybe crazy. Tony says their dad does not have all the answers and that
he wants to explore on his own. He is doing what he believes in, but he is a
little scared. The guidance counselor reminds the students about John Hayes,
a speaker they had heard earlier in the day. John's company designs and manufac-
tures artificial limbs and medical equipment. His father, a prominent physician,
had pressured John to go to medical school. John talked about his not wanting
to go to medical school, having arguments with his dad, feeling guilty, and searching for and finally finding a way to combine his mechanical and engineering
interests with the medical ideals he had admired while growing up. John feels
good about his career, but he made it clear that finding and starting out on his
own path had not been easy.

Growth toward a career choice and toward a vocational self-image is a
specialized part of a larger whole—the development of an identity as an independent adult. As we learned in previous chapters, developing from a dependent
infant into an autonomous adult is a process that will continue in various forms
throughout life. Although career exploration and career choice may occur at
different ages and at different times in the life cycle, we make most decisions
about how to earn a living in early adulthood, when we start the larger task
of separating physically from our family and becoming financially independent.

To lay the groundwork for successful independent lives and individual iden-
tities, young adults in our society are expected to work at separating intellectually and emotionally from their parents and significant others. As children or
even as adolescents, most of us relied greatly on the opinions of others in determining what to do and even how to do it. Because the rules and demands of

school and home have guided our lives for at least 18 years, some of us may be bewildered when we are suddenly told to figure out what we want to do with the rest of our lives. Faced with these decisions, some people may be tempted to rely on the feelings or ideas of someone else, sometimes even without knowing that is what they are doing. Others, who grow up in families where it is assumed that they will become a doctor or take over the family business, have a different problem. Instead of having too many options, they believe they have none. Although they may be aware of other attractive alternatives, they feel they can't disappoint their families. Most people who change careers in their 30s or 40s do so because they have realized that their first career was not really *their* choice but a choice made by or for someone else.

Thus, learning to separate your own ideas and feelings about your future from those of others who have helped to shape and influence you is crucial. Of course, complete separation is not possible—nor would we want it. We have learned important skills, attitudes, and values from our families, and we continue to learn from friends, employers, teachers, life partners, and others. What is important is being able to listen to and weigh these external opinions and feelings and decide whether they are comfortable or fit with our own feelings and plans. We have been taught from the time we were small not to let ourselves be pressured into doing things that are not in our best interest ("Don't talk to strangers." "Say no to drugs."). In career choice, this means learning how we can best utilize our interests, talents, and values in the world of work, and being able to consider the views and demands of others without turning choices over to them. Our job, then, is to keep sight of this perspective, which can sometimes be difficult. A true career option exists only if we know ourselves, if we are aware of but not totally guided by the wishes of others, and if we have found ways of successfully expressing ourselves through a specific major or occupation.

Part of the process of separation involves knowing what and who is controlling our feelings and influencing our options. We all start life as helpless infants, with what psychologists call an "external locus of control." We are totally dependent, and our behaviors and later our attitudes are determined by what others tell us is good or bad and/or what the consequences will be. As we grow into and through adulthood, our main developmental goal is to learn to be physically and psychologically independent, as well as interdependent with (rather than dependent on) others. In this process we are developing an "internal locus of control"—the ability to control ourselves, to act rather than react, and to examine and refine our own goals, attitudes, and values to ensure that they are ours, not "swallowed whole" from someone or something external. After we have made progress in this never-ending task of defining ourselves, we can come to a decision by considering our own wishes and realities and can reward ourselves internally and be comfortable when we have done something we believe in, regardless of its popularity. This is not to say that we should be insensitive to the feelings of others. It means simply that our first and biggest responsibility is to do a constructive job of living our own lives.

Stages of Development

Many theorists on the subject of human development have proposed ways of understanding and "mapping" the stages of growth. We will look at one of these theories particularly as it pertains to early adulthood and career decision making. (Don't forget homemaking. Motherhood is a job choice, although many women these days hold another job simultaneously.) As we discuss development, put what you learn in the context of your own experiences and feelings and try to determine the stage through which you are now moving. Remember that people will be at different stages for reasons that have little to do with age. The characteristics of your family life, your parents, the community you grew up in, and your experiences determine how you grow, and how fast. Later in this chapter we will discuss some things that hinder this growth and how they may be dealt with.

William Perry (1970), and Lee Knefelkamp and Ron Slepitza (1976), developmental theorists who have specifically studied college students, say that all of us go through four general stages (actually nine, counting substages, but all the details are not important here) before we are able to make commitments based on our own well-informed and independent decisions. In the first stage, *dualism*, we view the world in terms of black or white, good or bad. "Right" is determined by what others think. In other words, decisions in this stage are based on external factors such as social stereotypes and the desire to do the right thing in the eyes of others. People who begin a career search with this outlook may believe there will be "only one right job" for them and that someone (a counselor) or something (a test or the approval of others) will tell them what it is. Such individuals are apt to have made a career choice early in their lives without much consideration or struggle and will give it up only with considerable frustration and a strong sense of personal failure. People who think dualistically will have difficulty completing the career decision process comfortably if they are forced to start over, because they focus on what others think (and often get conflicting information) and do not know what they themselves feel or think. To relieve their frustration, they may be tempted to make a dependent decision that may not fit them as they continue to grow.

As we move toward the second stage of development, *multiplicity*, we gradually become more aware of multiple possibilities for ourselves but remain interested in finding the "right" way of doing things, with the rightness of a choice still being guided primarily by the beliefs and wishes of others. Thus, instead of making a singular choice early in life to keep with a family tradition or expectation, people in the multiplistic stage may consider several academic or occupational possibilities. Nonetheless, they search through each possibility with the goal of finding the singular choice based on some external standard or process, not on their own needs and desires. Vocational explorers who continue to move on through this stage without making a premature decision, or one that is based solely on intuition, will continue developing their abilities to explore both themselves and the world, while tolerating ambiguity, confusion, delay, change, and anxiety about the future and the risks inherent in choices. They realize that information is incomplete, that there are no guarantees, and that they will nonetheless be responsible for what they choose and all its results. They are moving toward a planful decision, having realized that a dependent decision would mean giving up control over the choice and that an intuitive decision would mean "leaping before they look."

As we become more aware of our selves and of our own needs and feelings, we realize that we need to develop a process of analyzing and synthesizing information so that we can be flexible enough to work within the confusion and change engendered by continuous new information and be able to match and integrate internal and external sources of information. People who make decisions early in this stage may make an intuitive decision. They are beginning to understand themselves and they see more choices than does a dualist, but they may be afraid of the delays and risks involved in a planful decision and may attempt to jump ahead by doing what "feels right" without considering relevant external information.

As we move toward a greater ability to comprehend information both about our selves and about the environment, we enter Perry's third stage of perception and growth: *relativism*. Now we realize not only that there are many possible options but also that their rightness is not absolute but relative to our own upbringing and beliefs, our cultural conventions, and the laws and codes of our society. We begin to synthesize our own internal signals with information from the environment and to develop a personal decision-making process. We are able to see the need for the rules of family and society, which bind us together and keep order, but also the need to realize that sometimes being true to our inner selves may require us to go against some set of external values, even though it may produce discomfort or conflict.

The final stage of development, *commitment in relativism*, occurs when we become comfortable enough with the risks and responsibilities of our own adulthood to make a planful choice, knowing that it is not foolproof or in some cases even permanent. It represents the integration of internal and external voices and the realization that the only way we can impose order on the multitude of external options and "right" answers is by choosing, believing in ourselves, and actively working to make the life that we want. The ideal personification of this last stage, which most of us don't reach in our lifetimes, is someone like Gandhi or Martin Luther King Jr., who developed such an advanced sense of commitment and personal values that they found constructive ways to defy laws and even death to stand for what they believed. As psychologist David Matteson (1975, p. 226) so aptly put it, "To come of age is to realize that the creation of values lies in our own hands. We now wear the masks of the gods."

Commitment in relativism can be confusing and risky, because as the name implies it means a self-directed choice made among multiple feasible alternatives. As with most things, however, there is a positive side. The act of commitment allows us to free the energy devoted to deciding and use it to deepen and expand our area of choice, which leads to increased self-confidence and a sense of anticipation about the future. And although having several attractive career choices makes deciding harder, it allows us to do contingency planning. If our primary choice is not feasible, must be postponed, or ceases to interest us, we have a range of acceptable options to fall back on. We can plan our education so that if we want to make a career change at some point, several paths are open to us. This is usually a wise strategy, because even if we do not change internally the job market may. In the 1990s, with large groups of jobs regularly being created or becoming obsolete through changes in the economy, farsighted people are opening their minds to all possible interests and opportunities, filing them away for future reference.

Interpersonal Influences

The problems that most of us will encounter when we grow into relativism and commitment are not likely to be great problems of moral principle, but rather the daily discomforts that come with exercising independent thinking, feelings, and behavior. There is anxiety associated with examining ourselves and our realistic opportunities—we may find problems or limitations we prefer to ignore. There is risk involved in change, in trying new things, in committing ourselves to a decision with an uncertain outcome. Finally, there is the burden of responsibility for the choices we make and their consequences.

A scary independent choice may seem especially difficult if others about whom we care disagree with our views. Conflict, or at least disapproval, may greet our tentative plans and make it more difficult for us to stick with them. Most of us have loved ones who want to be supportive but who nonetheless hold definite values and hopes for us—for example, that we be in a certain business or profession, mix with certain kinds of people, support a family (or take care of a family). They hold beliefs about what makes a "successful" adult—one who makes money, helps others, or acquires education or prestige. If we have a family of our own creation—a spouse and/or children—the problem becomes more complex, both financially and emotionally. We may experience conflict or guilt about taking time and money away from the family to pursue or change a career. Many times these loved ones feel let down because our choices are different and do not realize that they may really be expecting us to meet their needs instead of our own needs. Sometimes it is necessary, though unpleasant, to fight it out with those we love in order to resolve our discomfort and help them understand our reasoning and goals. This may lead to acceptance or compromise.

If you find that your initial announcement of career choices or interests causes consternation or conflict, you may need some time to think things through. Instead of perceiving the disagreement as a criticism of you or your judgment, try to understand the point of view of the others involved:

1. They may lack information about you or your choice.
2. They may believe that you are bucking an important family tradition.
3. Your choice may not fit their image of you.

4. They may think they have a better understanding of you or the world of work than you do.
5. Even though you've changed, they may still view you the way you were before.
6. They may believe that you should engage only in certain kinds of work because of your sex or ethnic background.
7. They may be disappointed because they think your goals are either too low or unrealistically high.
8. They may be afraid of losing you because you are becoming independent and are changing your views of life.
9. They may be concerned about the costs associated with your choice because they are footing the bill for your education or training.
10. They may be dependent on you financially or emotionally and fear your plan will jeopardize their current way of living.
11. They may be upset about the time or attention this choice will take away from the family.

Then consider your own feelings and attitudes. If you respond defensively because you have strong feelings that will interfere with your perspective, you may want to take some time out, or to talk with someone supportive to get yourself calmed down and more confident before renewing discussions with your loved ones. When you do return to your significant person or group to work at resolving the differences, try to do the following.

1. *Select a comfortable place to discuss your plan.* A public setting such as a park or a restaurant can be a good place to share your decision. It can help you feel relaxed, create the atmosphere of a special occasion, and encourage a sense of mutual understanding.

2. *Be positive, clear, and calm in presenting your choice.* Know yourself and what you want to do and can do. Use accurate, current, and unbiased career information to back up your decision and show that it is realistic and carefully thought out. Express your views positively and with enthusiasm.

3. *Be open to learn from what others say.* Invite their reactions without losing sight of your own objectives. Be willing to change your mind if you find that you have not seen things as fully or clearly as you had first thought.

4. *Be willing to listen to others.* Acknowledge the feelings and interpretations of others before challenging them. Put yourself in the other person's frame of mind and let him or her know that you are trying to understand their point of view without compromising your own objectives.

5. *Be patient.* It may take a while for the other person to change his or her views. Plant a seed of thought and nourish it over time with additional facts and observations. Knowing how they usually behave can help you understand their challenge until they are willing to see your side.

6. *Build on your commonalities* and agreements *and minimize your differences.* This should be done honestly and openly, not in a shallow, camouflaging way. Show that you are not in total disagreement about everything.

7. *Accept responsibility for your part of the conflict.* If conflict arises, don't blame or placate others—talk about it instead.

8. *Act assertively.* Express your needs and feelings in a nonjudgmental, responsible way. Identify the source(s) of disagreement (probably where interpretations differ) and discuss strategies for moving beyond them. For example, it's quite possible that the pressure to live up to a family tradition would make you feel angry and disappointed. Stating what you feel and what causes you to feel that way, and asking that the family not have such fixed expectations of you, is an assertive way of dealing with the situation. Another assertive technique is to keep the discussion focused on the choice to be made, rather than letting it drift into an argument about personalities or past disagreements. If you have a job and/or a family of your own, you can be assertive by suggesting acceptable compromises. You may be able to do what you want to but change your job, timetable, or other plans to minimize time and money pressures on yourself and on others.

The flowchart in Figure 6-1 gives a step-by-step example of how a hypothetical student, Suzanne, might deal with a family's reactions. Of course, not all such situations have an "ideal" outcome. If you think you are falling into self-defeating behaviors or avoiding conflict, you can turn to someone more objective to help sort things out. If you believe you have said and done all you can to resolve the issue and find that the people who are important to you are still upset, you may feel that you must choose between a harmonious relationship and your career. At this point you also have some sorting to do and may need help to see all sides of the problem. It is important to consider the feelings of people you love, especially if it is someone, like a spouse, who may have to share directly in the results of your decision. But if you are thinking of compromising in your decision because of someone else's opinions, it is crucial to examine both yourself and their feedback carefully. To avoid long-term problems with your career satisfaction, your choice must be made not because you are afraid of someone else's reaction but because it is in your best interests and is comfortable for you.

Myths

Another thing that makes it more difficult for us to grow into a planful career commitment is the number of myths that we encounter—and believe—about career decisions. These are learned during our early development, when we are still seeing things dualistically and depending on external sources for "right" answers. Some of the earliest myths we encounter are hard to recognize because they may be based on values, beliefs, and attitudes we learned from the family. For example:

1. Everyone must climb the ladder of success, even if it means doing things that are not interesting.
2. Go where the money is, regardless of what kind of work it involves.

Behavior →	Interpretation →	Feelings →
Suzanne announces at a family dinner that she is leaving teacher education to major in business.	Her father and husband are both college professors with Ph.D.'s. They feel she is abandoning a family tradition of careers in education. Her mother and her husband feel that a business career won't combine well with motherhood.	Family members feel hurt, angry, disappointed, worried that Suzanne is making the "wrong" choice. She feels the same things.

Behavior →	Interpretation →	Feelings →	Behaviors →	Outcomes
Her family tells her she is making a mistake. Her father tells her she is choosing a materialistic career that won't benefit society. Mom and husband warn that she will not have the time or energy to spend with her children that a teacher would.	Suzanne may make several interpretations, leading to different feelings and behaviors: (a) I'm letting my family down.	She feels: Guilty, selfish.	Continues with education but is unhappy.	Trains for a career she doesn't like, resents her family's interference, and later has to change careers.

(b) **My judgment is bad.**	Self-doubt, anxiety.	Worries, vacillates, asks for advice.	Loses valuable time and confidence, is uncertain about whatever decision she makes.
(c) **Motherhood is only compatible with certain careers.**	Trapped, fearful about future.	Avoids a decision, studies less, and goes out more.	Loses time, grades drop, ends up on probation, and cannot change majors.
(d) **My family doesn't care what I want.**	Angry, hurt.	Rebelliously changes her major and remains angry at the family.	Goes into business at the cost of anger and strained relationships. Unresolved resentments later interfere with her career.
(e) **I need to work at clearing this up.**	Hopeful, but worried.	Thinks and does research to confirm and improve her ability to explain her decision.	Talks out decision, listens to family arguments, works out compromises. She will try business but keep them informed and be alert for problems.

FIGURE 6-1 Sharing a decision with others: What can happen.

3. Work is the only way to personal fulfillment.
4. We should respect tradition and maintain different types of work for men and women.
5. I must choose between really having a career and having a family.
6. Women shouldn't compete with men for jobs, especially jobs that involve creativity, managing others, and decision making. Because they are passive, emotional, and respond to things intuitively, women just aren't equipped to handle such situations.
7. If I lose a job to a woman, it means I'm inadequate as a male.
8. If my spouse has to go to work, it means I've failed as a husband.
9. If I say no to what others expect of me, I am insensitive and unlovable.

Messages our families send us about work—such as what meanings and rewards work should bring, or what sexes (or other groups) should do what jobs—need to be recognized and examined for what they are: someone else's ideas. If we subject these messages to the light of our own personal conclusions, feedback from others, and information about the world of work and still feel comfortable with them, then we may want to incorporate them into the set of beliefs we hold—out of choice, not because we feel we must conform to outside expectations. Developing our own choices and ideas is central to the process of becoming an independent adult. This means that we cannot always do what others expect and still be true to ourselves.

The current workplace reflects the reality that many jobs once thought to require physical strength can be done effectively by women using other skills. While not usually equal to men in physical strength, women now are doing such jobs once reserved for men as firefighting, operating heavy equipment, and police work on the beat.

Current surveys suggest that work satisfaction and success at work mean different things to different people. Many people indicate that the recognition and satisfaction gained from work are more important to them than money. Surveys about work satisfaction reveal that there is another group of people who say they work only "for a living" and that their primary satisfaction in life comes from leisure activities or family. Clearly there is no "right" answer.

Other myths that emerge from our early years come from dualistic, dependent ways of looking at situations. They include:

1. The choice of a major or occupation is irreversible. Once you make it you cannot change your mind.
2. There is a single right career for everyone.
3. It is not okay to be undecided, because being undecided is a sign of immaturity.
4. Nobody else is undecided. I'm all alone.
5. I know other people who have known what they wanted to be since childhood. Something's wrong with me because I can't be that way.
6. Life is always fair.
7. Life is always unfair.

8. Somewhere there is a test that can tell me what to do with the rest of my life.
9. Others know what is best for me.
10. Somewhere there is an expert who can tell me what to do.
11. If you can find out what you are interested in, you will automatically do well at it.

Most of these myths are kept alive when people do not gather more information and when they cling to old views out of fear of change. These myths suggest that everything is black or white and that there is some way of discovering the one "right" career. Moving into the multiplistic stage by increasing our knowledge both of ourselves and of the world enables us to see more options, shades of grey, and ways in which different things are right for different people.

Some 30 to 50 percent of entering college freshmen change their majors at least once by graduation. Although this may cause some short-term aggravation and inconvenience, it prevents much long-term dissatisfaction and shows that a choice is not irreversible, that it is all right and even common to be undecided. Undecidedness or change is a natural part of life because we are continually growing and acquiring new information. Sometimes the wisest decision a person can make is not to decide—temporarily.

There are 20,000 occupations in the U.S. Department of Labor's *Dictionary of Occupational Titles*, grouped according to skills. Skill and interest inventories confirm that many jobs can be grouped together in different ways because of certain things they have in common. This suggests what is indeed happening more and more in the world today: as individuals grow and the economy changes, many people will move into areas related to—or even far afield from—their original jobs. In other words, we need to remain open to expanding our list of acceptable options if we are to continue to grow in our careers.

This complexity also indicates why it is impossible for any test or expert to tell us what is right for ourselves. At best, these external aids can help us discover our interests, skills, and attitudes and how they may relate to certain career directions. In spite of continued improvements in vocational testing and in research on career choice, statistics show that the best predictor of what occupation a person will choose is what that person has said he or she will do. Our best path is to explore how realistic our wishes and interests are and whether our skills and interests match. Interest does provide motivation to acquire skills, but it does not guarantee that those skills will be acquired. A satisfying career is one that blends our skills and interests as well as other aspects of ourselves, including our work values and personal aspirations. Sometimes it is tempting to cling to myths because they give us an excuse to avoid the effort and responsibility involved in researching and making our decisions.

Still other myths are difficult for us to let go of because they strongly influence our feelings about ourselves. They too are easy to hide behind when reality is frightening. Such myths are:

1. If things don't go the way I expect, it means that I'm a failure.
2. In order to have a feeling of worth, I should be and must be thoroughly competent, adequate, intelligent, and achieving in all possible respects.

3. People are either successful or complete failures in their career pursuits. There's no in-between.
4. I'm unhappy when I think about selecting a career goal, because things external to me make me that way.
5. A person should be in total control of his or her career.
6. You must thoroughly analyze all aspects of a choice before you implement it; otherwise you're not really prepared.
7. The world of work is changing so rapidly that you can't really plan for the future.
8. If I get away from the pressure to decide—if I take a year or two off from college—I'll be able to make a better decision.

Like many of the myths already mentioned, these myths too are fed by our self-doubts and unrealistic expectations. Many things in the world cannot be predicted. The only thing we really have control of is ourselves. Things in the school of experience are learned by trial and error. If we cannot bounce back and learn from problems, if we run away from our problems or blame them on externals, we cannot grow. Myths 6, 7, and 8 above are especially handy rationalizations for avoiding the risk that comes with making a commitment. There is only so much we can know or control, and time will not change the fact that in order for us to move forward, a decision must be made and implemented, despite all its uncertainties.

Integrated Career Choices

The conflicts, doubts, and changes we encounter in examining ourselves and in leaving behind the myths and the dependent decisions may be difficult, but they are not negative. They are part of the solution, necessary vehicles for growth. We must move through the stage of "right" answers and the stage of confusion to the realization that we create our own options and answers by choosing from available alternatives those that fit us. To accomplish this, we must examine our values, beliefs, interests, abilities, opportunities, and relationships. In developmental terms, integration means taking the internal (self-knowledge: attitudes, values, needs, feelings, interests, and abilities) and the external (the realities of the workplace, the opinions of others, the changing environment) and making them work together.

If this process, represented in Figure 6-2, is short-circuited, we are left without the ability to make (and appropriately change) decisions and commitments. Going through all the steps of gathering information about ourselves and the world of work and considering all the elements is difficult and sometimes discouraging. Doing this while still holding on to our dreams and ideals, being realistic without being cynical, accepting external limitations gracefully, and managing our own feelings requires courage and consistent effort. But when

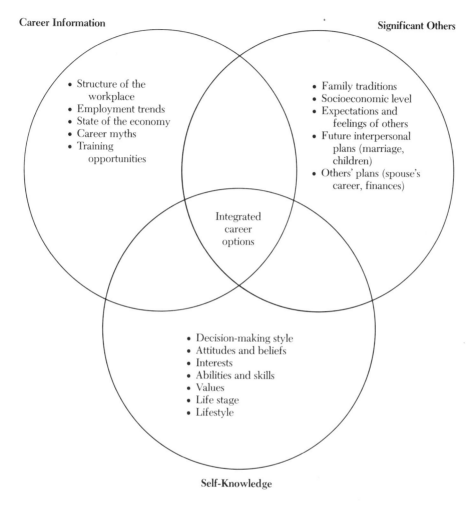

Career Information

Significant Others

- Structure of the workplace
- Employment trends
- State of the economy
- Career myths
- Training opportunities

- Family traditions
- Socioeconomic level
- Expectations and feelings of others
- Future interpersonal plans (marriage, children)
- Others' plans (spouse's career, finances)

Integrated career options

- Decision-making style
- Attitudes and beliefs
- Interests
- Abilities and skills
- Values
- Life stage
- Lifestyle

Self-Knowledge

FIGURE 6-2   Self-knowledge, career information, and the dreams of significant others: three factors to consider in developing integrated career options.

this process of integration is completed, we will be able to make and enjoy our best adult decisions and commitments.

Career Roadblocks

Read the following vignettes. For each situation, brainstorm ideas for solutions. Write them down. (Remember, brainstorming means just throwing in all ideas without evaluating them.) Then take the ideas and evaluate their pros and cons. Notice whether they seem dualistic, multiplistic, or relativistic. Note who is influencing the decision-maker and whether you think that influence is legitimate. See whether you can spot any ideas based on career myths. You do not have to find a solution, but try to determine what you think is the best solution and why.

1. Pat is a homemaker who wants to return to her career. She and Bob have two small children. When they started their family, both agreed that preschool children need a full-time mother. Bob still feels that way, but Pat has been home three and a half years and feels as if the business world is passing her by.

2. Leland wants to return to school and retrain himself in order to get out of a job he does not like. However, the program he wants is full-time for two years, which means that he, Candy, and their son would have to live on her income as a secretary. This would result in a greatly reduced lifestyle and a smaller place to live, among other sacrifices. Candy wants Leland to be happy, but she is upset about these drastic changes. She doesn't understand why he took the job in the first place if it wasn't the right job for him.

3. Dennis and Susan are married and have just finished graduate school. Susan is a veterinarian specializing in large animals and has two likely offers, both in wonderful rural settings in the Midwest. Dennis is an expert in high-tech electronics, and his best opportunities are in highly populated areas like Boston or New York.

4. Tanya is a senior in college who has won a fellowship to go on for a Ph.D. She is surprised but thrilled and feels that under the circumstances she can postpone her family until she has her doctorate and is established—say, age 32 or so. Her fiancé, Harley, is against this. His parents were older when he was born, and he has always planned to have his children when he is young. He is hurt because he believes that a family should come first; he feels that Tanya can return to school when the children are older.

5. Jay was recently passed up for a promotion at age 46. He makes good money but realizes that he will never go any higher in the company. He doesn't get along with his new boss. He wants to quit and turn his hobby of toymaking into a mail-order business. His wife, Glenda, is fearful about the financial risk. She thinks she is too old now to start working, and they will soon have two children ready for college.

6. Pearl is the head of a large data-processing department that is facing cutbacks. She must lay off one of the following employees. Which one should she let go and why?
    a. A recently hired new college graduate who catches on quickly but has no experience.
    b. A 59-year-old woman who has been there 30 years. She is not energetic but is careful and thorough.
    c. A 32-year-old woman who is a good worker but who is absent frequently (from a crucial job) because of a handicapped child.
    d. A 33-year-old man who has one of the less essential jobs in the department but is a close friend of the company's owner.
    e. A new immigrant who has some valuable technical expertise but takes extra time because of difficulty with the English language.

Letter to _____

Prepare a letter about your career plans to the person or people who are most important to you—your parents, spouse, fiancé, children, or friends. Use the following points as guidelines:

1. What I have learned about myself—interests, abilities, values, and what I need and want from a career.
2. What I have learned about the world of work and how it applies to me.
3. What career alternatives I have chosen and why.
4. What questions I have about how others might perceive my choice.
5. What myths or prejudices I think my loved ones and I might be subject to.
6. Why I might be nervous about sharing my feelings and ideas.
7. What kind of response I hope for.
8. Areas in which I would welcome advice.
9. What I plan to do next.

If you need more clarification regarding where you stand or what to tell others about your potential career commitments at this point, additional exercises are available in Appendix F. One, entitled "When Others Challenge Your Career Choice," takes you through the process of communicating with family members about your decisions, like Suzanne in Figure 6-1. The other, entitled "Removing Myths and Beliefs That Block Effective Career Decision Making," will help you identify and correct myths and misconceptions that may create internal roadblocks in your decision process.

Identifying Pathways and Roadblocks

There are three sources of information and potential interference that have to be considered for a balanced decision. These three (see Figure 6-2 on page 123) are career information, significant others, and self-knowledge. Use the following exercise to evaluate where you stand on each of these.

1. Which of the three areas do I know the most about?

_____

What is there in this area that I still need to work on to increase my understanding? _____

2. Which of these areas do I feel best or most confident about? (This is not necessarily the same as question 1. Consult your feelings, not your knowledge base.)

_____

_____

Why do I feel good about this? _____

_____

3. Which area do I know the least about? _____

_____

What things can I do to learn more about it? _____

_____

How do I plan to do this? _____

_____

_____

_____

4. What area do I feel most scared or uncertain about? _____

_____

Why? _____

_____

What can I do to feel better about this? _____

_____

5. What one thing, if changed, would help me the most? _____

_____

What (if anything) can I do about it now? _____

_____

6. What strengths do I know I have that I can fall back on? _____

_____

_____

6. How can I use these to help in areas where I have problems or limitations?

References and Resources

Carney, C. G., and Reynolds, A. (1985). *When others challenge your career choice: Strategies for conflict resolution.* Columbus: Ohio State University, Counseling and Consultation Service.

Knefelkamp, L. L., and Slepitza, R. (1976). A cognitive-developmental model of career development: An adaptation of the Perry scheme. *Counseling Psychologist, 6*(3), 53–58.

Matteson, D. R. (1975). *Adolescence today: Sex roles and the search for identity.* Homewood, IL: Dorsey Press.

Perry, W. G. (1970). *Forms of intellectual and ethical development in the college years.* New York: Holt, Rinehart, & Winston.

CHAPTER SEVEN

Finding a Job
Is a Job!

When nothing else seems to help, I go and watch the
stone cutter hammering away at his rock,
perhaps a hundred times without a crack
showing in it. Yet on the hundred-and-first blow
the rock will split in two, and I know that it was
not only that blow which split it, but all that had
gone before.

—*Jacob A. Riis*

5:30 P.M. "It's been a long and frustrating afternoon," Mr. Edwards thought as
he picked up his briefcase and walked out of the interviewing room of the college placement office. He'd interviewed five students since he had arrived on
campus that morning, but he hadn't found the right combination of enthusiasm,
style, and experience essential for the position. Rich, the first candidate, seemed
to be job shopping and wasn't goal directed in his approach. The second, Barbara,
was bright and interested in the position and was minimally qualified for it but
wasn't well rounded. She had spent a lot of time studying and had neglected
opportunities to work during the summer and engage in the social/cultural
aspects of college life. Robert, the third, had a poorly prepared resumé, complete with whiteouts. The fourth, Cheryl, was overly anxious, made little eye
contact, and either misunderstood questions or ignored them in her effort to
sell herself. Roseann, the last student, had the confidence and experience for
the position but didn't want to relocate, sure death for someone who wanted
to work her way up in the administrative structure of a national organization.

As he was walking to his car, his mind drifted to the legendary football coach
Vince Lombardi, who is quoted as saying, "If you aren't fired with enthusiasm
you will be fired with enthusiasm." Mr. Edwards decided to put it another way—
"If you aren't fired with enthusiasm, you won't be hired with enthusiasm." His
train of thought continued: "I just wish they'd prepare earlier and think more
about what they want ahead of time. It would save them a lot of disappointment and me a lot of time. I hope things will improve tomorrow."

As he found out later that night during dinner with some other interviewers,
every profession has its quirky and humorous side; and employment interviews
are not excepted from strange twists of events. The conversation turned to an
article one of them had seen in the Columbus, Ohio, daily newspaper the *Columbus Dispatch* (July 19, 1989). Mike Hardin, a feature writer, described some
humorous events he had been told about by some corporate interviewers. One
interviewer described a candidate who answered each question using a different
voice of a Looney Tunes character. Another applicant jumped up during the
interview, knocked over his chair, and asked the interviewer, "Does my beard
scare you?" She said it didn't, but he did.

Other tales included a top executive who was told by a female candidate
that her professional goal was to replace him. Another top executive told of a
bald candidate who excused himself from the interview and returned a few
minutes later wearing a hairpiece. There were also tales of a candidate who sat

through the interview listening to a Walkman, a candidate who swore his loyalty by saying he would get a tattoo with the company logo if he got the job, another who called his therapist for advice on a tough question, one who bolted from the interview to run home and turn off the stove he had left on, another who kept her raincoat on in a failed attempt to avoid revealing that she had forgotten to put on her skirt, another who had forgotten to zip his fly, and one who fell over when he stood up at the end of the interview because his foot had fallen asleep.

Although Mr. Edwards laughed at the stories, he realized how disappointed some of the applicants he had interviewed that day would be when they received a letter of rejection from him.

All of these stories about interviewing disasters share a common theme: a primary reason why students have difficulty in securing a job is their inability to communicate their interests and talents effectively to an employer. To avoid this pitfall, we encourage you to start preparing for your job search well in advance of your senior year—ideally, during your freshman year, when you may be seeking part-time and summer jobs—so you can refine your approach before graduation. While it is true that a temporary job may involve less personal investment than a "real," long-term job, there are some important similarities between the two. If you recognize and capitalize on these similarities, the odds are that you will be more satisfied as you pursue your career goals.

Profiting from Experience

Temporary and long-term work share common opportunities to learn and to demonstrate new skills. The newspaper route you may have had when you were younger provided chances to learn how to deal with the public, to sell a product, to manage money, and to organize time around work tasks. Think about the rainy days when you were forced to demonstrate perseverance and "intestinal fortitude"!

As noted in Chapter 5, it is wise to investigate and consider any appropriate volunteer or cooperative educational experiences that may be available through your college. Such experiences are a rich source of occupational information. They provide opportunities to confirm and develop your skills and to make contact with potential employers.

Because the skills you demonstrate in temporary jobs can be applied to long-term settings, it helps to catalog your past work experiences. Include in your list any involvements you have in student and community organizations while in school. Making this list will help you recall and pull together the bits and pieces of your work-related experiences. A simple way of doing this is to use an index card, such as the one shown on page 131, to record each of your learning experiences on the Personal Skills Inventory at the end of this chapter. Catalog past jobs, and begin now to keep a current record of new experiences as they occur.

Temporary and long-term jobs also involve similar job-search processes. Unless you worked in your family's business, you had to do some job campaigning to locate any jobs you have held.

Activity _____

Place (address) _____

Dates _____ Supervisor _____

Salary (if any) _____

Description of duties:

Skills I demonstrated:

Interests I expressed:

Values I lived up to:

Generally speaking, the major difference between campaigning for temporary jobs and campaigning for more permanent jobs is that, since a greater commitment is being made in the latter, a longer and more formalized procedure is usually required. Resumés must be prepared, cover letters transmitted, and formal interviews conducted. If you wait until near graduation to develop your formal job-hunting skills, you will probably experience some distress about the process and feel rushed. After all, it is a new situation that requires development of new skills. While practice may not make perfect, it does a lot to create self-assurance, prevent mistakes, and relieve the anxiety of a job campaign. Consequently, this chapter is written to help you learn formal job-search skills that can be used while applying for temporary or volunteer work prior to graduation as well as for permanent jobs when you graduate.

The Traditional Job Campaign

To conduct an effective job campaign you will need to answer four questions:

1. What do I want to do?
2. When will I begin?
3. Where do I want to work?
4. How will I go about getting a job?

What Do I Want to Do?

Narrowing down and learning about the possible answers to this question has been your goal up to this point. Cornerstones of this decision are your personal qualities and your self-image. These include preferences, attitudes, beliefs, values, interests, and skills. You have expressed them in your work history, self-assessment activities, Holland personality types, ideal job description, lifestyle preferences, daily decisions, and interaction with others. They are in turn affected by your history, experience, decision and planning style, life stage, and choice of lifestyle. When it comes to making and implementing tentative commitments, attention must be paid to specific preferences, such as work location, environment, and level, to the training and experience needed, and to the balance between what you must give to the job and what you will get out of it. Many of these issues can be clarified by the search for occupational information and opportunities.

When Will I Begin?

This question has two parts: When do you want to start to work? and When will you begin your job campaign? Starting at the end first—a date for starting work—will allow you to plan time to conduct a thorough job campaign, one that will permit you to explore a variety of options under minimal time pressures. While there are no precise rules for how much time you may need to spend preparing for and conducting a job campaign, remember that planning ahead will produce better results. For example, if you are thinking about working at a national park for the summer, you might start writing for information during the preceding fall. Then you have at least five months to explore your options and another five months to conduct a formal job-search process.

Where Do I Want to Work?

Having clarified a personal direction and decided how much time you need for your job campaign, you can begin the task of identifying and evaluating specific work opportunities. These opportunities can be identified in a variety of ways: friends and relatives, newspapers and trade journals, professional associations, offices, government and private employment services, and direct contact with employers. Take advantage of the placement office on your campus. Your placement officer can help you locate jobs, help you polish your written application materials and interviewing skills, and match you with employers who are recruiting students on your campus.

Once a list of potential employers has been generated, the actual task of job campaigning can be started. The traditional way of doing this involves preparing a resumé that summarizes your background, then sending the resumé, with an accompanying cover letter, to prospective employers in hopes of securing a follow-up interview. During the on-site interview, a mutual negotiation process occurs. You and the employer balance your individual wants and needs against each other's aims and objectives. More will be said about this shortly.

A bit of preliminary research about each organization you are thinking of contacting can help you present yourself (on paper and personally) in a way that stands out in a large pool of applicants. It can also boost your confidence and help you prepare for subsequent job interviews. Gather as much information as you can about the employers that interest you. Use company brochures, Dun and Bradstreet reports, public financial information (including salary information, which is vital in negotiating employment conditions), and word-of-mouth insights from friends, family, your college adviser, and your placement officer. All this can give you a picture of a firm's economic stability and growth potential.

Most job applicants use a mass-mailing procedure, sending the same resumé and cover letter to all employers, regardless of how the companies differ. While this approach can have some success, it may not catch an employer's eyes as effectively as a cover letter that shows you have done your homework and know about the employer's enterprise. The background information you have gathered to identify potential employers can be used in tailoring your cover letter to an employer's needs. Although most students use the same resumé with different cover letters for different employers, some attempt to create a cover letter and resumé for each employer. There are no clear rules about this, and we know of no evidence to support either approach. The best advice we can give is to choose an approach that best suits your own style and the amount of time and money you are willing to spend in preparing your resumé.

The knowledge you have about employers can also help you make decisions about whether to send out applications in the first place. After all, employees hire employers too! In making such initial decisions, it is helpful to prepare a list of criteria for evaluating employers. Some criteria you may wish to use include the size of the organization, its location, its history and image, its products or services, its administrative and promotional structure, its atmosphere and attitudes toward employees, and its future prospects—in short, the same requirements you would use to evaluate a full-time job. Specific guidelines for preparing a cover letter and resumé are provided later in this chapter. You may also wish to use Richard Bolles' 1981 book *The Three Boxes of Life* to identify other ways of locating employment information.

A Novel Approach to Job Campaigning   John Crystal and Richard Bolles (1980) have developed an alternative approach to the traditional job search just discussed. As with the traditional approach, they advocate that you start your job campaign by identifying the type of work you want to perform (the skills and interests you want to make use of through your work). After you determine what you want to do, they suggest that you identify the specific geographical location where you want to live. You can do this by making up a list of criteria for your ideal living and working environment (size of the community, weather preferences, terrain, leisure and cultural opportunities) and then identifying the place or places that most closely match these criteria. Once you have decided on a particular place, Crystal and Bolles suggest that you visit it to conduct a job campaign. The local telephone company can assist you in the early exploration process by sending you copies of directories for communities that interest you. Directories, also available in public libraries, can be used to explore community resources and to identify and contact potential employers. Visiting different areas can be an expensive way to find a job, but one way to offset the costs is to use the job campaign as a working vacation by visiting areas of interest during free time prior to a job search.

Crystal and his associates suggest that two steps be taken in contacting employers in your preferred environment. *The first step is to conduct a community survey.* This requires that you locate at least one work setting where your talents can be utilized and attempt to set up an information-gathering interview with the person who makes decisions about personnel in that setting. Such persons might include vice-presidents, managers, and personnel directors, but not clerks and receptionists, who simply implement decisions. The information-gathering interview is used to explore in a personal way the atmosphere of the company, its plans for the future, and the specific needs of the employer. The idea is to gather and share information, *not* to secure a job. Remembering this can alleviate your anxieties about applying for a job and provide valuable insights into the organization. At the end of the information-gathering interview, you can ask the person you have interviewed for names of other individuals in similar positions who can be contacted for additional informational interviews. These persons are then contacted and interviewed in a similar manner until the entire community has been canvassed.

A thorough informational-interviewing campaign will cover most of the employers who may have jobs of the type you wish to pursue. This can lead to two important outcomes. (1) You will know where the potential but hidden jobs are (Richard Irish [1987] suggests that up to 80 percent of the jobs in the United States are hidden) and (2) you will know which companies offer the work atmosphere that most appeals to you. Having this knowledge, you can eliminate undesirable prospects and pursue more desirable ones.

The second step in this process is to develop a prospectus to submit to desired employers. The prospectus should include your observations of the positive aspects of the employer's setting, your projections of the employer's needs, and the special qualities you have to offer to fill those needs. In essence, you are writing your own job description—a contract that is open to mutual negotiation. After the employer has had time to read your prospectus, you should recontact him or her and set up an interview to present your case, a task that requires a considerable amount of self-confidence and sensitivity to others.

How Will I Go About Getting a Job?

The paperwork process of conducting a job campaign traditionally has required that you prepare three documents: (1) a background resumé, (2) a cover letter to accompany the resumé, and (3) follow-up correspondence after the employment interview. Guidelines for each of these activities are provided in the paragraphs that follow.

Contents of a Resumé

A well-written resumé briefly outlines the highlights of your educational and work history. Try to capture the reader's interest by demonstrating that you have the background to succeed in the position for which you are applying. Preparing an effective resumé is a creative effort; plan on writing several drafts and experimenting with several formats to develop an approach that best suits you. An outline of the contents of a resumé and examples of the different types of resumés follow.

Identifying Information   Your name, address, and telephone number. Both a permanent and a temporary address may be included.

Job Objective   The job objective identifies the responsibilities, challenges, and work activities that you wish to assume. Use job titles or descriptive phrases to specify the particular job or kind of job you are looking for. You may wish to state entry-level as well as long-range goals. The *Dictionary of Occupational Titles* may be helpful in locating appropriate job titles as well as in putting into words the range of duties sought.

Educational Background   List of schools attended, dates, degrees, diplomas, and certificates, with emphasis on the highest level achieved and special training pertinent to your job objective.

Experience or Work History   A summary of your work experience describing the nature of the work, job title, name of employer, and inclusive dates of employment. Work experience relevant to your job objective should be emphasized. Since most students have little or no relevant experience, it is important to list all summer, part-time, and significant volunteer positions.

Military Record   A brief statement of your service obligations, if any, or your service experience, if your tour of duty is completed. If your work history and your educational background were mostly military, include your military experience and training under the previous headings.

References   It is satisfactory to state simply that references will be supplied on request. However, if you are registered with a placement office and have a complete credential/job-placement file, reference should be made to the availability of your confidential data from that office, noting its full address and telephone number. A job application may ask for two or three people who can be contacted as references, so before beginning your job campaign, identify those people, ask permission to use their names, and obtain complete addresses and phone numbers.

Personal Data   Include early background (if it is significant), hobbies, and other activities. Do not include personal characteristics such as age, sex, marital status, or physical disabilities. Your employer will ask for this information after you are hired.

Date, Statement of Availability   These items are optional, but it is desirable to date each resumé as you distribute it and to mention when you are available for work.

Resumé Suggestions[1]

1. Your resumé should be confined to one page if possible. Few college students have had enough experience to justify more than that. If you are one of those few, however, do not hesitate to use the space you need to tell your story, but do not go beyond two pages.

2. Experiment with the arrangement of headings and text so as to find the best total appearance and readability. Use capital letters and underlining sparingly. Use indentation as a means for identifying separate items. Organize material so that facts and categories can be found easily by the reader.

3. Balance the material on the page so that the total effect is pleasing to the eye. Leave sufficient margins so that the page does not look crowded. Fill the page, so that there will not be excessive space at the bottom..

4. Be consistent in the use of graphic display techniques. Do not use indentation in one section and underscoring in the next.

5. As you edit your material, keep in mind your intended purpose. Eliminate unimportant details, and stress accomplishments you are proud of. Write and rewrite until you are satisfied that your descriptions are factual and positive statements of your experience, giving promise of potential and continued growth.

6. You may write in complete sentences or in partial sentences, as long as your meaning is clear. The test is whether your text is readable and understandable. Use simple words that convey exactly what you mean. Use punctuation marks intelligently.

7. It is not necessary to use the first-person pronoun unless the text does not make sense without it. Since you are writing about yourself, verbs will imply the "I" as the subject of your sentences. Use of the third person in referring to yourself is not acceptable unless it is contained in a quotation by another person.

8. Use the present or active tense when you refer to activities in which you are currently engaged (for example, supervise, manage, develop), but anything previous to current activity must be referred to in the past tense.

9. Avoid the use of slang, professional jargon, and clichés. Do not abbreviate. Employers who have to take time to interpret what you are saying will probably not bother.

---

[1]Items 1–11 are from *Career Development for the College Student* (pp. 89–90), ed. by P. Dunphy, 2nd ed., 1973, as adapted from *The Resume Workbook: A Personal Career File for Job Applications* by C. Nutter, 3rd ed., 1970, Cranston, RI: The Carroll Press. Copyright 1973 by The Carroll Press. Reprinted by permission.

10. Consult a dictionary for correct spelling. Mistakes reflect on your education and therefore on your qualifications.

11. Before you type your final copy, have someone else react to it. Your family and friends or your school placement officer may be able to offer suggestions. Consider your own reaction after setting it aside for a day or two. Would you hire the person described in this resumé?

12. Have your resumés reproduced by a reputable copy or printing service.

13. When contacting an employer through the mail, *always* enclose a resumé with a typed letter of introduction. (See the section on cover letters that follows.)

Types of Resumés

Chronological Format

If you believe that your most recent educational or work activity is your most important activity, place it first on your resumé. Other experiences you have had should then be listed in order of occurrence, starting with the most recent and ending with the most distant. Include the starting and ending dates to show how long you were involved in each educational or work activity.

This format is probably the most common, especially for job seekers with limited experience. Because of its logical sequence, it is easy to follow and allows the reader to trace your educational and work history rapidly.

Before you begin writing a chronological resumé, jot down all your educational and work experiences. Then go back and select only those that are directly related to the job you are applying for. This method will help you avoid the common pitfall of losing the most significant aspects of your work history in a web of unessential facts and dates and unimportant jobs.

Functional Format

The functional approach highlights the function or title of the positions you have held. In preparing this type of resumé, remember that your goal is to place your most significant work experience immediately before the employer. Job titles and specific duties are highlighted to support your qualifications for the job. While you should include names of employers and dates of employment with the descriptions, remember that they are secondary to the functions or positions you wish to emphasize.

This approach will be especially useful as you gain more experience, because it allows you to highlight part-time, temporary, and volunteer work in your career field more effectively than you would be able to do with a chronological resumé.

Analytical Format

In the analytical approach, you may emphasize particular vocational skills or specialized knowledge by grouping your background experiences according to their common features. Since you will be doing this to demonstrate their applicability to a specific job, you will probably need to overlook chronological sequence and specific job titles in preparing an analytical resumé.

Imaginative Format

The imaginative or creative format is probably the most difficult type of resumé to prepare and the most risky to use. The general goal of this approach is to stand out from other applicants in some unique way because of the appearance of your resumé. Applicants who use this type of resumé may include aspects of the other approaches to resumé preparation in new and unique ways, or they may create an entirely new format for highlighting their work history. Putting together a new style of presentation requires a considerable amount of planning, creative writing talent, and a willingness to violate established norms. Common creative or dramatic methods of preparing imaginative resumés include unique graphic displays, headlines, colored paper or ink, and direct quotations from former employers or teachers.

Employers in the creative or artistic fields, such as advertising, theater, and art, are most apt to appreciate this type of resumé. Companies that are conservative in their orientation may decide that because you stand out so much they will leave you out. If you elect to try this type of resumé, find out as much about each employer's style of conducting business as you can beforehand.

The sample resumés that follow highlight the career path of a Mitchel Livingston. As you read each resumé, notice how Livingston uses the four different types of resumés described above to accomplish different job objectives. Note also how he emphasizes different aspects of his work history in each resumé, thus demonstrating to employers that he has the skills and experience required to be successful in the position he is applying for.

Examples of Resumés
Chronological Format

Mitchel D. Livingston
565 South Spring Road
Westerville, Ohio 43081
(614) 890-9751 (home)
(614) 422-6091 (work)

CAREER OBJECTIVE

Chief Student Affairs Officer

EDUCATION

Michigan State University; Ph.D. in Higher Education, College Student Personnel; 1980.

Southern Illinois University; M.S. in Higher Education, College Student Personnel; 1971.

Southern Illinois University; B.S. in Physical Education; 1969.

WORK EXPERIENCE

7/80–Present   Dean of Student Life, The Ohio State University. Provided leadership for 11 offices that serve different student populations.

11/75–6/80   Director of Residence Services, The University of Iowa. Provided leadership for all university-owned and operated residence halls.

11/74–11/75   Director of Residence Halls, Oakland University. Administrative responsibility for all university-owned and operated residence halls.

9/71–11/74   Assistant Director of Residence Halls, Oakland University. Responsible for student life programming, security, and discipline.

10/70–6/71   Administrative Assistant to the President, Southern Illinois University. Provided administrative support in the Office of the President.

10/70–6/71   Residence Counselor, Southern Illinois University. Administrative responsibility for a 17-story residence hall.

10/69–8/70   Assistant Area Head, Southern Illinois University. Duties included student life programming and discipline.

INTERESTS

Ancient history, tennis, and carpentry.

March 1990

Functional Format

Mitchel D. Livingston
565 South Spring Road
Westerville, Ohio 43081
(614) 890-9751 (home)
(614) 422-6091 (work)

CAREER OBJECTIVE

Chief Student Affairs Officer

WORK EXPERIENCE

Dean of Student Life:
Budget, staff, and plan all Student Life Office functions. Provide leadership for the Offices of Greek Affairs, International Student and Scholar Services, Disability Services, Student Organizations and Activities, Black Student Programs, Commuter Student Affairs, Judicial Affairs, Alcohol Education, Hispanic Student Programs, Women's Services, and Forensics and Debate. Other responsibilities include student leadership training and development, Student Life research, Student Affairs orientation, Welcome Week, OSU/Michigan Weekend, and other campus-wide events.

Represent the Vice Provost for Student Affairs on various university committees, meetings, events, and act as the senior Student Affairs officer in his absence.

Teach "Introduction to College Student Personnel Work" and "Practice of College Student Personnel Work" as an Adjunct Professor in the College of Education.

The Ohio State University   7/80–present

Director of Residence Services:
Planned and directed all functions of University-owned and operated residence halls, food service, student development programming, maintenance, and business administration. Managed family housing (799 apartments) and auxiliary enterprises such as vending for the entire university, public cafeteria operation in residence halls, food service catering for off-campus organizations, and summer conferences, camps, and workshops.

The University of Iowa   11/75–6/80

EDUCATION

Ph.D.   Michigan State University; December, 1980
Major: Higher Education, College Student Personnel
Minors: Labor Industrial Relations and Management Science

M.S.   Southern Illinois University; June, 1971
Major: Higher Education, College Student Personnel
Minor: Psychology

B.S.   Southern Illinois University; June, 1969
Major: Physical Education
Minor: Psychology

PROFESSIONAL ASSOCIATIONS

American College Personnel Association

National Association of Student Personnel Administrators

The Ohio State University Minority Faculty and Staff Association; President 1981–1983

AWARDS

Outstanding Young Men of America; 1981

Meritorious Service to the Hispanic Student Body; The Ohio State University; 1981

Outstanding Leadership Award; Romophos-Sophomore Honorary; The Ohio State University; 1981

Meritorious Service Award to Students in Biological Sciences; The Ohio State University, 1980

NCAA athletic scholarship; Southern Illinois University; 1964–1968.

REFERENCES

References are available upon request.

Analytical Format

Mitchel D. Livingston
565 South Spring Road
Westerville, Ohio 43081
(614) 890-9751 (home)
(614) 422-6091 (work)

CAREER OBJECTIVE
Chief Student Affairs Officer

QUALIFICATIONS

MANAGEMENT AND SUPERVISION: As Dean of Student Life at The Ohio State University, eleven separate offices that provide programs and services for different student populations were developed into an organization joined by a common philosophy of student development. Implementation of management by objectives as the planning, management, and evaluation system is central to the effective and efficient operation of this newly created office. Supervision of 11 professional staff.

Reorganized the residence hall program at the University of Iowa. Key to the reorganization was the establishment of three assistant directors who assumed comprehensive administrative responsibilities for functionally related areas. Essential to the reorganization was the development of a common operating philosophy as well as the establishment of planning and management systems. Supervision of 25 professional staff.

As Assistant Director of Residence Halls at Oakland University, problems of staff morale, decreasing occupancy, racial conflict, and quality of life were resolved. Strategic planning measures were implemented over a three-year period which reversed the problems previously identified. Supervision of 5 professional staff.

FINANCIAL PLANNING AND DEVELOPMENT: Integrated financial and program planning through a common management system. Responsible for the distribution of $1 million for support programs and services provided by eight different offices. Also served as the primary administrator of four successful grant proposals that were designed to enhance the quality of student life.

Prepared specifications for an $11 million budget in the Residence Services department at the University of Iowa. Budget plan was based on projected occupancy, inflation rates, and anticipated program changes.

Developed specifications for a $2 million budget in the residence hall department at Oakland University. Budget plan was based on occupancy, inflation rates, and anticipated program changes.

PROGRAMMING: Developed the Affirmative Action Seminar Series to increase executive level participation in the letter and spirit of affirmative action activities. The goal of this program was accomplished through six university-wide seminars.

Implemented a peer support program designed to assist high-risk students who are admitted to the University. The goal of this program was to reverse the 50% attrition rate after the first year for minority students.

Provided leadership in the development of a major student/faculty/staff program called Project Unity. This program was dramatically effective in terms of reducing racial conflict in the residence halls. Project Unity was guided by the philosophy of bringing conflicting parties together to work toward common goals and objectives.

INSTRUCTION: Adjunct Assistant Professor, College of Education. Taught the introductory courses for Master's students in the Student Personnel program at The Ohio State University.

Co-taught the capstone course in the Student Personnel program. The purpose of the course was to assist graduates with the transition from student to professional employee.

EMPLOYERS

The Ohio State University; Columbus, OH 43210; 1980–present

The University of Iowa; Iowa City, IA 52240; 1975–1980

Oakland University; Rochester, MI 48063; 1970–1975

EDUCATION

1980   Ph.D. in Higher Education, College Student Personnel; Michigan State University

1971   M.S. in Higher Education, College Student Personnel; Southern Illinois University

1969   B.S. in Physical Education; Southern Illinois University

Imaginative Format

Mitchel D. Livingston
565 South Spring Road
Westerville, Ohio 43081
(614) 890-9751 (home)
(614) 422-6091 (work)

PHILOSOPHY

Despite our limited behavioral knowledge, the college must recognize that even its instructional goals cannot be effectively achieved unless it assumes some responsibility for facilitating the development of the total human personality.

A student is not a passive digester of knowledge elegantly arranged by superior curriculum design. A student listens, reads, thinks, studies, worries, hopes, loves, and hates.

A student engages in all these activities not as an isolated individual, but as a member of overlapping communities which greatly influence the student's reaction to the classroom experience.

To teach the subject matter and ignore the realities of the student's life and the social systems of the college is hopelessly naive. (Committee on Higher Education, 1968).

BACKGROUND

Michigan State University; Ph.D. in Higher Education; College Student Personnel; 1980. Southern Illinois University; M.S. in Higher Education; College Student Personnel; 1971. Southern Illinois University; B.S. in Physical Education; 1969.

Worked in a variety of Student Affairs positions at Southern Illinois University while completing the Master's Degree. These positions included Assistant Area Head in Residence Services, Resident Counselor, and Administrative Assistant to the President. After completing the Master's, accepted the Assistant Director of Residence Hall position at Oakland University in Rochester, Michigan. Immediately enrolled in the evening doctoral program in College Student Personnel at Michigan State University. Completed course work in five years and was subsequently promoted to Director of Residence Halls at Oakland. In 1975, left Oakland to assume the Director of Residence Halls position at the University of Iowa. Completed graduation requirement while serving in this capacity.

In 1980, accepted the Dean of Student Life position at The Ohio State University and am currently serving in this capacity.

THIS IS WHAT I CAN OFFER YOUR UNIVERSITY

A philosophy of Student Affairs work that is integral to the mission of your university.

Over 16 years of professional experience in Student Affairs positions of increasing responsibility.

Expert managerial and supervisory skills.

Proven competence in financial planning and development with multi-million dollar budgets.

Creative programming based on assessed student needs and interests.

Effective teaching skills that are grounded in developmental pedagogy.

A love for working with students and a belief that education can make all the difference in the world.

REFERENCES

References are available upon request.

The Cover Letter

An important rule of thumb in corresponding with employers is that each time you send a resumé it should be accompanied by a cover letter. Your cover letter allows you to introduce yourself to the employer by indicating why you are writing and what you can do for his or her organization. It briefly highlights your qualifications for the position and suggests a follow-up interview so you can more fully present your background experiences. Suggestions for preparing a cover letter and a sample cover letter follow. Typed cover letters always look more professional and present your resumé better than handwritten letters.

Unless you have been advised to correspond directly with your potential supervisor through a referral from another employee in the company or a job-search firm, it is best to direct your initial correspondence to the director of personnel in the company. Even though some popular books on job campaigning suggest that you go around the personnel director, research surveys conducted by the Administrative Management Society have shown that most employers still prefer that applicants start with the personnel office.

Correct Style and Content for Cover Letter

Box 1945
The Ohio State University
Columbus, Ohio 43204
October 25, 1990

(allow 2 or 3 spaces)

Mr. George McCormick
Director of Personnel
American Manufacturing Company
124 North Evans Avenue
Chicago, Illinois 60645

Dear Mr. McCormick: (use name)

Opening Paragraph   State why you are writing, name the position or type of work for which you are applying, and mention how you heard of the opening.

Middle Paragraphs   Explain why you are interested in working for this employer and specify your reasons for desiring this type of work. If you have had experience, be sure to point out your particular achievements or other qualifications in this field or type of work.

Middle Paragraphs   Refer the reader to the enclosed resumé, which gives a summary of your qualifications, and/or to whatever media you are using to illustrate your training, interests, and experience.

Closing Paragraph   Prepare an appropriate closing that paves the way for an interview by asking for an appointment, by giving your telephone number, or by offering some similar suggestion that will facilitate an immediate and favorable reply. Ending your letter with a question encourages a reply.

Very truly yours,

(always sign)

Fred A. Summers

Enclosure   (if enclosing a resumé, note it)
            (top and bottom margins should be equal)

Sample Cover Letter

2707 South Standard Avenue
Columbus, Ohio 43214
November 1, 1990

Ms. Jane R. Jones
Personnel Officer
Burke Technological Center
6401 Laughton Street
Los Angeles, California 90103

Dear Ms. Jones:

This morning's Los Angeles Times carried your advertisement for a "college student who is looking for a challenging and interesting summer position in a national
park." With my educational background, practical experience, and willingness to
work in an interesting position that offers a real challenge, I am sure I can be of
value to your service.

Next February I shall receive my Bachelor of Science degree from The Ohio State
University, where I have majored in public recreation.

For the last six years I have worked at a variety of part-time jobs: waiter, customer
service assistant, and assistant activities coordinator for the local YMCA. During the
past two years, I have gained working experience which will be very valuable to
your organization. Details of these jobs, my education, and other information may
be found on the enclosed resume.

I know that I can fill the challenging position you have open, and I would appreciate an opportunity to meet with you at your convenience to discuss in detail my
qualifications and future potential with your company. I may be reached every
afternoon at (614) 267-9200, extension 32; or any evening at (614) 261-1282.

Sincerely yours,

(*signature*)

James Shivley

Enclosure

The Employment Interview

Whether the traditional or nontraditional approach is used in establishing job
leads, the step that follows is the same: the employment interview. The employment interview is an opportunity for you and an employer to meet, to exchange
information, and to evaluate what each has to offer the other. As in any conversation between people, no two interviews are identical. Nevertheless, four common stages or components of an interview have been identified by the College
Placement Council—the opening, inquiry, matching, and closing.[2]

---

[2]Adapted from *The Campus Interview—Are You Ready?* (audiotape) with the permission of
the College Placement Council, Inc., copyright holder.

The Opening

During the first few minutes of an interview, there will be greetings and introductions, handshakes, and seats taken. Small talk that appears to be unrelated to the business of securing employment may occur. This stage will allow you to relax a little, to get accustomed to the interview situation, and to develop some initial impressions of the interviewer's style. This part of the interview is usually brief.

The Inquiry

A large number of questions are asked during this stage of the interview. The interviewer will try to obtain a clear understanding of your education, previous experience, achievements, short-term goals, and long-term aspirations. He or she will use a variety of questions to secure this information. Some may be very direct and require specific responses, but others may be more open-ended, providing you with an opportunity to emphasize your skills and interests. Although many questions may be directed to you during this phase of the interview, you should plan to ask some questions of your own as well. It is important for your own planning to clarify with whom and for whom you will be working, what you may be expected to do, and where. Your questions will also demonstrate how much research and thinking you have done concerning the position and the organization. A useful guide in choosing questions is not to ask questions that you yourself would be unwilling to answer.

The Matching

Matching occurs in two ways. The first screens you into a company by accentuating the skills, interests, and needs you have that are consistent with what a potential position demands and provides. The second screens you out of a company by identifying factors that reflect differences between what you want and what the employer has to offer. Both types of matching are operating during the interview. The purpose of both is to recognize and project how your specific skills and goals might relate to specific job responsibilities and opportunities.

The Closing

Interviews may last for a few minutes or for several hours. Initial interviews will often be brief, with follow-up interviews taking considerably more time. Regardless, the main purpose of this last part of the interview is to specify what the next steps in the selection process are and who is to take the initiative. At times you may be asked to take additional placement tests, undergo a physical examination, or return for further interviewing at another time, possibly with different people or at a different location. At other times the interviewer may indicate that the selection procedure is complete and that you will be notified as soon as a decision is reached.

According to Edgar Schein (1978, pp. 103–104), an authority on career development in organizations, the employer must learn several things about you during the interview:

1. Does the person have the *skills* and *experience* to do the job?
2. How will the person *fit* into my organization? Does he or she possess the style of work, attitudes, values, and personality that will blend with our organization? Can the person conform to the norms of our organization without sacrificing creativity and individuality?
3. Will the person easily *learn the ropes* and *make a contribution* to our setting, and possibly improve it?
4. Is the person capable of and invested in *learning* and *growing* as an independent contributor and possibly as a leader?

Schein suggests that you learn at least six things about an organization during the campus and on-site interviews.

1. Will I have the opportunity to *test myself* in the job? Is it challenging? Do I have the skills to do it? Can I take the pressure it may involve? Is it a position that I will enjoy?
2. Will I be *considered worthwhile*? Will I be given a chance to show what I can do? Will I be able to make a contribution and have it appreciated? Will I be liked and appreciated as a person?
3. Will I be able to maintain my *integrity* and *individuality*? Can I be part of the culture of the organization without violating my values or standards? Can I fit in without losing sight of who I am and what is important to me in life?
4. Will I be able to have a *balanced life*? Can I enjoy my leisure-recreational and social pursuits and still feel that I am working hard enough to satisfy myself and my employer?
5. Will I *learn and grow*? Will by colleagues and supervisors be the kind of people who provide me with new ideas and opportunities? Will I be supported if I decide to take classes or seminars to continue my professional growth?
6. If I become a member of the organization, will I *meet my own ideals* and *feel good about myself*? Will I be proud to be a member of the organization?

From Edgar Schein, *Career Dynamics*, © 1978, Addison-Wesley, Reading, Massachusetts. Pages 103 and 104 reprinted with permission.

Often the person interviewing you is not solely responsible for determining who will be hired, and other candidates may still be waiting for an interview. In either situation, the status of your application cannot be decided until all the interviews are completed and the results of the selection process have been reviewed by everyone involved. Consequently, you may leave the interview with the feeling that you really do not know where you stand. The truth is that at the moment probably nobody else does either!

Preparing for the Interview

Information about yourself and the prospective employer is only a portion of what is necessary for effective interviewing. What you know about yourself and the employer must be communicated confidently, clearly, and concisely. These skills can best be enhanced through practice.

One way of practicing for an interview is to imagine that you are the interviewer. What kinds of questions would you ask of an applicant for a position in your organization? Frank S. Endicott, former director of placement at Northwestern University, asked this question of recruiters for 92 companies. He found that the interviewers asked 50 common questions.[3]

1. What are your long-range and short-range goals and objectives, when and why did you establish these goals, and how are you preparing yourself to achieve them?
2. What specific goals, other than those related to your occupation, have you established for yourself for the next ten years?
3. What do you see yourself doing five years from now?
4. What do you *really* want to do in life?
5. What are your long-range career objectives?
6. How do you plan to achieve your career goals?
7. What are the most important rewards you expect in your business career?
8. What do you expect to be earning in five years?
9. Why did you choose the career for which you are preparing?
10. Which is more important to you, the money or the type of job?
11. What do you consider to be your greatest strengths and weaknesses?
12. How would you describe yourself?
13. How do you think a friend or professor who knows you well would describe you?
14. What motivates you to put forth your greatest effort?
15. How has your college experience prepared you for a business career?
16. Why should I hire you?
17. What qualifications do you have that make you think you will be successful in business?

[3]From *The Northwestern Lindquist-Endicott Report* by Victor R. Lindquist, Northwestern University Placement Center, Evanston, Illinois.

18. How do you determine or evaluate success?
19. What do you think it takes to be successful in a company like ours?
20. In what ways do you think you can make a contribution to our company?
21. What qualities should a successful manager possess?
22. Describe the relationship that should exist between a supervisor and those reporting to him or her.
23. What two or three accomplishments have given you the most satisfaction? Why?
24. Describe your most rewarding college experience.
25. If you were hiring a graduate for this position, what qualities would you look for?
26. Why did you select your college or university?
27. What led you to choose your field of major study?
28. What college subjects did you like best? Why?
29. What college subjects did you like least? Why?
30. If you could do so, how would you plan your academic study differently? Why?
31. What changes would you make in your college or university? Why?
32. Do you have plans for continued study? An advanced degree?
33. Do you think that your grades are a good indication of your academic achievement?
34. What have you learned from participation in extracurricular activities?
35. In what kind of work environment are you most comfortable?
36. How do you work under pressure?
37. In what part-time or summer jobs have you been most interested? Why?
38. How would you describe the ideal job for you following graduation?
39. Why did you decide to seek a position with this company?
40. What do you know about our company?
41. What two or three things are most important to you in your job?
42. Are you seeking employment in a company of a certain size? Why?
43. What criteria are you using to evaluate the company for which you hope to work?
44. Do you have a geographical preference? Why?
45. Will you relocate? Does relocation bother you?
46. Are you willing to travel?
47. Are you willing to spend at least six months as a trainee?
48. Why do you think you might like to live in the community in which our company is located?
49. What major problem have you encountered and how did you deal with it?
50. What have you learned from your mistakes?

If Endicott's list of questions isn't enough of a challenge for you, consider a list of the "ten toughest business questions" that executives ask of applicants for leadership positions. The list was developed by Joan Detz, a writer and lecturer on communication topics, for *New Woman* magazine (January 1989, p. 132).

We have modified her list to better suit college students entering a job after graduation.

1. *The hypothetical question*: "Suppose you were given an assignment during your first week on the job and couldn't meet the deadline. What would you do?"

Ms. Detz suggests that you try to avoid doomsday situations like this because they lead to an endless cycle of "what if" follow-up questions. Don't focus on what you would do if you failed; focus on what you will do to make sure that your efforts are a success.

2. *The yes-or-no question*: "Will you be able to do this job on your own, right away?"

Ms. Detz advises that you not be hasty with a "yes" answer but respond with "From the information I have now, it looks like things should go smoothly. However, I may need to consult with you if the situation changes or if I need more resources to manage it successfully."

3. *The what-do-you-think-the-other-guy-thinks question*: "How do you think your supervisor will view your leaving your present position?"

Avoid being a mind reader. Instead, you might respond with "My supervisor has agreed to write a reference letter for me, so she apparently understands my need for a change and my decision to advance in my career. If you have any questions about my performance, you might ask her directly."

4. *The ranking question*: "What do you think are the two or three most important concerns of people who are entering the type of position you are applying for?"

This question presupposes that you have a great deal of familiarity with the position and other applicants and are able to speak with confidence regarding the careers of others. Don't answer for others; speak for yourself, and point out that opinions will no doubt vary from applicant to applicant.

5. *The nonquestion question*: "I've enjoyed reading your credentials but don't think your background matches with our needs."

This form of resistance to your application is a challenge that should not go unanswered. Ms. Detz advises that you turn it into a question such as "You wonder how I can best serve you in the job. Let me tell you what makes me the best candidate for it. . . . "

6. *The off-the-record question*: "Between you and me, is this college really the best place for me to be looking for someone to fill this position?"

Although questions such as this may seem to provide you with an opportunity to openly express your frustrations with your academic experiences at your college (if you have any), it can come back to haunt you in two ways. First, secrets shared in confidence have a way of getting out. Second, if you answer the question, you will be in an awkward position of gossiping about someone else and may create some doubt about your loyalty to your employer. Therefore, we advise you not to tell the interviewer anything "in confidence" that you wouldn't share openly in public. Instead, focus on how your background experiences will be of benefit to the employer.

7. *The A-or-B orientation question*: "What is more important to you, salary or job?"

If you are like most students, you want a job that pays adequate salary and provides an opportunity for long-term professional growth. You need not exclude one to get the other; you should feel free to say "Both are important to me as opportunities to. . . . "

8. *The why question*: "Most college students are alike. Why should I hire you for the position?"

Ms. Detz advises that when you hear the word *why*, begin to put yourself in the interviewer's shoes. Think about what the employer needs and what you can do to fill those needs. For example, "Judging from the job description and our conversation, I gather that you are looking for someone who is a self-starter, can set goals, and isn't afraid of a challenge. I'm that kind of person. Let me tell you a bit more about how I've demonstrated those qualities in my studies and outside employment."

9. *The false-premise question*: "I notice you have had a series of short-term positions. I wonder why. Can't you keep a job for a long period?"

If you don't immediately challenge or correct a false-premise statement, it will continue to haunt you during the interview. Be firm in your response and say something like "In my desire to make my resume brief and easy for you to read, I did not describe my reasons for leaving the positions I have listed. I'm sorry that it has left you with an inaccurate impression of my background and want to thank you for bringing it up so I can provide you with more complete information. Let me explain more fully why I left each position and what I gained from working in it."

10. *The open question*: "So tell me about your last job."

Open-ended questions provide a golden opportunity to show why you are an attractive applicant for the position. Anticipate the opportunity and prepare for it by preparing in advance a short summary statement of how you utilized your interests, values, and skills to complete your assignments successfully on your last job and to enrich your preparation for the job you are presently seeking.

You might start your summary statement with "My last job required that I be able to _____ . I was successful at it because I was skillful at _____ and enjoyed _____ . It also gave me an opportunity to do the following things that are important to me in a job. These are the qualities I will bring to your position."

As you can see from these lists of common questions, employment interviewers cover a variety of topics, ranging from your preparation for and commitment to the job to your preferred lifestyle. As part of your preparation for the job interview, we would encourage you to read through the list of questions above, single out some that are difficult for you to answer as well as some that are easy, and mentally rehearse your responses to them. You may wish to write the questions down or record them on tape. Respond to them out loud. Taping your answers may help you to hear how you present yourself to others. You may also find it helpful to sit down with one or two friends and practice interviewing one another. One person can serve as the employer. The other can observe the interview and critique your performance. When practicing for an interview, keep in mind that how something is said may be as important as the content. Your tone of voice, gestures, eye contact, and posture convey as much about you as what you say.

Interview Suggestions

Many factors contribute to effective interviewing. Listed below are a few important tips.

Preparation

Know yourself. Have a clear understanding of your most prominent assets and goals and how these may be communicated. Know the organization. Be familiar with its products, priorities, and problems, and how your skills can contribute to its goals.

Write down the time and place of your interview and the interviewer's name. Be sure you can pronounce the interviewer's name properly. Have in mind a list of questions that you would like to have answered about the position and the firm during the interview. Be sure you are on time for the interview or, better yet, try to arrive a few minutes early so you can relax and mentally rehearse your plan for the interview.

Physical Appearance

Let basic good taste determine how you dress. Wear clothing that you feel will represent you well and will convey an image of which you are proud. Above all, be neat and clean. Maintain a relaxed and alert posture. When listening or speaking to an interviewer, maintain eye contact.

Speaking Style

Be honest and be yourself. Speak clearly and with enthusiasm, and at a pace and volume that can be easily heard. Emphasize your strengths and be ready to support statements with examples. Be sure you understand the question before you answer it. Listen—pause—then respond. Ask questions. Remember that the interview is a two-way street. As you approach the interview, remember that the purpose of the interview is not to intimidate you or put you through an ordeal (although occasionally an interviewer will do that). The interview is the most efficient way for you and an employer to get to know each other in a short period of time. Recognize that you have qualities and attributes that will make you a valuable employee and that an employer would not be meeting with you if he or she were not interested in the possibility of hiring you. Approaching an interview with confidence derived from an understanding of what may occur, from knowing yourself and being informed, and from prior practice will make the employment interview a valuable and rewarding experience.

Know Your Rights and the Employer's Rights

In their attempts to get answers to their questions about each other, employers and employees are expected to play fair with one another—that is, to demonstrate mutual respect and ensure that their questions are related to the job and to the applicant's skills. The problems that women, minorities, older individuals, and the physically challenged have experienced in the past have indicated that the problem of employment discrimination cannot be overcome with simple goodwill. Consequently, state and federal governments and the College Placement Council have developed a set of guidelines for employers and applicants to abide by during the job selection process. It is important that you know these guidelines as you enter your own job campaign.

During the interviewing and selection process, you and the interviewer are expected to treat each other fairly and with dignity and respect. The employer should fully and truthfully inform you about the organization and the particular duties and rewards of the position. Conversely, you should fully and truthfully tell the employer about your qualifications for the position and your professional plans. While the employer may dictate the general format (relaxed and casual or stressful and highly directed) and the length of the interview, you should be given the opportunity to present your interests, talents, needs, and plans in a manner that is most comfortable for you. Both of you may refuse any request that is unreasonable or inappropriate without feeling that doing so will cause distrust or conflict. You may also expect to be screened on the basis of your abilities rather than your age, race, sex, marital status, national origin, or physical handicap. The employer, on the other hand, can make decisions about your fit for the job based on your job-related skills, interests, values, and plans. Finally, you should also remember that interviewing for the job does not guarantee that you will be offered the position, nor does it guarantee the employer that you will accept it.

Table 7-1 sets out guidelines for questioning applicants for employment. These guidelines were developed by the Ohio Civil Rights Commission under the Ohio Fair Employment Practices Act. They parallel federal guidelines that have been developed by the Department of Employment Security of the U.S. Department of Labor, so they probably apply to your state as well. Read through the guidelines carefully to get a good understanding of what questions may legally be asked of you during the selection process. It is especially important to realize that while a prospective employer must not ask you certain questions, you may be required to provide such information—for example, a picture, your race, your sex, or your age—*after* you are hired, to help the employer provide affirmative action information to the government or for security purposes within the organization.

TABLE 7-1   Questioning Applicants for Employment

Inquiries before hiring	Lawful	Unlawful
1. *Name*	Name	Inquiry into any title which indicates race, color, religion, sex, national origin, handicap, age, or ancestry
2. *Address*	Inquiry into place and length of current address	Inquiry into foreign addresses which would indicate national origin
3. *Age*	Any inquiry limited to establishing that applicant meets any minimum age requirement that may be established by law	a. Requiring birth certificate or baptismal record before hiring b. Any other inquiry which may reveal whether applicant is at least 40 and less than 70 years of age
4. *Birthplace or national origin*		a. Any inquiry into place of birth b. Any inquiry into place of birth of parents, grandparents, or spouse c. Any other inquiry into national origin
5. *Race or color*		Any inquiry which would indicate race or color
6. *Sex*		a. Any inquiry which would indicate sex b. Any inquiry made of members of one sex but not the other
7. *Religion/creed*		a. Any inquiry which would indicate or identify religious denomination or custom b. Applicant may not be told any religious identity or preference of the employer c. Request pastor's recommendation or reference
8. *Handicap*	Inquiries necessary to determine applicant's ability to substantially perform specific job without significant hazard	Any other inquiry which would reveal handicap

(continued)

TABLE 7-1 Questioning Applicants for Employment (*continued*)

Inquiries before hiring	Lawful	Unlawful
9. *Citizenship*	a. Whether a U.S. citizen	a. If native-born or naturalized
	b. If not, whether applicant intends to become one	b. Proof of citizenship before hiring
	c. If U.S. residence is legal	c. Whether parents or spouse are native-born or naturalized
	d. If spouse is citizen	
	e. Require proof of citizenship after being hired	
10. *Photographs*	May be required after hiring for identification purposes	Require photograph before hiring
11. *Arrests and convictions*	Inquiries into conviction of specific crimes related to qualifications for the job applied for	Any inquiry which would reveal arrests without convictions
12. *Education*	a. Inquiry into nature and extent of academic, professional, or vocational training	a. Any inquiry which would reveal the nationality or religious affiliation of a school
	b. Inquiry into language skills, such as reading and writing of foreign languages	b. Inquiry as to what mother tongue is or how foreign language ability was acquired
13. *Relatives*	Inquiry into name, relationship, and address of person to be notified in case of emergency	Any inquiry about a relative which would be unlawful if made about the applicant
14. *Organizations*	Inquiry into organization memberships and offices held, excluding any organization the name or character of which indicates the race, color, religion, sex, national origin, handicap, age, or ancestry of its members	Inquiry into all clubs and organizations where membership is held
15. *Military service*	a. Inquiry into service in U.S. armed forces when such service is a qualification for the job	a. Inquiry into military service in armed service of any country but U.S.

(*continued*)

TABLE 7-1   Questioning Applicants for Employment (*continued*)

Inquiries before hiring	*Lawful*	*Unlawful*
	b. Requires military discharge certificate after being hired	b. Request military service records
		c. Inquiry into type of discharge
16. *Work schedule*	Inquiry into willingness to work required work schedule	Any inquiry into willingness to work any particular religious holiday
17. *Other*	Any question required to reveal qualifications for the job applied for	Any non-job-related inquiry which may reveal information permitting unlawful discrimination
18. *References*	General personal and work references not related to race, color, religion, sex, national origin, handicap, age, or ancestry	Request references specifically from clergy or any other persons who might reflect race, color, religion, sex, national origin, handicap, age, or ancestry of applicant

Source: Questioning Applicants for Employment and Membership in Labor Organizations: A Guide for Application Forms and Interviews, 1990, Columbus: Ohio Civil Rights Commission. Copyright 1983 by the Ohio Civil Rights Commission. Reprinted by permission.

If an unlawful question is asked during the campus interview, let your college placement officer know so he or she can remind the interviewer what is and is not an appropriate question. Also remember that you share a responsibility to keep the interview focused on your ability to do the job; so don't volunteer information that is illegal or unrelated to your capabilities as a potential employee.

For further information about your rights as a job applicant, talk to your campus placement officer or contact the Civil Rights Commission in your state. Your placement officer can help you with questions about your rights and responsibilities and can suggest ways to deal with illegal questions asked during the interviewing process.

When Awkward Questions Occur

Planning and thinking about your personal as well as career goals and philosophies are an important part of interview and preparation. They help you to act rather than react when faced with difficult or unexpected questions. Open-ended questions such as "Tell me a story" or "Tell me about yourself" give the interviewer a chance to see how you operate in an unstructured situation. What is important is not that you come up with the most clever response ever given but that you handle the challenge calmly, thoughtfully, and honestly—no cute answers or stuttering panic. It is perfectly acceptable to say that you need a moment to organize your thoughts.

If asked about your previous job, don't be negative or bad-mouth your former employer, even if you did have a bad experience there. Just describe your previous responsibilities and what you learned from that setting, then focus on how the job you are applying for will advance your career objectives.

Another common difficult-to-handle question encountered (often by women) is a question on a topic that is technically illegal, such as plans for a family, age, religion, or ethnic background. One option is to refuse to answer or to remind the interviewer that the question is illegal. Although you are in the right, such a defensive response is likely to make a negative impression. When such a question is asked, you must make a quick asssessment of how the situation feels to you. If the job seems attractive, you may choose to give a pleasant (and perhaps vague) response that stresses your assets, such as plans for child care or the advantages of your maturity. Or you may wish to redirect the question and answer with regard to your skills and your commitment to your career. If you feel sufficiently comfortable with the interviewer, you could initiate a dialogue to determine what is behind the interviewer's questions and what the company's real concerns are. If you are seriously interested in the job, it is probably important to discover the attitudes and feelings behind such questions. If there is truly a prejudice in the organization about working mothers or people of a certain background, it may not be a place you want to work.

Follow-Up Correspondence

After an interview, and especially after an on-site visit, a brief written reply to your interviewer or host is appropriate. This correspondence may include a thank-you for the interview, a brief review of reactions to information you received, a response or follow-up to any specific requests made during the interview, and a request for any additional information desired.

A major goal of this type of letter is to demonstrate your interest and initiative and to keep your name before those who may be aware of future job openings. A sample follow-up letter is shown next.

Sample Follow-Up Letter

815 N.E. Seventh Street
Hibbing, Minnesota 55746
December 2, 1990

Ms. Jeanne Clarke
Associate Director of Personnel
Allied Products
Duluth, Minnesota 55806

Dear Ms. Clarke:

Thank you for the invitation and the opportunity to discuss the marketing position available with your firm in Duluth.

I was particularly impressed by the information you provided about the in-service training opportunities with Allied Products. Likewise, your incentive and evaluation programs would provide the kind of salary, benefits, and constructive feedback that are important to me at this point in my career.

I have been giving a great deal of thought to the options you presented for starting in a regional or division office. Since I prefer to live in a larger metro-politan area, the division office assignment would be my first choice. However, the range of duties to be performed at either type of office is compatible with my experience and interest. I am attracted to both opportunities.

I understand that your recruiting process for this position will take an additional two to three weeks. I look forward to hearing from you at that time.

Sincerely yours,

(*signature*)

Maryann J. Olson

When a Detour Is Needed

Regardless of what job-search method is used and how well you prepare yourself for an interview, inexperience and an increasingly tight job market make it difficult to get the ideal job on the first try. In fact, it appears that only a few students will secure their most preferred job right after they graduate. (Many of them later discover it is not their ideal job!) Statistics show that most people change jobs within two years of their first employment after college. This suggests that job shopping, like selecting a major, is a normal part of the ongoing process of career development beyond college. Consequently, it may help to alleviate job-search pressures by putting aside the idea that one should achieve the ideal job standard on the first job try. You should look at all jobs in terms of the opportunities for development they provide. To maximize your opportunities for growth in a tight job market, other work alternatives may have to be pursued, at least temporarily. The Vocational Contingency Planning (VCP) approach developed by Jeffrey Kleinberg (1976) provides an alternate route and expanded opportunities when things do not work out as we hoped.

VCP is a useful backup to the traditional and nontraditional approaches. Like the other approaches, it begins with identification of the specific work-related skills you possess. It is unlike the traditional approach, which emphasizes matching one's skills to specific job titles, and more like the nontraditional approach, which looks at how specific skills can be transferred or utilized across a number of work settings and occupational levels.

The VCP strategy assumes that through employee turnover (retirement, death, advancement, and change) all occupations will in time have vacancies. VCP enables you to compete strongly for these openings when they became available. Essentially it offers three strategies for obtaining a primary occupational choice at some time in the future, even if the choice is currently inaccessible. The three alternative approaches are derived from classifying occupations in terms of level, field, and enterprise, and from identifying the skills that various occupations share in common.

To illustrate, suppose your primary vocational choice, elementary public school teaching (a social occupation), were unavailable to you in the area where you want to work. VCP offers three options for using the social skills of a teacher: the level detour, the field detour, and the enterprise detour.

The Level Detour

You could seek a position in the teaching field at a level of responsibility below that of a full-fledged teacher, such as assistant or day-care center aide.

The Field Detour

You could seek work in a field that relates in some significant way to the work of a teacher: textbook sales, audiovisual equipment maintenance, school security, or community liaison work. One way to identify field-related occupations is to list occupations that a person in your primary occupation may have contact with during a normal day's activities.

The Enterprise Detour

You could seek a position in nonpublic school settings, such as teaching in a private, parochial, or military school, tutoring, educational activities for a private firm, or volunteer work in community or government settings. This detour approach depends on locating other settings where the same type of work can be found.

All these vocational detours allow you to

1. Build up a positive work history with good, solid references in work activities related to your primary occupational goal.
2. Make personal contacts with those who might eventually be hiring you.
3. Pursue advanced study and training concurrently with the detour work.
4. Offer a richer repertoire of skills than is typically presented by the fresh-out-of-college applicant.
5. Prepare for the detour with a minimal amount of effort and time.
6. Engage in temporary work that will support you financially as you continue to pursue your primary goal.

VCP is not a panacea for achieving your primary occupational goal in a restrictive and deflated job market. However, it can increase the odds that you will eventually be able to attain your occupational goal and that in the interim you will learn about your interests and skills and be exposed to many interesting job possibilities.

Three methods of job campaigning—traditional (page 131), nontraditional (page 133), and contingency (158)—were briefly presented in this chapter to illustrate the diverse ways a job-search campaign may be conducted. Each approach has advantages and disadvantages. Using aspects of each, you can develop a personal style that is most effective for you.

When You Are Out of Work

Not everyone can be in the enviable position of looking for the next job while still employed. At some time, after graduation or because of certain circumstances in your life, you may find yourself unemployed. Here are some tips on how to cope with job hunting in that situation.

First and foremost, STAY ACTIVE! Keep yourself busy. Taking a part-time job will fill your time, make some money, and provide an opportunity to meet new people. Part-time or temporary work will also give you some time to spend in your job search—time to make contacts, write letters, interview, and make telephone calls. Many employers are sympathetic to the plight of the young person looking for a first job. Saying that you are working part-time on a temporary basis while you look for a good job demonstrates that you are assertive and enterprising. And if your part-time job is in a field that is related to your ultimate career goal, so much the better.

When you find yourself out of work, be prepared to pursue any and all leads that might land you a job. Letters, telephone calls, and personal contacts can be important parts of your job search. As a general rule, the job searcher will have to make 30 contacts with potential employers before getting a nibble. You can alleviate some of the anxiety by setting a goal of making 30 contacts in a month, rather than feeling that you *must* have a job in two weeks. Decide to be an active agent in your job search, not passively dependent on newspapers and employment agencies. Go out and look for a job—don't wait for a job to come your way.

Personal Skills Review

Throughout this text we have stressed the importance of being able to identify and capitalize on the work-related skills you have acquired in order to identify and pursue a career objective effectively. We have also pointed out the benefits of a thorough skill assessment in developing a job-search strategy. This will allow you to pursue a number of work alternatives in different levels, fields, and enterprises flexibly.

Skill identification is especially important when you are conducting a job campaign. It allows you to put your best foot forward through correspondence and job interviews. Employers need to know that you are not only interested in a job but can also demonstrate that you have the appropriate skills for it!

We often think that the only skills and experiences that employers will be interested in are those we can tie to formal educational, training, and work experience. Actually, we have had abundant opportunities in our leisure time and social pursuits to acquire solid skills that can be used in work settings. Being a member of a family, for example, can provide opportunities to observe how a mini-corporation (the family enterprise) manages its resources, utilizes lines of communication in decision making, and negotiates differences in styles and opinions. Given this, it will be important to attend to the learning opportunities you have had on all sides of your lifestyle triangle. This can be done by using the card file suggested at the beginning of this chapter or by identifying where and how you acquired the skills you noted in the self-assessment inventories provided in Appendix B. This approach can be especially helpful if you have limited work experience or have "stopped out" from work. Other useful approaches to identifying your skills can be found in the books by Bolles and Haldane listed among the resources at the end of this chapter. Regardless of how you approach the identification of your skills, it is important to be able to specify what the skill is and where and when you learned it, so that you can accurately present your qualifications to employers.

You may conclude that you have some skills of significant quality and value that were learned in informal settings or were self-taught: cooking or child care in the home, bookkeeping for a club or group, running a local hospital benefit, photography for friends or a school paper, botany learned at city park classes. The origins of these skills may sound unprofessional, but they can often be legitimized by imaginative additions, such as statistics, samples, or letters of recommendation. The hospital bazaar experience may look more professional diagramed on paper, detailing such things as your duties, the number of people you supervised, and the amounts of money handled. If your skill produces a portable product, bring a portfolio of your best work. If your product is not portable, it may show off well in photographs or drawings. If you have performed a service (cooking, child care, bookkeeping, photography) for individuals or groups in the community, or learned a skill from someone (the park director), ask for a letter of recommendation describing or confirming your skills.

Personal Skills Inventory

The following Personal Skills Inventory is designed to help you identify and pull together all the skills you have acquired. These include skills from your education or training and work experiences, as well as your leisure and recreational pursuits and your interactions with family and friends.

The inventory requires that you clearly describe the specific skill you wish to share with an employer and the context in which you acquired it. Examples are provided to stimulate your thinking. We also encourage you to go back through the skill items in the self-assessment inventories in Appendix B to generate other skills for your list. If, for example, you indicated that you have a strong skill in "operating office machines," a "conventional" skill, you would try to identify on the personal skills inventory where and how you acquired that skill and describe which machines you know how to operate.

PERSONAL SKILLS INVENTORY

Learning Context	The Skills
Where I learned it	Describe the specific skill in terms of what it is, where you learned it, and when you learned it.

From education or training

1. In my secretarial sciences curriculum at my technical college, I acquired specific skills in running a duplicating machine, a desk calculator, and a dictaphone. Other "conventional" skills that I acquired include . . .

2. _____

3. _____

4. _____

From work experiences

1. In order to pay for my education, I worked part-time at night selling shoes. This gave me the opportunity to develop special and "enterprising" skills in meeting others, assisting them in meeting a specific need, and dealing with customer complaints. It also helped me acquire "conventional" skills in maintaining an inventory, exchanging money, and record keeping.

2. As a result of my being employed, I learned how to keep a balanced budget to meet my own educational objectives. Thus, I am very familiar with the skills of setting priorities and long-range planning.

3. _____

4. _____

From leisure/ recreation pursuits

1. I like to fish, and during high school I learned how to tie flies for fishing, an "artistic" and "realistic" skill. I became so proficient at it that I soon was able to set up a profitable part-time business selling them. Through this experience I learned how to produce a quality product to meet a public demand, to manage a stock inventory, and to plan and manage a budget. I also learned how to relate to customers effectively. All these are "enterprising" skills.

(continued)

PERSONAL SKILLS INVENTORY (*continued*)

Learning Context   The Skills

2. As captain of my YWCA baseball team, I learned how to support and encourage others, to give advice, and to present their views to people in authority (the coaches). These are primarily "social" skills.

3. _____

4. _____

From kinship/ friendship activities

1. During the summer of my junior year in high school, both my parents became quite ill for a month. Since I was the oldest child, I had to assume the responsibility for managing many household activities. Working with my relatives, I learned how to plan schedules, project a family budget, negotiate difficult situations with others, and supervise the activities of others (my younger brother and sister). These managerial skills fall into the "social" and "enterprising" categories.

2. _____

3. _____

4. _____

Some Challenging Situations for the Interviewee

Imagine yourself as Mila, Jack, or Karyn in the following situations.

1. While Mila is in the placement office scheduling an appointment for an interview with a campus recruiter, another student interrupts. He says he can't wait for his turn to make an appointment because he has to leave for home in 15 minutes to sing in a wedding. He also says he wants an appointment "Next Monday at 10 A.M.," at the same time and with the same employer that Mila wants to see.

2. During his meeting with a campus recruiter, Jack notices that the interviewer seems distracted. Her questions seem to have no direction and she jumps from topic to topic without paying attention to what Jack has said. When Jack asks about specific aspects of the job, the interviewer says, "I'll get to that later," but she hasn't yet.

3. Karyn made it through the campus interview and is now being interviewed at the federal agency where she wants to work. It has been a good day.

She likes the people she met, and the position will be an ideal place for her to start her career. Over lunch, the person who may be her supervisor starts asking her questions about her family background, religious practices, and marriage plans.

Review each situation. What employee rights are being violated in each case?

Some Challenging Situations for the Interviewer

Imagine yourself as Ms. Creps, Mr. Morrow, Mr. Smout, or Mr. Garlie in the following vignettes. As a responsible interviewer, how would you respond to each situation?

1. Ms. Creps is interviewing a recent graduate for a position as an administrative assistant in a small firm. The student begins to talk about her immigrant family and the religious teachings of her college.

2. Mr. Morrow, personnel director for a local school system, has advertised an opening for administrative assistant to the principal. Mr. Morrow's secretary has been preparing the candidate's files. As she files one candidate's resumé, she notices that it includes a picture of the person and his date of birth.

3. After a lengthy search, Mr. Smout has offered a position to a recent graduate who has considerable work experience in the field. The candidate initially accepted the position, but has just called to decline it because he got a better offer elsewhere.

4. Mr. Garlie just found out that an employee he has been supervising for a year lied about his criminal record during his job interview.

References and Resources

Harden, M. (1989, July 19). On job interview, some go far out to make an impression [In Essence column]. *Columbus Dispatch*, p. 1E.

Schein, E. H. (1978). *Career dynamics: Matching individual and organizational needs.* Reading, MA: Addison-Wesley.

Traditional Approaches

Corwen, L. (1988). *Your resumé: Key to a better job* (3rd ed.). New York: Arco.

Jackson, T. (1983). *The perfect resumé.* Garden City, NY: Anchor Press.

Jackson, T., & Mayleas, D. (1981). *The hidden job market for the 80s.* New York: New York Times Book Co.

McDaniels, C. (1978). *Developing a professional vita or resumé.* Garret Park, MD: Garret Park Press.

Powell, C. R. (1981). *Career planning today.* Dubuque, IA: Kendall/Hunt.

Nontraditional Approaches

Bolles, R. N. (1990). *What color is your parachute?* Berkeley, CA: Ten Speed Press.

Bolles, R. N. (1981). *The three boxes of life.* Berkeley, CA: Ten Speed Press.

Crystal, J., & Bolles, R. N. (1980). *Where do I go from here with my life?* New York: Seabury Press.

Haldane, B. (1975). *How to make a habit of success.* Washington, DC: Acropolis Books.

Irish, R. K. (1987). *Go hire yourself an employer* (3rd ed.). New York: Doubleday.

Kleinberg, J. D. (1976). Vocational contingency planning in a recession. *Vocational Guidance Quarterly, 24*(4), 366–367.

Lathrop, R. (1989). *Who's hiring who.* Berkeley, CA: Ten Speed Press.

Planning for work. (Undated). *Catalyst* (New York).*

Your job campaign. (Undated). *Catalyst* (New York).*

*Resources dedicated to expanding employment opportunities for college-educated women who wish to combine career and family responsibilities. For more information, write *Catalyst,* 14 East 60th Street, New York, NY 10022.

CHAPTER EIGHT

Work Adjustment and Career Expansion

When your work speaks for itself,
don't interrupt.

—*Henry J. Kaiser*

It is the end of the lunch hour in the cafeteria of a large corporation, and individuals and groups straggle back to their work areas. Three friends from the secretarial pool walk together toward the south end of the building, laughing and chatting. Debbie had been angry all morning at Evelyn, whose personal calls and sloppy filing had made a difficult morning worse. Debbie was scared of losing a friend, but she remembered what she had learned in assertiveness training about not allowing unresolved anger to build up. So she told Evelyn how she felt during lunch. Evelyn was a little defensive but understood Debbie's concerns and told her she had had a fight with her husband before work. This honest exchange felt good, and it made Marian decide to confide in her two friends. She had recently expected a promotion to a department that had lost a secretary, but she did not get it. She feels it is because she is African American. She knows she can file a claim with the personnel department or the Equal Employment Opportunity Commission but does not want to jump to conclusions, since this was her first try at promotion. The three friends talk it over and agree that Marian should start by going to the "powers that be" in the department where she applied and expressing her disappointment. Her goal is to find out why she wasn't chosen and what she can do to improve her future chances. This will help Marian and will also call attention to her ambition in a positive way.

Two men have stopped in the rest room after lunch and are sharing their experiences. Tom is unhappy with his job, which is no longer challenging, but feels stuck. He knows he hasn't done enough to promote his successes or to network within the company. He realizes that if he starts now it will take years. Tom is angry at himself, knowing that if he'd been looking ahead five years ago, he could have gone to school at the company's expense. Andrew is 59 and has been asked to take early retirement due to cutbacks. The financial package is good, but Andrew feels that without his job he'll feel useless and bored. He hasn't really developed any interests or plans for retirement because it has always seemed so far away.

Heading away from the cafeteria in the opposite direction are a man and woman in deep conversation. Stuart, a sales manager approaching middle age, is very satisfied with his current progress. He's not expecting an upward move anytime soon, but he has been included in more meetings and golf games and feels he is moving toward the influential "inner circle" of higher executives who control the important promotions. The young woman with him is his assistant, who is still learning the ropes. Stuart had really disliked the idea of training someone fresh out of college who, he thought, would be idealistic and resist the politics, pragmatism, and tradition that make the business world different from a textbook. But Phylis surprised him. She has good people skills and common sense. Without intending to, Stuart has become her mentor. He enjoys giving her advice and encouragement and watching her blossom. He is proud that management has noticed how she stands out.

People in work settings are all different. They are constantly adjusting and learning and are all at different stages of personal and career development.

We are all students of one another and of our surroundings, constantly looking for clues about how others react to us and what behaviors are appropriate. It is a survival mechanism—no doubt a part of us at birth—that helps us adapt to our environment.

Usually we are only dimly aware that we are "fortune telling," probably because our predictions are fairly accurate and require little conscious thought. It is the unexpected event, the situation we could not anticipate, that reminds us that our trust is often based on "mind reading" and assumptions.

The change may be small—someone does not show up as usual—or it can be large, as when one travels to a new place. Our antennae go up regardless, looking for new clues and guidelines for dealing with the new situation. Until a balance is again established, we are likely to feel uneasy, even in conflict, about who and where we are.

Successful employees recognize that the workplace is really a mini-society that sends out a constant stream of information about what is expected of its members and what the rules and limits are. Some of the rules are explicit, as in a job description or a personnel handbook, but many codes are revealed only in subtle patterns of behavior—in the ways workers dress, how they speak, topics of conversation, informal leadership patterns. Together, these subtle clues create an organizational climate, a bond that maintains the stability of the work setting and allows us to learn behaviors through which we can meet our needs and achieve our goals.

The Sixth Skill: Work Adjustment

The first five of the six career-planning skills mentioned earlier in this book should be second nature to you by now. All five—decision making, self-assessment, information gathering, integration, and job-search strategies—will be useful in job performance and expansion. In order to use them effectively to stay employed and grow with a job, a final skill—work adjustment—must be learned. The same people-reading skills discussed in reference to job interviews and job choice will be needed in dealing with your work environment and co-workers.

Researchers have found over many years that, after "lack of specific job skills," the primary reason people are not hired (or lose their jobs) is the inability to get along with others in the work setting. This implies that to perform effectively in a new environment, one must look for and learn the hidden rules of behavior for getting a promotion and dealing with co-workers on a day-to-day basis. For example, a Roper poll of nearly 2,000 adults (*USA Today*, December 4, 1985) showed how such rules can vary according to the setting in which one works. Those contacted by the poll were asked how people got ahead in their organizations. According to the respondents, success in government organizations is gained primarily by knowing the right people (58 percent). Intelligence (29 percent), aggressiveness (20 percent), hard work (13 percent), and creative ability (9 percent) appear to be less important qualities. People working in business settings indicated that aggressiveness was most important (38 percent), followed by intelligence (34 percent), hard work (33 percent), and knowing the right people and creative ability (31 percent each). (Several reasons were presented, and respondents could check more than one, so the total percentage for their particular work setting could be more than 100 percent.)

Besides learning these hidden rules for advancement, it is necessary to negotiate successfully the complex maze of daily interactions with your peers. This involves learning the social pecking order, dress habits, conversational customs, and individual roles. (Does your group of co-workers have a "gossip," "snitch," "mother hen," "swinging single," "scapegoat," or an informal leader?) Fitting comfortably into a changing work group involves learning to interact pleasantly with and be tolerant of all kinds of people, but it often requires much more than that. Many situations require that each work group member do part of a total job, which means that members agree on the goals and methods of operation and must be able to depend on one another. This requires working together, giving and taking directions, and sharing ideas and credit—which in turn require patience, kindness, tolerance, discretion, tact, and, when all of the above fail, the ability to handle conflict.

When Conflict Occurs

Despite many commonalities that people share in a work environment, they differ greatly in the ways they approach their jobs. These differences are most likely to stand out when workers are under pressure, when their responsibilities are not clear, or when their personal expectations or needs are violated. All three situations often lead to conflict. Conflict situations offer ideal opportunities for clarifying personal differences and for team building. In fact, people sometimes engage in conflict to bring themselves closer together.

Regardless of the origin and content of the conflict, some simple guidelines (some of which have been suggested by psychologist Harriet Goldhor Lerner in her book *The Dance of Anger* [New York: Harper & Row, 1985]) may prove helpful for you if you become embroiled in a conflict at work:

1. Do not let differences build up. Deal with them as they occur, or you will run the risk of confusing several issues.

2. Deal with the other individual directly. Dr. Lerner advises that you not create a triangle with a third person who must carry your secret frustration. By the same token, you can avoid unnecessary stress and confusion by refusing invitations to become involved as a third party unless it is clearly a part of your job and you have the support of both parties to help them resolve their conflict.

3. Avoid personalizing the issue by placing blame or name calling. If the conflict is related to a colleague's behavior, be sure to keep the focus on the specific behavior, not on the individual's personality. Notice, for example, how

"When you extend your lunch hour without notifying me, I find myself frustrated because I can't live up to my commitments. Please let me know when you're planning on being late in the future so I can schedule around it" differs from "You ———. You'll never learn. You made me miss my appointment. Wait till I tell your supervisor."

4. Do your homework. Plan ahead and try to identify at least one positive alternative for correcting the situation, and plan on inviting other alternatives from the other person involved. That way, you will have a better sense of control over yourself, and you'll be less likely to sound or feel as if you are blindly lashing out.

5. "Speak in your own voice," suggests Dr. Lerner (p. 204). Don't bring in an anonymous third party by saying something like "Other people agree with me that you are. . . ." Doing so isn't fair, raises anxieties, and doesn't help. Use "I" statements, such as "I want," "I need." Let others speak for themselves.

6. Whenever possible, use humor and focus on the positive aspects of your differences as a way of relieving tension and supporting the other person's efforts at change.

7. Plan time for a follow-up review of the changes made so that any new problems can be dealt with in the future.

8. Don't try to go up the chain of command unless you cannot resolve the matter directly through the steps we have suggested. Dr. Lerner notes that if you do go to a superior, you should find out what the appropriate procedures are and inform the person with whom you have been in conflict about your plan.

Adjusting to a Work Environment

In addition to learning how to get along smoothly with all kinds of people in an organization, successful work adjustment usually requires learning to handle some aspects of the work environment and duties.

A major cause of job failure, according to Dunphy (1973, p. 126) is "the inability to accept the job for what it is, rather than for what the new employee thought or hoped it would be." The transition to a new work environment requires time and effort. You may not immediately understand why your company does something in a certain way. What works in practice may not always coincide with what you learned in school. And of course your employer presented the best side in the interview, just as you did. You may find certain routine or unpleasant duties associated with your job description that you had not anticipated. Some of the problems of romanticizing a job can be avoided by looking at the world of work as realistically as possible and by determining what you want and don't want in a job so that you can ask accurate questions about those things in a job interview.

For those who are beginning their first job, no matter how carefully you have searched and how realistic your job choice is, you will have to face the major challenge of accepting and adjusting to a work setting that is very different from life with your parents or in school. All the things we have discussed—

your environment, your image, and your ways of relating to others—will probably need to be modified. Having an employer or supervisor overseeing and/or evaluating your work will be a new and at times anxiety-producing experience.

The greatest single adjustment problem of new employees is making the transition from classroom learning to job experience. Moving on your own from taking tests, supervised lab experience, or even apprenticeship to doing what you have been learning about is a big step. You will be expected to correct your own mistakes, overcome job problems, and pat yourself on the back. You may not get criticism or reassurance from others as often as you did in school. In a career, unlike the classroom, you will be missed if you oversleep, take a day off, or leave early. You will be responsible not just for understanding the theory behind a situation but also for making it work.

In learning what responsibilities are involved in your job, you may discover that it calls for things you did not learn in class and must learn on the job. A primary example of such a skill that cannot be learned from books has already been discussed—the art of getting along with all kinds of people, including some who are very different from you or whom you may not even like. You will also need patience. You may not get a raise or a promotion every time you think you deserve it, and your hard work will not always be appreciated. Nor will you be able to change everything you think should be changed. You may not have as much responsibility or voice in some matters as you would like, at least at first.

A work situation can be fun, informal, and comfortable, but it is also scheduled and structured. Your part in the organization is taken seriously by everyone. Your first job will be a world of new responsibilities.

Be an Effective Communicator

Another skill that employers mention often is effective communication. You will need to know how to communicate at many levels. The first level involves the basic skills of which we are all aware: reading, writing, and speaking. Almost all jobs require oral communication. Many require reading written communication —correspondence, reports, memos, minutes, newsletters, and public relations information. You will need to understand the principles of clear communication: organizing your ideas, making yourself understood, being tactful, persuading, and using vocabulary and grammar correctly. For written communication, clear and logical organization and correct spelling and punctuation are essential. To make friends and to hold your own among colleagues, you will need more informal communication skills, such as confiding, confronting, using appropriate humor, and keeping confidences.

The second group of common skills required are less obvious. Their purpose is to help in expressing oneself. Self-expression means telling people what we believe, what we want, and where we stand. This is what gives us "personality" and attracts others who are like us. It also sets boundaries by letting others know what we value, what we won't tolerate, and how we feel. We also reveal much about ourselves nonverbally, including things we may be trying to hide.

Since nonverbal communication is a fact of life, it is important to understand your attitudes and feelings and be as honest as you can about yourself. When people have interpersonal problems or get unexpected reactions from others, it is often because they have a negative attitude that they are unable to hide successfully.

One unique problem that almost everyone who works must face is the need to communicate clearly and successfully with a supervisor or boss. Problems may arise if the boss is a poor communicator or is prejudiced, angry, or incompetent. Unfortunately, the problem still belongs to the employee, who must persevere to find out what the boss wants. Many of us also create our own problems with bosses because we have anger at authority figures that originated in our relationship with our parents. If you suspect this is a problem for you, try to be aware and objective, or you may see problems in your work relationships where none exists.

The third communication arena is that of transcending personal and cultural differences. There are many immigrants now living and working in the United States; their backgrounds may differ from those of native-born citizens, and for many, English is a second language. Other countries are also buying and building businesses and factories here (like Honda) and hiring U.S. citizens into jobs supervised by foreign-born managers.

Another difference that becomes evident in studies of communication is that between men and women or between majority- and minority-group members. In groups, meetings, and classes, majority-group men tend to talk more than women and minorities, talk longer, and interrupt more frequently and are validated more by discussion leaders. This problem is worse in traditionally male-dominated fields or corporations. Women and minorities need to be prepared to deal with this and to meet it with confidence and assertiveness rather than hostility. Majority-group males also need to be sensitive to these differences and change their behaviors accordingly.

Your success in your career will thus depend on what you do and don't say and how you express yourself in an increasingly diverse workplace that requires many forms of communication.

Manage Your Time Wisely

Still another important work-adjustment skill is the wise management of your time. For most employees, especially those who work on tight time schedules, the old cliche "Time is money" is the primary mode of operation. According to employment expert Robert Hall (cited by reporter Rick Ratliff in an article entitled "Time Theft Up, Researcher Claims," *Columbus Dispatch*, July 17, 1989, p. 2B), you can create problems for yourself with a time-conscious employer if you become a "time thief" who wastes time on the job. Who is a "time thief"? According to Hall, they are fairly easy to identify because they constantly socialize with other employees, make excessive personal phone calls, fake illness or take unwarranted sick days, take inordinately long lunch hours and coffee breaks, frequently arrive late and/or leave early, conduct personal business or engage in activities related to other employment while on the job, look busy while doing nothing, and create a need for overtime by doing their production slowly during normal working hours. If you find yourself engaging in such behaviors, try to find out why. Are you bored with your job and need a new set of challenges? Are you a victim of the "push-pause syndrome"—doing things rapidly for a brief period of time, then slowing down greatly for a long period—and need a more balanced work load? Do you need to transfer to a work setting that allows for more flexible use of your time and greater control of your work schedule? By asking yourself such questions, you may be able to identify needed changes that you can make, perhaps with input from your supervisor, to make your time and that of your employer more productive and enriching.

Understanding and Managing Stress on the Job

Stress has become a familiar term and a well-researched concept as the fast-moving 20th century draws to a close. It is easy to see stress as something caused externally, a problem, rather than what it is—a fight-or-flight reaction, an internal psychological and physiological response that living things produce when faced with change or danger. Risks and problems, including positive risks like marriage or a job promotion, often cause stress. Stress is not something that can be avoided. It is a part of meeting life's challenges that must be accepted and managed constructively.

Tension Equals Energy

The anxiety that accompanies new experiences, expectations, conflict, and even happiness is a physiological message to us that we have needs or concerns that are not being addressed. This anxiety stresses us, and our systems generate energy to deal with the challenge. Our job is to identify our needs and figure out how we can satisfy them. Sometimes the cause of our discomfort and the solution are obvious and easily resolved ("I'm hungry; I'll eat" or "I disagree; I'll argue"). Often, however, the need or problem is hard to identify or the solution is delayed or unavailable ("I don't know why I feel angry at my boss" or "I love this work, but the pay is too low"). Then we will need indirect strategies for dealing with anxiety, such as a relaxation exercise, jogging, or a talk with a friend. Since a great deal of potential energy builds up along with our feelings and concerns, we must learn to recognize any self-defeating behaviors we may use to reduce this pressure (being late to work, drinking too much, kicking the dog) and find ways to convert the energy into positive action (confronting the situation, finding a "detour," planning a long-term change).

How Much Is Enough?

Another interesting finding that consistently appears in the research is that the removal of all stress is not helpful. If too much stress is bad for us, so is too little. We perform best at a certain optimal (moderate) level of stress, where we are stimulated enough to be "on our toes" but not enough to be panicked or discouraged. At this optimum level of stress, we are able to do the job described above: convert the tension and energy into a creative motivator. Burnout occurs only when there is too much or too little stress (Levi, 1972).

Our level of stimulation is not the only determinant of stress. Our effectiveness depends on (1) our level of stimulation or arousal, (2) our talents and capabilities, and (3) the nature or difficulty of the work (Gmelch, 1983). And our stress level depends as well on our perceptions and beliefs. In other words, stress is influenced not only by our capabilities and by job difficulty but by our perceptions of our abilities and of the problems that lie ahead. So, it is important to know yourself and have an objective view of the job. If you do, you can more accurately answer such questions as the following: (1) Is the job too easy or too difficult for me? (2) Will I be comfortable with the people, circumstances, and rewards? (3) Do I have enough skills and experience? An unrealistic level of confidence can put you in a stressful situation that might have been avoided, while too little confidence could cause you to pass up an "ideal job."

It takes effort and alertness to keep aware of your personal "stress index" because the possibilities for falling outside of this optimal stress zone are numerous. For example, most of us have experienced overstimulation or overwork, which results in exhaustion or illness, hasty and shortsighted solutions, and low self-esteem (feelings of failure). But many people do not realize how stressful understimulation is. Lack of variety, challenge, or excitement results in decreased motivation, boredom, fatigue, frustration, and dissatisfaction (Gmelch, 1983), which also have an adverse effect on job performance and self-esteem. To decide how closely your abilities, interests, and goals match an unknown job, you must evaluate job difficulty—both quality and quantity of work. (Can I do this? How much can I do? Is what they are asking realistic?) You must also learn what kinds of things bother you (I hate to be indoors on nice days) and how many of these stresses are built into a particular job. (As a teacher, I will be indoors on a lot of nice days, but I'll be out at 3:30 and all summer. And I can take the students on field trips.) The optimal level of challenge in any area of a job is that which is just beyond our reach: a stretch but not an impossibility.

Strategies for Stress Management

Fortunately, just as there are multiple sources of stress, there are many ways of dealing with it. The prerequisite is to understand yourself, your job, and the concept of stress, so that you can identify the source of the problem as well as your own needs and feelings. Knowing your goals and priorities is crucial in converting your tension into constructive action.

Taking Care of Yourself   It is most important to examine the part our attitudes, behaviors, and choices play in any problem rather than blame our discomfort on something external (the boss, the economy) that we cannot change. We can help maintain good health and attitudes by pursuing recreation, hobbies, relaxation techniques, and so on. Continuing education that will help us avoid obsolescence or will prepare us for a career shift will also help us remain optimistic.

To some extent, we can alleviate stress through appropriate changes in our environment. We may be able to get help from our boss or transfer to another department. A feeling of being overwhelmed can be helped by breaking a large project into smaller parts and by delegating responsibility (this can be difficult if we are anxious to have everything perfect). Finally, if we want change—internal or external—in a job or career, we must take the initiative.

Taking Risks   Be willing to try new things and to stretch a bit beyond your present capabilities. Don't be afraid to ask for responsibilities in areas that interest you, to try creative solutions, or to ask for help if you are overwhelmed. Discuss feelings of stress and strategies with your boss—he or she has surely experienced them too.

Taking Responsibility   Avoiding stress doesn't just mean knowing our limits; it means making sure others know them. It means saying no and speaking up for our needs in a constructive, nonthreatening way. It means we don't take responsibility for others, but we do take responsibility for our health, happiness, and commitments.

Part of your responsibility is identifying sources of stress in order to work with them, and that means knowing where to look. The obvious stresses have been discussed—orienting to a new job and work climate; forming new relationships; dealing with conflict and, possibly, discrimination; pleasing your superiors while taking up for yourself. However, much more subtle stresses are with you throughout your working life. In any career, you must make decisions daily, balancing numerous factors, including your own self-interest. You are constantly working to move toward new goals through job skills and networking, and every new stage in your career development brings new challenges. Change, a constant source of anxiety, is always with you. Other stresses come from intangible things. You may find that although you like a job, the company may have a poor ethical climate (for example, widespread discrimination) or may expect you to do things that go against your personal beliefs. Or you may be uncomfortable with your colleagues' attitudes or values. If you have negative feelings about your job, don't talk yourself out of them; try to determine the source.

Taking Control   This is the "bottom line" of stress management. Highly stressed people do not feel in control. Staying in control means using all the strategies we have just mentioned, in addition to looking ahead and anticipating other challenges to be mastered. It means knowing where you are going and why, and how you plan to get there. It means knowing what things distress you and limiting your exposure to them or learning how to deal with them. It means saving your energy for important issues. It means knowing your feelings, goals, and values so you can deal with disappointment, change, or conflict without "cutting off your nose to spite your face." It means being able to recognize early warning signs of stress in yourself and taking action to understand the problem and make changes before it becomes a catastrophe (Gmelch, 1983).

Stress is an unavoidable part of being human; of growth, change, and getting what we want. A moderate level of stimulation is most comfortable. If there is too much or too little (or we perceive that there is), stress results. Stress creates energy, and we must learn to convert it to motivation and action instead of letting it get out of control. We can minimize and use stress best by matching ourselves to a job for which we are well suited and by using stress-management techniques that emphasize caring for ourselves, taking risks and responsibilities, and remaining in charge of ourselves—our feelings, priorities, goals, and choices—even when things are . . . well, stressful.

Balance Your Career and Family Roles

As indicated by research and statistics cited in earlier chapters, today's young couples often believe they can have it all—two challenging careers; a tidy home; gourmet meals; time to ski, golf, or travel; and, for some, children. In 1990, 25 years after the advent of the women's movement, many changes have been made in the structure of marriage and family. It is now becoming clear, however, that having it all demands high energy, motivation, cooperation, strategic planning, and organization. Such a lifestyle exacts a physical and emotional price even when it is going smoothly: guilt; regret over leaving young children; less time for self, spouse, or partner; frequent exhaustion. When something goes wrong in this carefully orchestrated system—a sick child or babysitter, one person feeling overworked, cash flow problems—the stress level can go from manageable to acute. There are no easy answers for these dilemmas, but it does help to anticipate the presence of stress and know in advance that you will need to develop clear priorities, open communication, long-term commitment, and flexibility before you can successfully combine career and family.

Effectively Handling Performance Appraisals

Another important element in adjusting to a work setting is the way you handle evaluation of your work by superiors. Supervisors can appraise performance on the job through a variety of methods. The way they approach the evaluation may be a matter of personal preference, organizational policy, or a combination of the two. The most informal manner is the pat-on-the-back, "You're doing a good job" approach, which may or may not be tied to specific areas of performance. Generally speaking, with this approach you know you are doing well, but you may not know in what specific areas you are excelling or how your performance might translate into a salary increase later on. A variation is the "management by exception" method, in which you do not receive an evaluation unless you are doing poorly. Here, you don't know how well you are doing, and you are made aware of only your mistakes.

Many organizations require more formal and concrete feedback about an employee's performance, most often prior to the end of a six-month probationary period and yearly after that. The supervisor may be asked to rate the employee on a form that is used to evaluate all staff members in comparable positions. Common areas in which employees are evaluated include job knowledge, achievements/accomplishments, planfulness/thoroughness, creativity/originality, problem solving/decision making, ability to get along with others, communication skills, and ability as a supervisor/leader.

Companies that use this type of evaluation may ask the supervisor to compare your performance in these dimensions with that of other employees in a similar position or with an objective performance standard. Space usually is also provided for the supervisor to summarize overall performance and suggest how you can enhance the quality of your work. How much input you have into your evaluation may depend on your supervisor's personal preferences. One supervisor may simply give you a written copy of your evaluation to review and sign without much discussion. Another supervisor may ask you to rate yourself on the form prior to the evaluation session and may spend some time with you comparing both ratings in an effort to reach a consensus about your performance. It will be helpful to find out in advance how you will be evaluated so you can optimize your input—either by giving your supervisor needed information before the evaluation or by preparing to present your best case during the evaluation.

Another approach to evaluating your performance is called "management by objectives" or "management by results." Under this approach, you meet with your supervisor to develop an action plan that describes what you expect to accomplish during a particular period of time, how you will accomplish it, and by what target date. You will be expected to review your progress with your supervisor from time to time. Your performance evaluation is based on how effectively you have accomplished your objectives. There are still other approaches to evaluate your performance. We encourage you to find out early during your employment how you are going to be evaluated so that you can be prepared to present your strengths, weaknesses, and accomplishments in the most constructive manner.

Regardless of the format that is used, an effective performance appraisal process is designed to keep you "on target" in meeting your job assignments and to be sure that you are effectively adapting to the organizational culture. You can utilize the process to your best advantage if you present your successes to your supervisor as they occur (memos can help here) and ask for suggestions and guidance when it is most appropriate (but don't overdo it). Listen carefully to the feedback you receive. Be sure you understand it, and translate it into action steps you can take to improve your effort. You can also help yourself by preparing a list of your accomplishments and of questions and issues you would like to discuss with your supervisor at the evaluation meeting. If the feedback you receive is not accurate, be sure to correct it in a positive manner by providing more objective evidence (for example, memos documenting your success) in a diplomatic but assertive manner. Remember, though, that your supervisor will set the standard for your performance based on his or her experiences and expectations, so be prepared to find that even though you believe you have been doing a good job, your supervisor might have higher standards.

Methods for awarding salary increases will vary from organization to organization. Some settings provide the same percentage increase for all staff regardless of their performance (this is often purely a cost-of-living increase); others will award increases strictly on merit; still others will combine a cost-of-living increase with merit; and others will combine cost-of-living and merit increases with market-adjustment increases that are designed to keep the salaries of staff in certain fields competitive with those of other organizations. Knowing the general procedure used for determining how staff salary increases are awarded will take some of the mystery out of your adjustment period in the organization.

Developing a Strategy for Personal Affirmative Action

If you are a female or a minority member, you will have some additional—or, at any rate, different—kinds of adjustments to make, as well as additional opportunities and advantages. Several laws prohibit discrimination in training, hiring, promotion, and wages on the basis of such factors as sex, race, and age. The best places to look for employment if you wish to take advantage of this trend are large companies or companies with federal contracts, where the laws are more strictly enforced. Look also at any company where an employer is personally responsive to these affirmative action guidelines.

If you are hired by a company where female or minority employees are not numerous, you need to exercise extra care in orienting yourself. Be yourself. Do not go to extremes to blend in *or* to emphasize your differences. And it is especially important to accept the existing situation, if it is essentially a fair one. Do not demand special treatment, and do not go on a crusade to change attitudes if your presence seems to be resented. Be friendly and give your co-workers time. Because of this new legislation, competition is much stiffer today for white males, and it is not surprising that some of them resent it. So if you encounter angry reactions, do not be oversensitive. Try your best to make friends with colleagues that you like, since informal gossip and lunchtimes can be the best sources of important information and contacts for promotion in a large organization.

If you feel that you are being discriminated against within the organization once you settle in your job, there are several places where you may seek assistance. Unless you have a trusted lawyer or supervisor, the best source of information is the Equal Employment Opportunity Commission. Before making a complaint, be sure that you have facts and dates to back up your accusations. Keep written notes on all conversations and events that you believe demonstrate discrimination against you.

If you are a minority member, a female, or an older person who is hired into a situation where you are a pioneer—a tradition breaker—tread carefully. Everything that has been said applies especially to you. Be as responsible as you can, move cautiously, and listen and watch carefully for those clues discussed earlier that convey behavioral norms. Try not to be negative or defensive. By responding to your situation with care and sensitivity, you can help to open more jobs like yours to a larger segment of the population. These new changes in employer policies are a great step forward, and now is just the right time to take advantage of them and to support this broadening of equal opportunity in American society.

A Taboo Topic: Personal Harassment in the Workplace

The workplace reflects the diversity that exists in our changing society. Consequently, organizational cultures are evolving to accommodate greater variability in individual styles of relating, personal values and lifestyles, and physical capacities. Attitudes that are based on stereotypes and outdated information are being challenged, and individual behaviors that reflect outmoded thinking are being called into question. In fact, the U.S. Equal Employment Opportunity Commission reports that about 13 percent of the lawsuits they filed during 1985–1986 involved claims of sexual harassment.

Despite the more general changes in society and particular work settings where a commitment to social diversity is evident in the policies and practices of the organization, personal harassment still occurs. Sometimes the harassment is enacted without the perpetrator's awareness that the behavior is inappropriate, and often without its being reported by the victim for fear of reprisal or embarrassment.

As we observed in Chapter 3, because of the past "scripting" and real differences that each of us has, old attitudes run deep about male/female roles and ethnic differences. Thus, the problem that women experienced with sexually aggressive adolescent males during high school and college may continue into the work setting, often in more subtle ways. Better grades or a promotion may be promised if a person is willing to engage in a sexual liaison with someone who is in a position of power. Suggestive comments may be made about a person's manner of dress, walk, or voice. Sexual and off-color jokes may be told to test a person's tolerance of a sexual put-down. The continuum of sexually oriented activity of this type may start with a glance or gesture, a whistle, or a comment with a double meaning, move toward a direct proposition, and end with touching, a forced embrace, or coerced intercourse. And the slur or attempt at intimidation need not only be about sex; it can be focused on a person's ethnicity, religious preference, physical capacity, or age. Regardless of how the harassment occurs, one person's attempt to assert power has violated another's right to work in a setting that is free of unwanted attention, coercion, or ethnic put-downs.

How extensive is the problem of harassment in the workplace? We were not able to locate studies of ethnic harassment but were more successful in getting some information about the prevalence of sexual harassment in the workplace. Citing several surveys conducted in the early 1970s, the Project on the Status and Education of Women of the Association of American Colleges reported that 70 to 90 percent of female workers have been harassed on the job.

If you encounter harassment on the job, remember that harassment is not likely to stop if you try to ignore the behavior. You must confront it in a constructive way if you want the behavior to stop. The Project on the Status and Education of Women of the Association of American Colleges suggests that you follow four steps in confronting harassment.

First, *speak up and act assertively* when the incident occurs. Say no firmly, directly, and clearly—for example, "When you say such things you offend me and make me uncomfortable." If the other person didn't realize that the behavior was offensive, your feedback may stop it. If not, at least you will have asserted yourself and preserved your self-esteem and dignity.

Second, *keep a record* of what happened, where it happened, when it happened, who was around to witness the event, and how you responded. These records will be of great help if you need to make a formal complaint later. Tell someone such as a peer or colleague about the event. Ask whether the person has had a similar experience with the harasser, and ask if he or she will back you up if you file a complaint. Harassers often make abusive comments and overtures to more than one person; thus, you may find that you are not alone in your concern.

Third, *find an advocate,* such as an affirmative action officer, personnel specialist, or mental health professional who can support you emotionally as well as counsel you on organizational and legal procedures for managing such situations.

Fourth, *write a letter* to the harasser that clearly and succinctly states your case. Mary P. Rowe wrote an article entitled "Dealing with Sexual Harassment" for the *Harvard Business Review* (May–June 1981) that provides useful guidelines for composing such a letter. She suggests that the letter be written in three parts.

The first part provides a concise, factual account of what happened, as you experienced it, without any evaluation. The focus should be on specific behaviors exhibited by the other person (for example, words and physical gestures such as touching), along with the time and place in which they occurred.

Use the second part of the letter to describe your reactions to the other person's actions: what you thought and how you felt about it.

The third part should briefly, clearly, and directly state how you want the other person to change—for example, "I want you to stop saying (or doing). . . ."

To ensure that the person receives the letter, deliver it directly or send it by registered or certified mail. Keep a copy for your files, but don't send a copy to someone in authority, at least not at first. Give the harasser a chance to change. If that doesn't work, you may use the letter to document any attempt at retaliation by the other person, to file a formal complaint later, or as part of a lawsuit.

If you find these steps difficult, it may be helpful to bolster your confidence by taking a course in assertiveness training or self-defense. Certainly, make sure that you draw as many supportive people around you as you can (trusted family members, colleagues, or a mental health professional) to advise and counsel you in case the situation becomes complex, drawn out, and conflicted.

Keep in mind, too, that even though you may expect your employer to be reasonable and fair, some unfair "hidden expectations" may exist in such a situation. Offenders who are in supervisory roles, or who are influential with management, tend to have more credibility than younger employees. Executives also tend to believe that a subordinate who cannot adjust to a supervisor's expectations has an "attitude problem" (is a "tattletale" or is "paranoid") and should be transferred within the organization or terminated. If you encounter such expectations, you will have to be patient and persistent and be mindful that it is wisest to follow the steps outlined above before requesting a personnel action by the employer or taking your case to court.

Avenues for Career Development within an Organization

We have already seen that occupations are organized according to the level of responsibility they require, the type of work performed, and the kind of enterprise or organization (see Chapter 5). Knowledge of these three areas is helpful because it shows how a person can apply his or her skills, interests, and values in a variety of settings, but it does not give specific details about avenues for career growth within a particular work setting. For charting the course of your career within a particular organization or across several organizations, you can use the Career Cone approach or the Career Roles approach.

The Career Cone

The first approach for charting your growth within an organization was developed by Edgar Schein (1971) of the Sloan School of Management at the Massachusetts Institute of Technology. He suggested that the best way to look at career advancement within a given organization is in terms of the "Career Cone" shown in Figure 8-1.

Schein's Career Cone illustrates the three ways of growing within an organization: inwardly, vertically, and horizontally. The first form of growth, *movement toward the inner circle,* is probably the least familiar of the three because it is not necessarily accompanied by a visible change in position or title. Also, unlike many forms of growth, it may not require that you develop new skills to be successful at it. Your progress on this dimension will be measured in terms of your interpersonal relationships, not necessarily in terms of your position. As a new employee you will have to prove to your supervisor that you can be trusted and are dedicated to accomplishing the goals of the organization. Your first test as a new employee will occur when your supervisor passes on to you your first organizational "secret," such as the reasons a particular decision was made, or who is "in" with the boss and why. The sharing of this secret may be a prelude to a request for help or support from you in carrying out certain actions or decisions. If you pass the first test, others will follow. The secrets

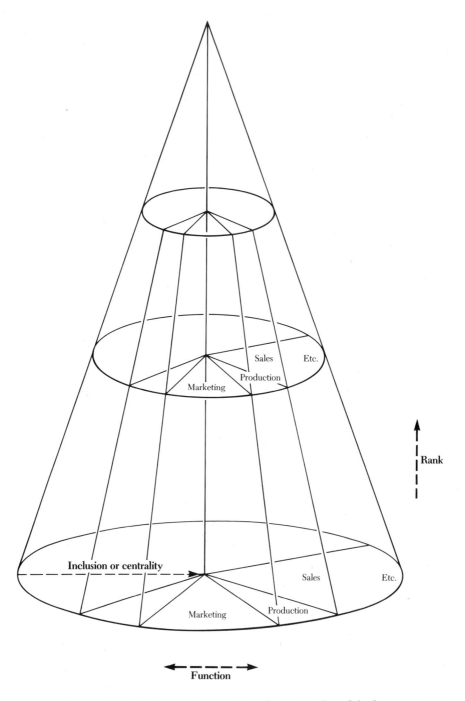

FIGURE 8-1 Schein's Career Cone: a three-dimensional model of an organization. Reprinted with permission from NTL Institute, "The Individual, the Organization, and the Career," by Edgar H. Schein, p. 404, *Journal of Applied Behavioral Science*, Vol. 7, No. 4, Copyright 1971.

that are shared will become increasingly important, and you will sense that you are becoming a more central member of the inner core of decision makers within the organization. Your status will thus depend as much on who you know as on what you do. Failure to pass this test of confidence may be costly: you may be passed over for a promotion or be an outsider to information that affects your work. But passing the test is not always the only, or even the best, choice. If you find yourself in an organization where sharing inside information puts you in a position that is morally or ethically uncomfortable for you, this may be the signal that you need to begin looking around for openings in other departments or in other organizations.

Generally speaking, the higher your position, the more access you will have to privileged information within the organization. Individuals at the top of the organization need more information to make decisions that are critical to the entire organization. Thus, movement toward the inner core is often accompanied by a promotional change in title. There are, however, a number of circumstances in which a trusted employee at the lower levels of the organization may be called on for input into key decisions because of specialized knowledge or informal leadership status.

The second form of growth, vertical *movement up the organizational ranks,* is probably the most familiar. Achievement by moving up the organizational ladder is a common standard for success to most Americans. We are all familiar with the story of the unskilled worker who through diligence and a willingness to acquire new skills is eventually promoted all the way to the president's chair. As a new employee, your potential for promotion within the organization will be measured in terms of your trustworthiness and your capacity to take on increasingly greater levels of responsibility for complex tasks and for supervising others. Your tolerance for stress and your willingness to continue your professional education will also play an important role in determining how successful you are at accomplishing this form of growth.

The third form of professional growth described by Schein involves a *rotation across a series of functions* within the organization. Rather than moving upward, you may move horizontally across positions at the same level. Many management-training programs use this form of growth as a means of exposing new employees to the different facets of an organization. As a new sales representative, for example, you may spend several weeks in the production department, then be rotated across other departments until you have been exposed to the inner workings of the entire organization. This short-term approach to horizontal mobility may also be the source of long-term growth for some employees. It's not uncommon to find an employee who has worked in several departments during his or her career, all at the same level of responsibility. A highly skilled graphics designer may be assigned to different departments, depending on the project that needs his or her expertise; a teacher may transfer among schools in the same school district; and an insurance agent may switch from life to auto insurance sales. In each of these situations, the employee is using the same set of transferable skills to perform related functions. A special advantage of making a series of lateral moves such as these is that it may put you in touch with new learning opportunities and keep you professionally fresh. When coupled with an active refinement of your management skills, a broad range of experience can also be a valuable asset when you are seeking a promotion or a new job.

Career Roles

The second approach to charting your growth within an organization is to look at the professional roles you may assume during your career. This approach was introduced in part in Chapter 4, where adult life stages were discussed. A number of writers (Dalton, Thompson, & Price, 1977; Schein, 1978; Tiedeman & O'Hara, 1963) have contributed to our knowledge of what happens to students during college and after they enter the labor force. Perhaps the easiest way of thinking about your career during college and beyond is to imagine yourself moving through seven roles over time: "student," "applicant," "apprentice/trainee," "colleague," "mentor," "sponsor," and "retiree." These seven roles are summarized in Table 8-1, which describes each role in terms of the central tasks and activities it involves and the major psychological issues it may create.

Each of the roles shown in Table 8-1 evolves over time as we gain new skills and insight into ourselves. You played the role of a *student* for many years, through formal and informal education. This role became more complex over time as you were asked to make more choices and assume greater levels of responsibility for your actions. Your initial career choices were probably based on a fantasy or on someone you admired, but then they came to be based on actual work experience, better occupational information, and higher levels of awareness of what you could do, liked to do, and believed you ought to do.

In the previous chapter, you became acquainted with the role of *applicant* for a professional position. This role requires that you focus your view from a general understanding of occupations to a more precise understanding of particular organizations and specific jobs. It also requires that you assertively engage in a process of locating positions, applying for them, and securing a position that best reflects your occupational self-concept. Since the job-campaigning process may contain much stress, frustration, and disappointment, it can teach you a great deal about how well you tolerate uncertainty.

The move from applicant to your first professional position as an *apprentice/trainee* is a bit like returning to your first days as a college student. It involves learning the ropes of the new setting, accepting the wisdom and guidance of others about how best to manage your responsibilities, building supportive relationships with others, learning to live with the difference between your fantasy about what life should be like in the new place and the reality of the situation, and overcoming the insecurity associated with being less skilled than others in some areas. More will be said about this role later in this chapter.

Unlike the shift from applicant to apprentice or trainee that occurs shortly after graduation, there may be no clear moment when a person moves from trainee status to that of a *colleague*. For people who have a considerable amount of work experience and a great deal of professional maturity, or who are working in a job that does not involve many complex tasks, the shifts may occur

TABLE 8-1 Seven Career Stages

	Stage 1	Stage 2	Stage 3	Stage 4	Stage 5	Stage 6	Stage 7
Role	Student	Applicant	Apprentice/ Trainee	Colleague	Mentor	Sponsor	Retiree
Central tasks	Developing and discovering one's values, interests, and abilities. Making wise educational decisions. Finding out about occupational possibilities through discussion, observation, and work experience	Learning how to look for a job, how to apply for a job, how to negotiate a job interview. Learning how to assess information about a job and an organization. Making a realistic and valid job choice	Learning the ropes of the organization. Helping others. Following directions. Achieving acceptance	Becoming an independent contributor. Finding a niche in the organization as a specialist	Training/ mentoring others. Interfacing with other units in the organization. Managing team projects	Analyzing complex problems, shaping the direction of an organization. Handling organizational secrets. Dealing with organizational politics. Developing new ideas. Sponsoring the creative projects of others. Managing power and responsibility	Adjusting to changes in standard of living and lifestyle. Finding new ways of expressing one's talents and interests
Major psychological issues	Accepting responsibility for one's choices	Assertively presenting oneself to others. Tolerating uncertainty	Depending on others. Dealing with reality, shock of what the organization is like. Overcoming insecurity	Reassessing original career goals in light of new self-knowledge and growth potential in the organization. Independence. Accepting responsibility for one's successes and failures. Establishing a balanced lifestyle	Assuming responsibility for others. Deriving satisfaction from the successes of others. If not in management role, accepting role of established professional and finding opportunities for lateral growth	Disengaging from primary concern about self or ownership to become more concerned with organizational welfare. Managing personal emotional reactions to high levels of stress. Balancing work and family, life planning for retirement	Finding satisfaction in one's past career accomplishments while being open to new avenues of personal growth

Source: Adapted from "The Four Stages of Professional Careers—A New Look at Performance by Professionals" by Gene W. Dalton, Ralph H. Thompson, and Raymond L. Price, 1977, Organizational Dynamics (Summer), pp. 19–42; and Career Dynamics: Matching Individual and Organizational Needs (pp. 36–48) by Edgar H. Schein, 1978, Reading, MA: Addison-Wesley.

rapidly, sometimes within several months. Others may take considerably longer to reach the new status. Regardless of how long it takes, the benchmarks for successfully moving into the new role are the same: feeling increased confidence and "belongingness" in the organization, being able to act as an independent contributor, finding and shaping a personalized professional niche in the organization as a recognized specialist, and developing a mentoring relationship with someone who is more senior in experience in position. As they make the transition, some employees spend time struggling with how best to balance their desire to assert their views of how things ought to be against the realities of past traditions and established policies. Assertively presenting new ideas involves using tact and diplomacy with colleagues and a willingness to take responsibility for one's successes and failures. The degree to which a person is effective in moving to the status of colleague often depends on how well he or she utilizes the help or advice of a supervisor or more experienced co-workers and on how well non-work-related pursuits are balanced against frustrations that occur in the work setting. The period of shaping one's niche may also be accompanied by a time of self-assessment in which one begins to ask, What does the future look like for me in this organization?

People who take on the role of *mentor* usually have a considerable amount of work experience and personal maturity and are viewed as established professionals. Such people derive satisfaction from training and supervising others through informal or formal means and may measure their own success by how they have helped others achieve rather than by what they themselves accomplish. Because they generally have a high level of knowledge and credibility with their peers, they often serve as bridges between staff and the upper levels of management. They may also be involved in making connections with other organizations. Such individuals are often in supervisory roles.

The *sponsor* role is usually associated with upper levels of management. People who fill this role are usually responsible for shaping the direction of an organization or a major segment of it. The skills for success in the sponsor role are complex: dealing with complicated problems, managing organizational politics, sponsoring the creative ideas of others, originating or promoting new directions for the organization, and managing personal reactions to high levels of stress. Such people must be willing to make quick decisions and to exercise their authority during crisis periods while having a long-range plan for accomplishing the overall mission of the organization. At different points in time, they may be a disciplinarian for an errant staff member, a referee in a staff conflict, a teacher of a new idea or approach that protects company policy, and a team leader. Also crucial to their success is the ability to work for long periods of time at high levels of involvement and the capacity for taking advantage of social and leisure activities for personal restoration.

The *retiree* role becomes part of the conscious thinking of many workers around the age of 40 as they examine the next steps in their career and realize that their current or next position may be the one from which they will retire. The central tasks for the retiree are to adjust to a new standard of living and lifestyle and to find new ways of utilizing interests and talents that may have been dormant during the working years. People who enjoy their retirement find satisfaction in past career accomplishments but remain open to new pursuits.

Our overview of the avenues for career development is now complete. We have a general picture of the workplace, and we have highlighted avenues for growth within particular work settings. In the remaining pages of this chapter, we will look at what you can do to promote your career growth more actively by pursuing professional development opportunities and by wise decision making.

Personal Development

When you take a job, you have entered into a contract with your employer. In return for your contribution of labor and talent, you receive wages and certain other benefits. Be aware, however, that you also work for yourself and that one of your goals during your career should be your own development. It may be helpful to start the process by identifying interests and skills that you have which your current position does not permit you to utilize. These could be of benefit to the organization, and your supervisor might be responsive to a well-presented statement explaining why you should be permitted to add new duties to your current responsibilities. Supervisors will tell you that they spend a good deal of time checking to see that employees do their required work. The person who completes essential task assignments and asks for more is likely to be a valued employee.

Years from now, there will be a vast number of jobs that do not exist today. The training you have now will not necessarily prepare you for jobs that will be around ten years from now. Throughout this book, however, we have emphasized that education, job training, and decision making are lifelong processes. Learning how to learn is an important skill, one that you should continue to use once you finish your formal education. Professional conferences, work friendships, journals, and news media help you keep up on what's happening in your field and in related fields. Many employers will pay for some or all of an employee's continuing education. You may find that taking some courses in areas new to you or volunteering will help you do your current job better, as well as prepare you for a better job.

Most employers will be as interested as you are in your personal and professional growth. The company benefits by developing talent within its ranks, with an eye to present competence and future promotion. Take advantage of opportunities that come your way. Increasing your skills and knowledge is a good way to enhance your value to an employer. Managerial obsolescence, which threatens managers committed to security rather than growth, is a major problem in business. By keeping current in your field, you can avoid becoming obsolete. Being concerned with your continued development will help you maintain occupational viability and vitality.

The major ingredient in the personal and professional development of many workers is their relationship with a *mentor*. The mentor, as discussed earlier, is often a boss or prestigious older colleague—someone you hit it off with who functions as a friend, teacher, and surrogate parent. This figure is a primary source of the nonacademic information and confidence that needs to be developed for successful work adjustment. From a mentor you can learn how to implement and apply ideas and to develop influence. The mentor relationship is usually personal enough that the new worker can request feedback, ask questions about other people, air misgivings, and get honest advice about how best to use the employment situation for personal development. The mentor also functions as a role model. By watching the way he or she deals with many situations, you can refine the use of all six career skills.

Female and minority employees may have more difficulty attracting a mentor or keeping such a relationship running smoothly. This may happen because such employees are not totally welcome in a particular work setting or because they seem different and old-timers are afraid of them. Since so many potential mentors are men, there are also some additional complications for females: beliefs that many men have about what behaviors are appropriate for women, teasing or gossip about the relationship, and the possibility of sexual attraction. There are no rules for handling these pitfalls effectively. Sensitivity to the mentor and to the work environment is called for. Although a mentor must essentially be a volunteer, you can invite the support of a potential mentor by asking questions or showing an interest in how that person's job is done. As with any other situation in a new work environment, patience and quiet observation are best at first.

It should now be clear that the skill of maintaining a successful career adjustment is composed of the ability to adapt to and grow along with shifts in the environment and changes in oneself. These include abilities for social interaction, communication, and continued learning, as well as regular use of the first five skills learned in this book—decision making, self-assessment, information gathering, integration, and job-search strategies. Keeping abreast of satisfaction and fit in any job requires that we regularly reassess our feelings, values, beliefs, goals, interest, skills, and experience—all of which accumulate and change over the years. We must also be sensitive to the job market and the economy and to changing requirements and possibilities of other jobs and new opportunities. Organizing this stream of new information within the structure of our decision skills should help us know when and how we wish to act to reach our evolving career goals.

Promotional Strategies

Your attention to personal development and growth will inevitably lead to expanded interests and abilities and a desire for new challenges. Depending on your development as an individual and the direction your company is taking, this need for change can be met in a variety of ways—for example, a move to another organization or another career area, a move up in your company's hierarchy, a lateral move to another area or department, or even just a move toward greater inclusion in decision-making processes that affect you (illustrated by

Schein's Career Cone). This can be as simple as asking to be included in policy-making or managerial meetings or as complex as a planned campaign to qualify and be considered for a certain promotion or job.

Whether you enter a job with the general goal of being promoted or are aiming for advancement to a specific position, there are professional and inter-personal tips and strategies that will help you to move along your planned path and to meet transitions and obstacles more smoothly.

1. Begin early to document your successes. When you offer good ideas, institute new policies, or contribute to the solution of a problem, put it in a written report as a memo or get it into the minutes of a meeting. Make sure the people who do the promoting get a copy, and keep a copy for yourself. Save letters of recommendation. If someone you trust commends or thanks you for a job well done, you may want to ask him or her to put it in writing and/or make sure your superiors hear the news.

2. Be sure that you fully understand the requirements and demands of your target position and are willing and able to meet them.

3. Build a system of formal and informal connections. Make an effort to cooperate with your supervisor and understand his or her problems. Do the same with others in higher positions who may be influential in choosing which people to promote. Keep in touch with friends you make in other areas and departments and in other companies. Besides enjoying their company, you may find that their shop talk and problems can provide valuable information about what to expect and about where job openings may occur. In the case of friends or mentors that you trust, let them know how things are going for you and what your future plans are so that they can put in a good word for you if the oppor-tunity arises. (You may be able to do the same for them.) Your immediate super-visor may be a good person to confide in, but not always. If you are uncomfortable about your relationship, if someone else is really making the decisions, or if you are after your supervisor's job, that is not the best person to choose as an ally. If you don't get along with your supervisor and think he or she will block your chances for advancement, you may want to plan for a lateral move to another area where the environment is more favorable.

4. When you have made a decision to try for a specific position or to make a move within a specific time frame, share this with your support group and suggest things you think they might do to help. Whenever it seems appropriate, share your goals with the people who will make the promotion or do the hiring. Present them with documentation of your work successes, your reasons for being interested in the change, and what you believe you can offer in the new position.

Although each person in our society is free to aim as high as his or her potential permits, striving to reach the top may not be that important. It can also be unwise. Being at too high a level puts constant pressure on you. Too much pressure may cause considerable stress and physical, emotional, and in-terpersonal damage. Reaching for ever-higher levels of achievement in order to please or keep up with others can thus become a trap if the work does not also provide personal pleasure and satisfaction.

To avoid reaching too high too soon, Cosgrave (1973) suggests that you may wish to start by defining the level where you will be most comfortable and setting a series of moderate goals for yourself. These goals will then act as a series of steps, which you master one after another. This method makes your distant goal more tentative and less overwhelming and gives you room for further investigation and redecision.

Beginning at a moderate level does not mean that you must stay there or that your talent is being wasted. One advantage of a job on this level is that you have an opportunity to learn the ropes and make mistakes in a situation where you are not ultimately responsible. The "whiz kid" who steps into a higher job in full view of the company brass is under much more pressure *not* to learn by trial and error.

Regardless of where you start or how high you aim, you will probably reach your ceiling. If your upward movement continues when that happens, you might find yourself at a level of responsibility that is beyond your competence or that you feel demands too much time and energy. Laurence Peter (1984) believes that this happens frequently and is a prime cause of inefficiency in our society. His "Peter Principle" is: "In time, every post tends to be occupied by an employee who is incompetent to carry out his/her duties." The remedy is to halt advancement just below this level.

It may be difficult to acknowledge that you have reached your ceiling when your present work is being done. You may go through a period of anxiety and uncertainty at this time in your career. The rewards of moving up in the hierarchy may seem to outweigh the problems—a trap of rising expectations. During such times, you will be faced with having to choose between moving up, moving across, or moving out.

Career Expansion: Moving Up, Across, or Out

Harriet Goldhor Lerner, author of *The Dance of Intimacy*, observed:

> All of us have deeply ambivalent feelings about change. We seek the wisdom of others when we are not making full use of our own and then we resist applying the wisdom that we *do* seek even when we're paying for it. We do this not because we are neurotic or cowardly, but because both the will to change and the desire to maintain sameness coexist for good reason. Both are essential to our emotional well-being and equally deserve our attention and respect.[1]

No work environment is ideal. Each has its peculiarities and problems. Even the job that approaches the ideal will be unsatisfying some of the time. Discomfort can be an important prelude to growth, but how do you know when it is time to look for a different position—to move up, across, or out? How frustrated,

---

[1]From *The Dance of Intimacy* (p. 11) by Harriet Goldhor Lerner, 1989, New York: Harper & Row. Copyright 1989 by Harriet Goldhor Lerner. Reprinted by permission.

bored, or disappointed must you be before you say "Enough is enough" and begin the process of change? These are difficult questions. There are no pat answers or formulas, only those that you find in yourself. There are, however, some areas to explore and questions to ask as you sort through your motivations to make a change.

Start with yourself, where the growth cycle begins and ends:

1. Do you want more money? More or less responsibility? A new set of tasks? A different lifestyle?
2. Have your career goals changed since you started at your job? If they have changed, how do they differ?
3. Are you a victim of the Peter Principle?
4. Last, but very important, how much of your dissatisfaction is due to your attitudes and behaviors, which will follow you to any job you choose?

Next, look to the organization:

1. Does it ask too much or give too little, leaving you feeling burned out and unappreciated?
2. Does the job have a negative effect on the other aspects of your lifestyle— your social life and leisure pursuits?
3. Has your employer made comments about your work performance falling off, indicating that he or she also sees that you are less involved in your work than before?
4. Is the employer supportive of your need for change, or is such change viewed as a threat to the status quo?
5. Is there an unresolved conflict at work that haunts you from day to day?

After you have explored these questions, look at the options you will have if you stay where you are: can you redefine your position (sometimes even the slightest alteration can make a big difference), or move to another one within the firm to save the benefits you have accumulated? Finally, look at the benefits of moving out. Where do you want to live? What work would you do there?

Before we discuss the process of changing jobs further, however, let us look at the whole idea of job change. Years ago employers tended to view with concern the employee who had a vocational history marked by several jobs. People tended to remain with the organization where they began work, moving up or across rather than out. While this is still often the case, today's American work force is more job mobile than ever before. Every year 10 percent of the labor force changes jobs. The average American can expect to change jobs at least three or four times during the course of his or her career.

The increased acceptability of job change, mid-life career change, and multiple careers has its roots in the social upheaval of the 1960s. During that period, the motivation for choosing a job ceased to be based solely on security. It expanded to include self-growth and personal satisfaction. As an outgrowth of social change, people now leave jobs for many reasons. Whereas people once stayed with a secure job unless they had extreme problems, it is now acceptable for them to change jobs because they realize they chose the "wrong" job, because they have changed, because the job has changed, or because they have done as much as they can in that job and are looking for a new challenge.

The prospective employee who can give a good explanation for seeking a new position is usually able to locate one. If your record as an employee is marked by frequent or directionless moves, however, you could experience difficulty looking for still another job. Informed decisions made in the early stages of your job search can help keep you out of a job that you may want to leave in six months.

Consider the advantages and disadvantages of available jobs. Be realistic about your strengths and limitations when you assess the requirements of new jobs. On the basis of adequate information, make a decision about what you would like to do and how you are going to do it. If possible, stay in your present position while conducting your job search—an employer is more likely to hire someone who already has a job. (The "interviewing for informaiton" approach is a useful way of searching out new prospects while maintaining control over your present job situation. So is taking on some job responsibilities that involve meeting the public or other people in your field.)

Regardless of what you do, your overriding goal should be to retain a balanced perspective on where you are, what you want to do, and how you will go about getting what you want. This requires that you be thorough and clear-cut in your approach to building your future. In this way you can increase the odds of saying to yourself in the future, "I have lived the way I wanted. I have enjoyed my career."

Promoting Constructive Change

Imagine yourself in the following situations:

1. You are a new employee. Your colleagues seem to think you are being given preferential treatment because of your gender, race, or social group membership. You'd like to change their attitudes because you don't think you are being judged fairly.
2. Your supervisor is making heavy demands on your time. You haven't been able to meet those demands without putting in a considerable amount of overtime. The pressure of the job has been causing you to cut back on leisure and social pursuits that are important to you. It doesn't look as though the situation will change in the near future.
3. You have a strong but unexpressed difference of opinion with a colleague about the way a project should be done. You've been holding back your opinion for several weeks, and it's beginning to distress you.
4. After a year on the job, you did not receive the raise you hoped for. You believe you deserve a raise and want to take steps to get it.
5. Your recent request for a promotion was denied, but you don't know why.
6. You've been doing the same job for five years and have recently been feeling bored and restless. You don't know why your feelings have changed, but you are becoming more and more distressed about your situation.

7. You are a departmental supervisor. Two of your employees have had a considerable amount of conflict recently. You'd like to change this situation as soon as you can because it's beginning to affect the morale of the entire staff.
8. You're going to retire in two years. How will you prepare for the change?

Choose two of the situations described above and apply them to your own career in the future. For each situation, try to identify its potential causes and outline a strategy for resolving or changing it. Use the procedure below to develop your change strategy.

1. What are the causes of this situation?

    a. _____

    b. _____

    c. _____

2. What is the worst possible way I could handle this problem?

_____

_____

_____

3. To change the situation to make it more constructive, I would have to alter my behaviors in the following ways. (Identify specific behaviors you would need to change.)

    a. _____

    b. _____

    c. _____

    d. _____

4. To change this situation to make it more positive or constructive, others would have to change their behaviors in the following ways. (Identify specific behaviors that they would have to change.)

    a. _____

    b. _____

c. _____

d. _____

5. How will you communicate your desire to change the situation to others?

   a. _____

   b. _____

   c . _____

6. How much responsibility will you take for promoting the change? How much responsibility will you share with others?

_____

_____

_____

7. Using the information from your answers to the questions above, list the specific steps you will take to create this change.

   a. _____

   b. _____

   c. _____

   d. _____

   e. _____

Self-Review Activity: How Much Have I Changed?

Turn back to the activity entitled "Where Am I in the Career Decision-Making Process?" at the end of Chapter 2, on page 27. Use the stages presented in the activity to summarize your progress thus far and to plan the next steps in the decision-making cycle.

References and Resources

Cosgrave, G. P. (1973). *Career planning: Search for a future.* Toronto: University of Toronto Press.

Dalton, G. W., Thompson, R. H., & Price, R. L. (1977, Summer). The four stages of professional careers—A new look at performance by professionals. *Organizational Dynamics,* pp. 19–42.

Dunphy, P. W. (Ed.). (1973). *Career development for the college student.* Cranston, RI: The Carroll Press.

Gmelch, W. H. (1983). Stress for success: How to optimize your performance. *Theory Into Practice, 22,* 7–14 (Columbus, OH: Ohio State University, College of Education).

Hughes, J. O., & Sandler, B. R. (1986). In case of sexual harassment: A guide for women students. Washington, DC: Association of American Colleges, Project on the Status and Education of Women.

Lerner, H. G. (1985). *The dance of anger.* New York: Harper & Row.

Lerner, H. G. (1989). *The dance of intimacy.* New York: Harper & Row.

Levi, L. (1972). *Stress and distress in response to psychological stimuli.* Elmsford, NY: Pergamon Press.

Peter, L. J., & Hull, R. (1984). *The Peter principle.* New York: Bantam.

Project on the Status and Education of Women. (1978, June). *Sexual harassment: A hidden issue.* Washington, DC: Association of American Colleges.

Schein, E. H. (1971). The individual, the organization, and the career: A conceptual scheme. *Journal of Applied Science, 7,* 401–426.

Schein, E. H. (1978). *Career dynamics: Matching individual and organizational needs.* Reading, MA: Addison-Wesley.

Tiedeman, D. V., & O'Hara, R. P. (1963). *Career development: Choice and adjustment.* Princeton, NJ: College Entrance Examination Board.

APPENDIX A

Experiential Exercises

A Personal Coat of Arms
Guidelines for a Personal Journal
Explorations in Lifestyle Choice
Decision-Making Vignettes
You, the Employer

A Personal Coat of Arms[1]

In years gone by, families created personal coats of arms to present themselves to others. These coats of arms often depicted some of the family history and beliefs and activities that were important to the family. This activity invites you to create your own coat of arms to introduce yourself to others.

On page 198 you will find a blank coat of arms divided into six sections. In each section, make a drawing that expresses your thoughts in response to the directions below. Do not use words, except in section 6. Your drawings can be simple, since they express your feelings.

1. In section 1, express in a drawing your own greatest personal accomplishment.
2. In section 2, express in a drawing your family's greatest accomplishment.
3. In section 3, express in a drawing one or two things that people who care about you have suggested you do for a living.
4. In section 4, express in a drawing the thing you like most about being a student.
5. In section 5, show in a drawing what occupation you would ideally want to enter—if you had the time, money, and opportunity.
6. In section 6, list the things you want most from work.

Guidelines for a Personal Journal

The personal journal is a diary designed to help you become more aware of yourself in the career-planning process and to help you integrate all your experiences.

Your journal should consist of two entries. The first entry, *What I did*, may cover a variety of activities, such as your reactions to class sessions, observations of and conversations with others about your work, ideas about your interests, abilities, and values, volunteer or work activities that you are pursuing, and conversations you have had with others about their career goals.

The second entry, *How I reacted to what I did and what it means to me*, should focus on the thoughts and feelings the activity stimulated in you. It should also tell what these reactions mean to you as you think about yourself in the process of exploring and defining a career objective.

[1]This exercise is adapted from S. B. Simon, R. C. Hawley, and D. D. Britton, *Composition for Personal Growth: Values Clarification through Writing.* Copyright © 1973 by Hart Publishing Company.

Personal Coat of Arms
for

_____

(Name)

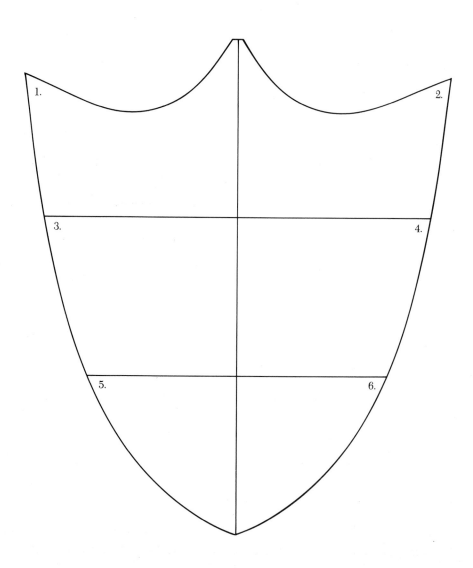

_____ Name

_____ Date

Personal Journal Entries for Week of   _____

What I did or what happened	*How I reacted*

_____ Name

_____ Date

Personal Journal Summary Self-Review
(What I have learned about myself
as I have developed my career plans)

Your entries need not be lengthy, but each should be made shortly after the activity has occurred. Each entry should reflect an attempt to integrate what you have experienced with your current thoughts about selecting a career.

On page 199 there is a blank sample journal page and a blank sample self-review page for you to copy into a notebook. Make a journal page (or as many as are needed) for each week and fill it out as discussed here. At the end of your career search, copy the Personal Journal Summary Self-Review into your notebook and fill it out.

Explorations in Lifestyle Choice

This set of exercises will help you gain a clearer idea of how you currently integrate your daily activities into your overall lifestyle and what needs these activities meet. The exercises give you an opportunity to become aware of how you spend your time, which activities you value, and how you express some of your personal needs and beliefs in the kinds of decisions you make about time. This will help you get a clearer perspective on your current life situation and how it relates to your career goals.

Exercise 1: Energy-Giving and Energy-Getting Activities

During a typical day, you no doubt have noticed that certain types of activities serve to restore your energy, refresh your mind, and relax you, while other activities seem to deplete your energy, exhaust you, and tire you out. In other words, the energy flow for any activity will be positive or negative.

Take five sheets of paper and head each with one of the activity categories in the Energy Flow Rating Scale box that follows. Then generate a list of activities that fit the criteria given in each heading. You should create as broad and as long a list in as short a time as possible. To do this, you will not examine each activity as you record it but will simply write down all ideas to make sure

---

Energy Flow Rating Scale

+ + = Activities that for me are very relaxing, refreshing, enjoyable

+ = Activities that for me are somewhat relaxing, refreshing, enjoyable

0 = Activities that for me are neither relaxing nor tiring, just "neutral"

− = Activities that for me are somewhat mentally tiring or exhausting

− − = Activities that for me are very tiring and exhausting

every possibility is covered. Once you have exhausted all your ideas, you can go back and review them and eliminate or combine some of them.

Next, apply the items to yourself during a typical week. Look at the list of activities you have generated and identify activities that best exemplify a typical week for you. Feel free to add items if you want to make your list more representative for you personally. Turn to Figure A-1 and record each activity you have listed over the appropriate energy flow category, + + to − −. This will help you gain a clearer perspective on the balance of a typical week in your life.

Once you have completed your list, ask yourself the following questions:

1. Is my typical week balanced the way I would like it to be?
2. Do I usually expend more energy than I receive? If so, how does it affect my general outlook on life?
3. Am I spending more time in pleasurable activities to the neglect of some important energy-spending tasks?
4. Do I build in rewards (energy-giving activities) after working hard at certain tasks?
5. If I wanted to alter the way I spend my time, what things would I give up or add on? Will I do it? Starting when?

Exercise 2: My Time Is My Lifestyle

Exercise 1 was designed to help you get a feel for how your energies flow in your interactions with your environment. The second activity will help you get a clearer picture of your current lifestyle—that is, the proportion of time spent in study/work, leisure/recreation, and kinship/friendship activities during a typical week.

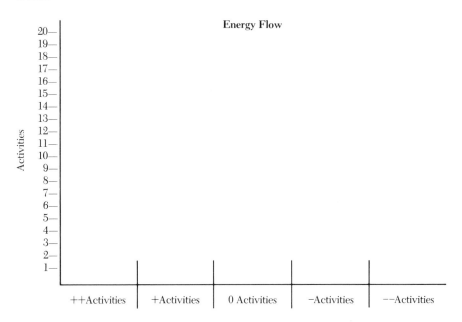

FIGURE A-1 Energy flow chart.

Take three sheets of paper and label as follows: "Study/Work Activities," "Leisure/Recreation Activities," and "Kinship/Friendship Activities." Record your activities during the next week on the appropriate sheets. At the end of the week, review what you have recorded and ask yourself the following questions:

1. Is this a typical week for me?
2. Is this the way I want to live in the future? If not, what would I change about my lifestyle? How would I make those changes? When?

To engage you more completely in the process of comparing the present with your future "ideal" lifestyle, draw two "lifestyle triangles" on a sheet of paper. Refer to the lifestyle triangle in Chapter 1 (page 8) to refresh your memory. Using data from the lifestyle survey you have just completed, first draw a triangle that represents the shape of your lifestyle now—that is, so many units of leisure/recreation on one side, so many units of study/work on the second side, and so many units of kinship/friendship on the third side.

After you complete this triangle, draw a second one that represents your ideal lifestyle, the one you want to shape through the choices you are making now. Compare the triangles and focus on how you can make the present more comfortable and on what you can do, starting now, to build toward your future ideal.

Exercise 3: Life Needs and Lifestyle Choices

As was described in Chapter 1 (page 6), Abraham Maslow suggested that each of our daily activities can meet one or several needs. Work, for example, provides money to purchase food and drink and to obtain shelter and security. It also provides us with opportunities to experience a sense of belonging, self-esteem, and self-realization. By reviewing how you spend your time during a typical week, you can begin to identify more clearly the needs that you are currently meeting in your life. When you do this, you may find that you wish to reprioritize some of your activities to meet some important needs that are not presently being met.

To complete this exercise, copy Figure A-2 on a sheet of paper and list the activities you engaged in during a typical week above the needs they appear to be meeting.

In reviewing the patterns of the needs you have met during a typical week, you may experience a desire to meet specific needs more frequently. Using the following list, identify these needs and plan strategies for increasing your likelihood of meeting them. (Use a separate sheet of paper if necessary.)

Needs I Would Like to *Meet More Often*	*Activities That Will Help Me* *Meet Them*

1. _____   A. _____

   _____   B. _____

                                                    C. _____

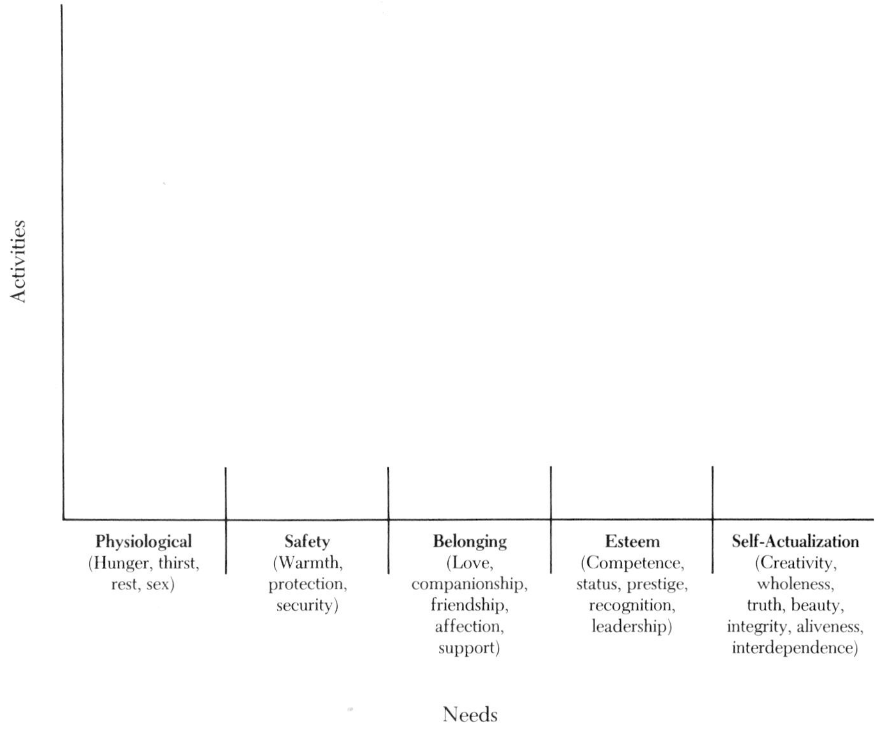

Activities (vertical axis)

| Physiological (Hunger, thirst, rest, sex) | Safety (Warmth, protection, security) | Belonging (Love, companionship, friendship, affection, support) | Esteem (Competence, status, prestige, recognition, leadership) | Self-Actualization (Creativity, wholeness, truth, beauty, integrity, aliveness, interdependence) |

Needs

FIGURE A-2   Life needs and lifestyle choices.

*Needs I Would Like to
Meet More Often*

*Activities That Will Help Me
Meet Them*

2. _____   A. _____

_____   B. _____

C. _____

3. _____   A. _____

_____   B. _____

C. _____

4. _____   A. _____

_____   B. _____

C. _____

Decision-Making Vignettes

Mark Manycredits

Mark Manycredits must declare a major, and he is having great difficulty making a decision. His real dream is to go to law school. His high school grade point average was 3.4, and his college grades are about the same. On interest tests he scores very high on law, and he loves debating and public speaking. But he is afraid he might not be able to succeed in law. His father says he will have trouble getting admitted to law school and being hired and that because he is African American he will have to do better than others to prove himself. His college adviser tells him the field of law is overcrowded anyway. If he tries and fails to get into law school, he will have a B.A. in political science, which won't really qualify him for any specific job.

Mark is also very interested in the possibility of being a medical technician, which he feels might be a less risky option. He has a cousin who is a lab technician, and he helped her one summer while doing volunteer work at the hospital where she works. She is well paid and has plenty of autonomy on the job. Mark's family believes that this second option is more realistic for him. They are struggling financially to help put Mark through college, and they don't want him to risk wasting those four years.

What should Mark do to resolve his problem in a planful way?

Helen and Harry Household

Helen and Harry Household have been married seven years. Helen is 30 and Harry is 32. They have two children, ages 4 and 6. Helen made good grades in high school and enjoyed studying. She got a scholarship from her hometown college but dropped out after two years because she was undecided about her major. She took a secretarial job, which she didn't really like, and soon afterward she met and married Harry. He has a B.A. in accounting and is just beginning to work his way up in a large firm. Helen has enjoyed doing volunteer work and being home with the kids, but now she feels ready to go back to school. She is anxious to get started soon because she feels she is getting older and because she has discovered several kinds of jobs she thinks she might like. Helen feels they could afford to put the 4-year-old in a preschool if they scrimped a little, or that she could go to evening classes while Harry babysits. She would prefer to go during the day so she could spend evenings with the family.

Harry wants her to wait until the children are older and he is making more money before she goes back to school. He's just beginning to enjoy having a little extra money for luxuries. He suggested that if Helen is bored at home she could look for another secretarial job for a few years. That way Helen could get out of the house and bring in a little money instead of spending it.

What should Helen and Harry do to resolve their problem in a planful way?

Molly Mathwhiz

Molly Mathwhiz has wanted to work with computers ever since she first saw one at a high school science fair. She can't decide whether to go away to a university and get a B.A. in computer science or to enroll in the two-year program at the technical college in her hometown. Molly's high school grade average is 2.9, but her math grades are much higher. Both schools she is considering have good programs in various computer areas, but her father wants very much for her to have a college degree. He believes that having a B.A. will help her get a better-paying and more prestigious job and that people will look up to her more if she has a college degree. Her high school boyfriend has a good job in their hometown and wants her to go to technical school rather than away to college so that they can get married and settle down.

Molly has some savings, but she will have to work no matter where she goes to school. She can probably get along on less money at tech since she can live at home. Molly would like to please both her father and her boyfriend, but the most important thing to her is to decide which degree would provide a better background and lead to more exciting job offers. She isn't sure she wants to get married right away, but everyone assumes they are engaged, and she's afraid if she goes away to school her boyfriend might meet someone else.

What should Molly do to resolve her dilemma in a planful way?

You, the Employer

Imagine yourself as a company personnel director who would like to hire a graduate of your college. If you are like most employers, you'll develop a rating scale that lists the qualities you will be looking for in the applicants. Although each worker quality is important, you will probably decide that some will have more weight in your decision than others.

The following list contains some of the reasons employers typically mention that they use for rejecting job applicants. Your task, as an employer, is to rank order them from most to least important to you. Use "1" to indicate the most important and "13" to indicate the least important worker characteristic for you.

Rank	*Quality*
a. _____	Inability to get along with people, little self-confidence, and little leadership potential
b. _____	Poor academic achievement, poor grades
c. _____	Lack of well-thought-out personal and career goals

(continued)

Rank	*Quality*
d. _____	No interest in the type of work my company performs
e. _____	Lack of personal initiative, enthusiasm, drive
f. _____	Inability to express oneself orally and in writing
g. _____	Unrealistic salary demands; not willing to work up from the bottom
h. _____	Poor personal appearance
i. _____	Lack of involvement in extracurricular activities
j. _____	No awareness of what my company is all about; has not read literature about it
k. _____	Not willing to travel or move
l. _____	Excessive interest in security and benefits rather than interest in job
m. _____	Inadequate preparation for the position being applied for

APPENDIX B

Self-Assessment Inventory*

Preference Inventory
Interest Inventory
Skill Inventory
The Summary Profile

People seeking assistance in planning their careers frequently say "I'm uncertain about what to major in or what career to pursue. Is there a test that can tell me what I should do with the rest of my life?" The question reflects a common but incomplete belief about the career-planning process. While it is true that a number of students have had their tentative educational and occupational goals confirmed by tests, there are many who have found that tests opened up new areas to explore rather than defining a single choice for them. Thus, tests can be used to narrow or to expand one's career options. Although we know that they may be helpful in these ways, it is also important to realize their limitations.

Just as hammers don't make good wrenches, tests don't provide useful aids to career planning when they are misused. Since tests sample around 10 percent of the 20,000 occupations that exist in our society, they provide only a limited view of the occupational possibilities for a particular person. Also, because most are heavily biased toward a person's past experiences, they can reinforce stereotypic notions about which fields men, women, and minorities should enter. For example, the woman who is thinking about entering a field traditionally dominated by men, such as engineering, will find her expertise as a secretary confirmed by the test but will not learn much about her potential as an engineer. The most beneficial use of a test in this situation would be to help her identify the interests and skills she will need to develop in order to become an engineer. It may involve some work on her part to pursue her new goal, but at least she'll have some suggestions on how to get there.

Another problem with tests is the way they are scored and interpreted. We remember most those experiences in which we have been actively involved: the poem we spent hours memorizing in grammar school, the recognition we earned for a job well done. In most occupational testing situations we are active only as long as we are taking the test. Computers and technicians score the results, and counselors interpret them for us. Because the expertise for scoring and interpreting the tests rests in someone else's hands, it's easy to feel mystified by the test. We may then passively absorb the results instead of gaining a better understanding of how we have developed our abilities and interests. Small wonder that researchers have found that most people forget the results of testing shortly afterward!

In sharing these points with you, our goal is not to turn you off to tests. Instead, we want you to recognize the limitations inherent in testing and to use the results wisely. It may be helpful to know that there are other, less complicated ways of assessing your personal qualities besides taking standardized tests.

One type of exploration involves examining the themes in your fantasies and aspirations and seeing how they match the requirements of different occupations. Similarly, you can make lists of activities that you enjoy and do well and look for commonalities among them that can be translated into work activities. You can also use self-scored inventories that tap into your interests, values, and abilities.

The self-assessment inventories that follow are divided into three main parts—the Preference Inventory, the Interest Inventory, and the Skill Inventory. They provide you with such an opportunity to review your work preferences, interests, and skills within John Holland's worker typology (see Chapter 3). The results of this inventory—the Summary Profile—can be used to generate educational and occupational areas for exploration that are consistent with your particular work personality.

Preference Inventory

According to John Holland, people tend to gravitate toward environments that match their work personality, and academic and work preferences tend to cluster around six common personality types:

1. *Realistic* people like to work with their hands, are often athletic, and tend to enjoy working outdoors with animals, machines, or nature.
2. *Investigative* people enjoy scientific types of activities in which they engage in research to test ideas or to develop new products.
3. *Artistic* individuals find that they most enjoy expressing ideas and feelings through writing stories and poems, painting, photography, sculpting, and physical movement.
4. *Social* people find satisfaction in teaching, counseling, assisting, and informing others.
5. *Enterprising* workers like to persuade, supervise, or lead others toward common goals or to sell an idea or product.
6. *Conventional* people most like activities that allow them to organize data, attend to detail, and check results for accuracy.

This activity allows you to compare your academic preferences with each of six types of worker personality. Your preferences are what you would ideally like to do if reality would permit.

On the pages that follow, you will find a number of college majors that will have varying degrees of appeal to you. You can indicate how much you prefer each major by circling a 3, 2, 1, or 0 next to it.

Circle "3" if you have a definite or strong preference for a major.
> *For example*: Engineering   0 1 2 ③
Circle "2" if you have a moderate preference for a major.
> *For example*: Medical technology   0 1 ② 3
Circle "1" if you have little preference for a major.
> *For example*: Anthropology   0 ① 2 3
Circle "0" if the major is not a preference for you at all.
> *For example*: Economics   ⓪ 1 2 3

Do not be concerned about whether you have the interests and skills to succeed in a particular major. You will review your interests and skills in the next two parts of this inventory. Because your first reactions will produce the most reliable index of your preferences, work rapidly and respond spontaneously to each major.

Be sure to circle a number beside each major before moving on to the next. Complete the entire inventory before you total your scores. That way, your responses will be fresh and will not be delayed by your stopping to calculate.

My "Realistic" Preferences Are in . . .

		0	1	2	3
1.	Agriculture	0	①	2	3
2.	Aviation	⓪	1	2	3
3.	Geology	0	①	2	3
4.	Industrial arts teaching	⓪	1	2	3
5.	Emergency medical technology	⓪	1	2	3
6.	Petroleum engineering	⓪	1	2	3
7.	Law enforcement	0	1	②	3
8.	Forestry	0	①	2	3
9.	Radiological technology	⓪	1	2	3
10.	Traffic technology	⓪	1	2	3
11.	Photography	⓪	1	2	3
12.	Dental ceramics	⓪	1	2	3
13.	Architectural drafting	⓪	1	2	3
14.	Marine surveying	⓪	1	2	3

"0"

$$\boxed{0}$$

$+$

Sum of circled "1s"

$$\boxed{3}$$

$+$

Sum of circled "2s"

$$\boxed{2}$$

$+$

Sum of circled "3s"

$$\boxed{}$$

$=$

Grand total of "1s," "2s," "3s"

$$\boxed{5}$$

My "Investigative" Preferences Are in . . .

1.	Economics	0	1	(2)	3
2.	Actuarial science	0	(1)	2	3
3.	Nursing	(0)	1	2	3
4.	Microbiology	(0)	1	2	3
5.	Dentistry	(0)	1	2	3
6.	Medicine	(0)	1	2	3
7.	Natural science teaching	(0)	1	2	3
8.	Medical technology	(0)	1	2	3
9.	Psychology	0	(1)	2	3
10.	Mathematics	0	(1)	2	3
11.	Computer programming	(0)	1	2	3
12.	Physician's assistant	0	(1)	2	3
13.	Aeronautical engineering	(0)	1	2	3
14.	Geography	0	1	(2)	3

"0"

$$\boxed{0}$$

+

Sum of circled "1s"

$$\boxed{4}$$

+

Sum of circled "2s"

$$\boxed{4}$$

+

Sum of circled "3s"

$$\boxed{}$$

=

Grand total of "1s," "2s," "3s"

$$\boxed{8}$$

My "Artistic" Preferences Are in . . .

1.	Medical illustration	(0)	1	2	3
2.	Fine arts	(0)	1	2	3
3.	Commercial art	(0)	1	2	3
4.	Music	0	(1)	2	3
5.	Library science	0	(1)	2	3
6.	Journalism	0	(1)	2	3
7.	English	0	(1)	2	3
8.	Foreign languages	0	(1)	2	3

9.	Industrial design	(0)	1	2	3
10.	Fashion design	(0)	1	2	3
11.	Dance	(0)	1	2	3
12.	Theater	(0)	1	2	3
13.	Interior design	(0)	1	2	3
14.	Landscape architecture	0	1	(2)	3

"0"

0

+

5

Sum of circled "1s"

+

2

Sum of circled "2s"

+

Sum of circled "3s"

=

7

Grand total of "1s," "2s," "3s"

My "Social" Preferences Are in . . .

1.	Cosmetology	(0)	1	2	3
2.	Occupational therapy	0	(1)	2	3
3.	Recreation leadership	0	(1)	2	3
4.	Dental hygiene	(0)	1	2	3
5.	Social work	0	(1)	2	3
6.	Guidance counseling	0	(1)	2	3
7.	Elementary teaching	(0)	1	2	3
8.	Paralegal assistant	0	(1)	2	3
9.	Probation officer	(0)	1	2	3
10.	Psychiatric aide	(0)	1	2	3
11.	Medical assistant	(0)	1	2	3
12.	Political science	0	1	(2)	3
13.	Television production	0	(1)	2	3
14.	Rehabilitation counseling	(0)	1	2	3

"0"

$$\boxed{0}$$

+

Sum of circled "1s"

$$\boxed{6}$$

+

Sum of circled "2s"

$$\boxed{2}$$

+

Sum of circled "3s"

$$\boxed{}$$

=

Grand total of "1s," "2s," "3s"

$$\boxed{8}$$

My "Enterprising" Preferences Are in . . .

1.	Accounting	0 ① 2 3
2.	Industrial engineering	0 ① 2 3
3.	Marketing	0 ① 2 3
4.	Real estate sales	0 ① 2 3
5.	Mortuary science	⓪ 1 2 3
6.	Park management	0 ① 2 3
7.	Radio/TV announcer	⓪ 1 2 3
8.	Fashion merchandising	⓪ 1 2 3
9.	Business management	0 ① 2 3
10.	Law	0 ① 2 3
11.	Flight attendant	⓪ 1 2 3
12.	Athletic administration	⓪ 1 2 3
13.	Camp director	⓪ 1 2 3
14.	Fire science management	⓪ 1 2 3

"0"

$$\boxed{0}$$

+

Sum of circled "1s"

$$\boxed{7}$$

+

Sum of circled "2s"   ☐

                       +

Sum of circled "3s"   ☐

                       =

Grand total of "1s," "2s," "3s"   ⬚ *7*

My "Conventional" Preferences Are in . . .

1. Personnel clerking   0 ① 2 3
2. Data processing   0 ① 2 3
3. Office machine technology   ⓪ 1 2 3
4. Medical secretary   ⓪ 1 2 3
5. Business education   0 ① 2 3
6. Orthodontics assistant   ⓪ 1 2 3
7. Office administration   ⓪ 1 2 3
8. Medical records technology ⓪ 1 2 3
9. Court reporting   0 ① 2 3
10. Bookkeeping   0 ① 2 3
11. Electrical technology   ⓪ 1 2 3
12. Finance   0 1 ② 3
13. Secretarial science   ⓪ 1 2 3
14. Mathematics education   ⓪ 1 2 3

"0"   ⬚ 0

       +

Sum of circled "1s"   ⬚ *5*

       +

Sum of circled "2s"   ⬚ *2*

       +

Sum of circled "3s"   ☐

       =

Grand total of "1s," "2s," "3s"   ⬚ *7*

Check to make sure you have circled a number (0, 1, 2, 3) next to each item. Then add the scores in each preference category and write the totals in the spaces provided. For example, in the "realistic" category you would total all the "1s" (if you had circled three "1s" the sum would be 3), all the "2s" (if you had circled three of the "2s" the sum would be 6), and all the "3s" (if you had circled three of the "3s" the sum would be 9). Next, add the three sums together to get your grand total for that category (from the above examples: $3 + 6 + 9 = 18$).

After you have determined the grand totals for each of the six preference categories, transfer those totals to the spaces provided below. (If, as in the example above, your grand total were 18 in the "realistic" category, you would write "18" above the "R" space provided below.)

Preference
Grand
Totals

5	8	7	8	7	7
R	I	A	S	E	C

Interest Inventory

The purpose of this activity is to allow you to compare your current interests with Holland's six worker personality types.

Below you will find a number of study and work activities that will have varying degrees of appeal to you. You can indicate how much you enjoy or are interested in each activity by circling a 3, 2, 1, or 0 next to each item.

Circle "3" if you have a definite or strong interest in the activity.
    For example: Making jewelry   0 1 2 ③
Circle "2" if you have a moderate amount of interest in the activity.
    For example: Selling insurance   0 1 ② 3
Circle "1" if you have little interest in the activity.
    For example: Installing vending machines   0 ① 2 3
Circle "0" if the activity has no appeal to you at all.
    For example: Running an Addressograph machine   ⓪ 1 2 3

Do not be concerned about whether you have the skills to perform a particular activity. You will review your competencies in the third part of this inventory. Because your first reactions will produce the most reliable index of your interests, work rapidly and respond spontaneously to each item. Be sure to circle a number beside each item before moving on to the next item. Complete the entire inventory before you total your scores. That way, your responses will be fresh and will not be delayed by your stopping to calculate.

My "Realistic" Interests Are in . . .

1. Routing aircraft, ships, trucks, or buses   0 ① 2 3
2. Installing, maintaining, and repairing computers or other computer machines   0 1 2 3

*3. Breeding pedigreed dogs, thoroughbred horses, or other animals ⓪ 1 2 3
 4. Landscaping yards and parks   0 1 ② 3
 5. Farming the ocean for fish and other sea products   ⓪ 1 2 3
 6. Building or repairing furniture   ⓪ 1 2 3
 7. Refining and demonstrating my athletic skills   ⓪ 1 2 3
*8. Enforcing laws to protect life and property   0 1 ② 3
 9. Creating blueprints for buildings, machines, or electrical equipment   ⓪ 1 2 3
10. Guarding the safety and feeding of wildlife   0 ① 2 3
11. Building houses or other structures   0 ① 2 3
12. Operating emergency, rescue, or fire-fighting equipment   ⓪ 1 2 3
13. Driving a truck, tractor, or bus   ⓪ 1 2 3
14. Building or operating radio or TV equipment   ⓪ 1 2 3

"0"   [0]

+

Sum of circled "1s"   [3]

+

Sum of circled "2s"   [4]

+

Sum of circled "3s"   [ ]

=

Grand total of "1s," "2s," "3s"   [7]

My "Investigative" Interests Are in . . .

 1. Investigating the occupations, style of living, or behavior of others   0 ① 2 3
*2. Experimenting with living plants or animals to explore the laws of growth or heredity   ⓪ 1 2 3
 3. Designing new forms of transportation or communication   ⓪ 1 2 3
 4. Designing experiments to create or to test new drugs, chemicals, or diets   ⓪ 1 2 3

*Items marked with an asterisk are from Occupational Interest Inventory. Copyright © 1956 by McGraw-Hill, Inc. All rights reserved. Modified and reproduced by permission of the publisher, CTB, 2500 Garden Road, Monterey, California 93940.

5. Designing buildings, bridges, or other structures   (0) 1 2 3
*6. Developing methods of long-range weather forecasting   (0) 1 2 3
    and prediction
*7. Operating an X-ray machine or other laboratory apparatus   (0) 1 2 3
*8. Examining the formation of mineral deposits and   0 (1) 2 3
    determining how they may be removed from the earth
9. Programming computers to solve complex technical problems   (0) 1 2 3
10. Studying the causes of or diagnosing and treating diseases   (0) 1 2 3
    and physical impairments in humans or animals
11. Navigating a ship or an airplane   0 1 2 3
12. Developing mathematical equations or chemical formulas   (0) 1 2 3
    to solve scientific problems
13. Studying the solar system   0 (1) 2 3
14. Investigating bodies of water, such as lakes, rivers, and oceans   0 (1) 2 3

"0"
$$\boxed{0}$$
+

Sum of circled "1s"
$$\boxed{4}$$
+

Sum of circled "2s"
$$\boxed{}$$
+

Sum of circled "3s"
$$\boxed{}$$
=

Grand total of "1s," "2s," "3s"
$$\boxed{4}$$

My "Artistic" Interests Are in . . .

*1. Playing musical instruments in a band, orchestra, or other   0 (1) 2 3
    musical organization and/or writing music
2. Designing floor plans and selecting furniture and color   0 (1) 2 3
    combinations for homes or offices
3. Illustrating or designing covers for books or magazines   (0) 1 2 3
4. Engaging in creative dance, ballet, or rhythmic gymnastics   (0) 1 2 3
*5. Drawing cartoons, comics, or caricatures of people   (0) 1 2 3
6. Writing short stories, novels, plays, or poetry   (0) 1 2 3
7. Using wood, clay, paint, or other materials to create   (0) 1 2 3
    art objects

*8. Doing creative photography   **(0)** 1 2 3

9. Conducting an orchestra or directing a play   **(0)** 1 2 3

10. Giving presentations or writing descriptions or criticisms of   0 **(1)** 2 3
sculpture, plays, books, movies, or music

11. Setting up art, merchandise, or museum displays   0 **(1)** 2 3

*12. Writing dialogue or commercial announcements for radio or   0 **(1)** 2 3
TV programs

13. Studying and interpreting foreign languages   0 **(1)** 2 3

14. Designing containers for commercial products   **(0)** 1 2 3

"0"

$$\boxed{0}$$

+

Sum of circled "1s"

$$\boxed{6}$$

+

Sum of circled "2s"

$$\boxed{}$$

+

Sum of circled "3s"

$$\boxed{}$$

=

Grand total of "1s," "2s," "3s"

$$\boxed{6}$$

My "Social" Interests Are in . . .

1. Supervising activities at parks or recreational facilities   0 **(1)** 2 3

*2. Taking care of children and assisting in their education   **(0)** 1 2 3

3. Helping people with their personal problems and   0 **(1)** 2 3
important decisions in life

4. Teaching or helping people to develop their talents   0 **(1)** 2 3
and interests

5. Teaching others how to care for themselves and improve   0 **(1)** 2 3
their health

*6. Advising parents about the rearing of their children   **(0)** 1 2 3

7. Coordinating health and social services for the public   **(0)** 1 2 3

8. Working with or helping in the treatment of sick, handi-   **(0)** 1 2 3
capped, or injured individuals

*9. Supervising the selection, placement, and promotion   0 **(1)** 2 3
of employees

*10. Visiting homes to help people who are in trouble or   0 **(1)** 2 3
need assistance

11. Teaching arts and crafts to others   ⓪ 1 2 3
12. Studying the customs and folkways of different societies   0 1 ② 3
    and cultures
13. Interviewing people for information about their beliefs   0 1 ② 3
    and habits
14. Helping others to develop their physical talents and   ⓪ 1 2 3
    athletic skills

"0"
┌─────┐
│ 0 │
└─────┘

\+

Sum of circled "1s"
┌─────┐
│ 6 │
└─────┘

\+

Sum of circled "2s"
┌─────┐
│ 4 │
└─────┘

\+

Sum of circled "3s"
┌─────┐
│   │
└─────┘

=

Grand total of "1s," "2s," "3s"
┌─────┐
│ 10 │
└─────┘

My "Enterprising" Interests Are in . . .

  1. Managing my own firm   0 ① 2 3
  2. Buying and selling stocks and bonds   0 ① 2 3
 *3. Buying merchandise for a large store or chain of stores   0 ① 2 3
  4. Managing the public affairs division of a corporation   0 ① 2 3
  5. Helping others to locate and secure equipment   0 ① 2 3
  6. Lobbying for the passage of a law   0 1 ② 3
  7. Settling disputes between labor and management   0 1 ② 3
 *8. Managing or directing a large enterprise or division of   0 ① 2 3
    a corporation
  9. Directing a social service or recreational agency   ⓪ 1 2 3
*10. Directing the sales policies for a large firm or managing ⓪ 1 2 3
    a group of salespeople
 11. Helping individuals plan their travels   0 1 ② 3
 12. Making announcements on radio or television   0 ① 2 3
*13. Investigating legal situations and interpreting the law   0 1 ② 3
 14. Managing and representing performers, speakers,   ⓪ 1 2 3
    and artists

"0"

$$\boxed{0}$$

+

Sum of circled "1s"

$$\boxed{}$$

+

Sum of circled "2s"

$$\boxed{}$$

+

Sum of circled "3s"

$$\boxed{}$$

=

Grand total of "1s," "2s," "3s" $\boxed{15}$

My "Conventional" Interests Are in . . .

1. Operating office machines   0 ① 2 3
2. Developing an accounting or filing system for a firm   0 ① 2 3
3. Posting bills for a large company   ⓪ 1 2 3
4. Planning or coordinating a conference or convention   0 ① 2 3
5. Assisting others in planning and managing their finances   0 ① 2 3
6. Classifying orders, figuring price quotations, and making out price sheets   0 1 ② 3
7. Keeping financial records   0 1 ② 3
8. Answering the telephone and giving information or routing phone calls   0 ① 2 3
9. Teaching business classes   0 ① 2 3
*10. Preparing payrolls, figuring commissions, and making salary deductions   0 ① 2 3
*11. Meeting clients, making appointments, and doing general office work   0 1 ② 3
12. Taking dictation and typing correspondence   ⓪ 1 2 3
*13. Making bookkeeping entries or keeping inventories   ⓪ 1 2 3
14. Studying how people managing their time and energies to complete work tasks   ⓪ 1 2 3

"0"

$$\boxed{0}$$

+

Sum of circled "1s"

$$\boxed{}$$

+

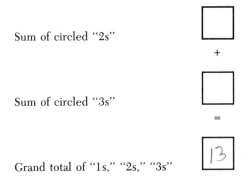

Sum of circled "2s"

+

Sum of circled "3s"

=

Grand total of "1s," "2s," "3s" |13|

Check to make sure you have circled a number (0, 1, 2, 3) next to each item. Then add the scores in each preference category and write the totals in the spaces provided. For example, in the "realistic" category you would total all the "1s" (if you had circled three "1s" the sum would be 3), all the "2s" (if you had circled three of the "2s" the sum would be 6), and all the "3s" (if you had circled three of the "3s" the sum would be 9). Next, add the three sums together to get your grand total for that category (from the above examples: 3 + 6 + 9 = 18).

After you have determined the grand totals for each of the six interest categories, transfer those totals to the spaces provided below. (If, as in the example above, your grand total were 18 in the "realistic" category, you would write "18" above the "R" space provided below).

Interest
Grand
Totals
   7   4   6   10   15   13
   R   I   A   S   E   C

Skill Inventory

"Jim and Julia are the math whizzes in our class." "Tina and Bill are the class leaders." Statements such as these are often used to group individuals according to a common skill that they possess, many times because they excel at that skill. While we may not be outstanding at a particular task when compared with our peers, each of us has skills that will allow us to function effectively at particular work tasks.

Like the preceding preference and interest inventories, this inventory requires that you look through several sets of skills and evaluate yourself on a scale that runs from 3 to 0.

Circle "3" next to an activity if you have a definite, strong
    skill in that area.   0 1 2 ③
Circle "2" if you have a moderate degree of skill in that activity.   0 1 ② 3
Circle "1" to indicate that you have enough skill to get by with   0 ① 2 3
    some help from others.

Circle "0" if you believe you have no skill at all in that
    particular activity.

ⓞ 1 2 3

When evaluating your skills, do not compare yourself with any particular reference group, such as other students or the general population. Rate yourself according to your own judgment of your ability. Be sure that each item has a number circled beside it before moving to the next item.

My "Realistic" Skills Are in . . .

*1.	Painting, varnishing, or staining wood or metal surfaces	0	①	2	3
2.	Working with wood using power tools, hand tools, or other woodworking equipment	⓪	1	2	3
3.	Working outdoors for long periods of time	0	1	2	③
4.	Putting together toys, furniture, or machinery that come unassembled	0	①	2	3
5.	Repairing furniture or other objects	⓪	1	2	3
*6.	Cleaning, adjusting, or repairing electric motors, sewing machines, or bicycles	⓪	1	2	3
7.	Completing tasks that require physical endurance or agility	0	①	2	3
8.	Making clothes or other wearing apparel from patterns	⓪	1	2	3
9.	Driving a tractor or a truck	⓪	1	2	3
10.	Reading blueprints or schemata	⓪	1	2	3
*11.	Doing odd jobs with a saw, hammer and nails, screwdriver, or plane	⓪	1	2	3
*12.	Making drawings with a compass, triangle, ruler, or other instrument	⓪	1	2	3
13.	Installing or repairing household electric circuits	⓪	1	2	3
14.	Constructing, planting, or cultivating rock gardens or making flower beds	0	①	2	3

"0"
┌─────┐
│ 0 │
└─────┘
   +

Sum of circled "1s"
┌─────┐
│   │
└─────┘
   +

Sum of circled "2s"
┌─────┐
│   │
└─────┘
   +

Sum of circled "3s"

$=$

Grand total of "1s," "2s," "3s"   7)

My "Investigative" Skills Are in ...

1. Mixing chemicals according to formulas   (0) 1 2 3
2. Experimenting with and creating recipes   (0) 1 2 3
3. Naming basic foods and telling why they are nutritious   0 (1) 2 3
4. Reading data tables, graphs, and charts   0 1 (2) 3
5. Setting up a scientific demonstration for a class or   0 (1) 2 3
   science fair
6. Understanding articles in newspapers and magazines about 0 1 (2) 3
   recent scientific breakthroughs
7. Describing the different classification systems for plants 0 (1) 2 3
   or animals
8. Reading topographical or navigational maps   (0) 1 2 3
9. Naming the different cloud formations   0 (1) 2 3
10. Using a microscope   (0) 1 2 3
11. Using a hand calculator   0 1 (2) 3
12. Interviewing others about their attitudes, feelings,   0 (1) 2 3
    and beliefs
13. Solving puzzles or figuring out how things work   0 (1) 2 3
14. Identifying the major constellations of the stars   (0) 1 2 3

"0"   0

$+$

Sum of circled "1s"

$+$

Sum of circled "2s"

$+$

Sum of circled "3s"

$=$

Grand total of "1s," "2s," "3s"   12

My "Artistic" Skills Are in . . .

1. Sketching, drawing, or painting; carving or sculpting objects   (0) 1 2 3
2. Creating new ideas and gadgets or expressing myself in original ways   (0) 1 2 3
3. Doing interpretive readings of stories, poetry, or plays   (0) 1 2 3
4. Impersonating the speech and mannerisms of others   0 (1) 2 3
5. Using the color wheel to mix colors or create color complements   (0) 1 2 3
6. Writing essays, stories, or poetry   0 (1) 2 3
7. Designing and making clothing   (0) 1 2 3
8. Singing or acting   (0) 1 2 3
*9. Arranging color harmonies and furnishings in a home   0 (1) 2 3
10. Learning a foreign language   0 (1) 2 3
11. Playing a musical instrument   0 1 (2) 3
12. Following the story line and message in movies, plays, and books   0 1 2 (3)
13. Performing ballet, tap dance, or gymnastics   (0) 1 2 3
14. Telling stories or jokes   0 1 (2) 3

"0" | 0 |

+

Sum of circled "1s" | |

+

Sum of circled "2s" | |

+

Sum of circled "3s" | |

=

Grand total of "1s," "2s," "3s" | 11 |

My "Social" Skills Are in . . .

1. Performing in athletic competitions   0 (1) 2 3
2. Planning social events   (0) 1 2 3
3. Entertaining others   0 1 (2) 3
4. Getting along with others who are different from myself   0 1 2 (3)
5. Teaching or tutoring   0 (1) 2 3
6. Explaining new ideas to others   0 1 (2) 3

7. Supervising children's activities   0 (1) 2 3
8. Meeting new people   (0) 1 2 3
9. Accepting and giving criticism   0 1 (2) 3
10. Helping others feel comfortable in new situations   0 (1) 2 3
11. Encouraging and supporting others   (0) 1 2 3
12. Working with others in a team effort   (0) 1 2 3
13. Determining the needs of others and helping them find solutions to their problems   (0) 1 2 3
14. Understanding other people's personalities   0 (1) 2 3

"0"

$$\boxed{0}$$

+

Sum of circled "1s"

$$\boxed{}$$

+

Sum of circled "2s"

$$\boxed{}$$

+

Sum of circled "3s"

$$\boxed{}$$

=

Grand total of "1s," "2s," "3s"

$$\boxed{14}$$

My "Enterprising" Skills Are in . . .

1. Organizing campaigns for candidates in school clubs or other social groups   (0) 1 2 3
2. Leading others   0 (1) 2 3
3. Entering new situations with ease and comfort   0 (1) 2 3
4. Interpreting changes in the economy   0 1 (2) 3
5. Persuading others to accept a new idea   0 (1) 2 3
6. Performing effectively in debates   0 (1) 2 3
7. Managing or supervising others in a work group   (0) 1 2 3
8. Selling products   (0) 1 2 3
9. Speaking on behalf of a group   0 (1) 2 3
10. Helping others resolve their disputes   0 (1) 2 3
11. Understanding how the legal system operates and how laws are passed   0 1 2 (3)
12. Finding and capitalizing on bargains and sales   0 (1) 2 3
13. Soliciting contributions to charities or political organizations   (0) 1 2 3
14. Giving speeches before large groups   (0) 1 2 3

"0"

☐ 0

+

Sum of circled "1s"

☐

+

Sum of circled "2s"

☐

+

Sum of circled "3s"

☐

=

Grand total of "1s," "2s," "3s"

☐ 12

My "Conventional" Skills Are in . . .

1. Operating office machines	0	①	2	3
2. Planning a personal budget	0	①	2	3
3. Organizing or filing materials such as records, class notes, stamps, or photographs	⓪	1	2	3
4. Keeping financial records	0	1	②	3
5. Typing, keypunching, or operating a calculator or office machine	0	①	2	3
6. Keeping an accurate checkbook	0	1	②	3
7. Organizing ideas or numbers so they are clear and understandable	0	①	2	3
8. Proofreading papers or records and finding the mistakes	0	1	②	3
9. Spelling and using punctuation and grammar correctly	0	1	②	3
10. Keeping accurate records	0	1	②	3
11. Examining or keeping budgets for businesses	⓪	1	2	3
12. Working in an office setting and doing a good job	0	1	②	3
13. Organizing my time to accomplish tasks	0	1	2	③
14. Acting as a secretary or treasurer in a club or organization	0	1	②	3

"0"

☐ 0

+

Sum of circled "1s"

☐

+

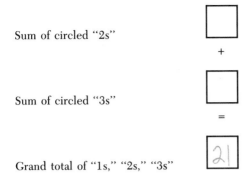

Sum of circled "2s"

\+

Sum of circled "3s"

\=

Grand total of "1s," "2s," "3s" **21**

As you did with the preference and interest inventories, go back and add the "1s," "2s," and "3s" you have circled for each skill category. Record the results in the spaces provided at the end of each category. After you have determined the grand totals for each of the six categories, transfer these totals to the spaces provided below. Record the grand totals in the appropriate spaces.

Skills
Grand
Totals

7	12	11	14	12	21
R	I	A	S	E	C

The Summary Profile

The final step in this self-assessment process will be to pull together a composite picture of your preferences, interests, and skills. This will allow you to look at your preferences, interests, and skills separately and to compare areas with one another.

To complete this process, write the grand total of your preference, interest, and skill scores in the spaces provided below. Then add the grand totals together to develop an overall composite score of your preferences, interests, and skills.

	R	I	A	S	E	C
Preference grand totals	5	8	7	8	7	7
	+	+	+	+	+	+
Interest grand totals	7	4	6	10	15	13
	+	+	+	+	+	+
Skill grand totals	7	12	11	14	12	21
	=	=	=	=	=	=
Overall composite score	19	24	24	32	34	41
	R	I	A	S	E	C

Finally, write the letters (R, I, A, S, E, C) that correspond to your *three highest* (including tied highest) composite scores in the spaces provided below.

Summary Profile: CES

√ S E C
√ E C S   √ C S E
√ E S C   S C E
√ C E S

Using the Summary Profile to Explore College Majors and Related Occupations

Turn to the majors finder in Appendix C and look for majors that correspond to the three letters in your summary profile. Be sure to rotate codes—for example, RIA, AIR, RAI, IRA, IAR, ARI. List the majors that have some appeal to you below.

1. _____Accounting_____
2. _____
3. _____
4. _____
5. _____
6. _____
7. _____
8. _____
9. _____
10. _____

Interpreting Your Summary Profile

Your summary profile can aid you in identifying college majors and related occupations to explore. In reviewing your profile, there are several other things to consider. Are your highest preference, interest, and skill scores matched with each other? In other words, are the majors that you prefer in line with the things you like to do daily and the skills you have? If your preferences, interests, and abilities correspond with each other, you will probably find it relatively easy to come up with a major and an occupation that utilizes certain common personal characteristics. If these three personal qualities do not match, you should look closely at why they differ and find a way of balancing them that is most comfortable and realistic for you.

For example, if the areas you prefer are not matched by your interests and skills, the majors you might ideally choose to pursue may be based on a standard (for example, a family value, stereotypes you have for certain majors or occupations, or the prestige you associate with different fields) that is not consistent with what you really enjoy doing and have the skills to do day in and day out. In this case, if you pursue your preferences, you may go through a period of frustration as you engage in activities that hold little interest for you and try to develop skills that coincide with your preferences. Another solution would be to accept the possibility that you may not be able to pursue your preferences and should select a field that is more consistent with your interests and skills.

If your strongest interests are not matched by your preferences and skills, you will be in a similar dilemma: you will need to find a way to balance the activities you enjoy most with your academic preferences and current skills. Again, the task is to figure out *what is most important to you.* If you give greatest weight to your interests, this may mean redefining your academic and occupational preferences and acquiring new skills to match your interests.

Finally, if your skills are in an area that differs from the area of your preferences and interests, it may suggest that there are some things you do well at but may not really invest yourself in on a continuing basis. For example, you may be good at a variety of office practices or "conventional" activities because you developed these skills to help you with your studies or for summer jobs, but you may not want to make a living with these skills on a permanent basis. Suppose your preferences and interests were in the "investigative" and "artistic" areas. You might consider the possibility of combining your interests and skills by utilizing your current skills in settings that are consistent with your preferences and interests—for example, in a medical or scientific setting or an advertising office—while you work to advance your education. In this way you can use your current skills to support yourself as you develop skills in areas that appeal to you.

Thus, how you balance these three personal qualities when they are not equally matched will require that you closely test out your ideals and dreams against the realities of your skills and resources and the requirements of different majors and occupations.

For some people, three or more letters in the Summary Profile might have an equal score. This type of profile can occur in two ways: (1) when all your scores are high, suggesting that you have diverse preferences, interests, and skills, and (2) when all your scores are low, indicating that you have not fully developed your preferences, interests, and skills.

In the case of equally high scores, you have several options to consider. You can look for majors and occupations that provide you with a great deal of diversity or seek opportunities to work across a variety of settings. You can also identify the specific preferences, interests, and skills you want to capitalize on and look for related majors or occupations. Or you can consider pursuing several fields during the course of your career, which will allow you to capitalize on your preferences, interests, and skills in different ways across time. Finally, you can explore the possibility of pursuing some activities that appeal to you at work and pursuing other activities outside of work through leisure and recreational pursuits.

A low profile with equal scores may indicate that you haven't had opportunities to try out the kinds of diverse activities that would allow you to identify your preferences, interests, and skills clearly. In this case you may want to gain more experience through volunteer work, classes, and part-time or summer jobs in areas that appeal to you. This type of profile may also suggest that you may

APPENDIX C

The College Majors Finder*
(For Use with the Self-Assessment Inventory)

Realistic Areas
Investigative Areas
Artistic Areas
Social Areas
Enterprising Areas
Conventional Areas

John Holland's approach to classifying worker personality types according to their common preferences, interests, and values was presented in Chapter 3. The self-assessment inventories found in Appendix B provided a way of identifying your own work personality type according to Holland's typologies. Chapter 6 described how the typologies may be used to classify work settings according to their common requirements and rewards. The Majors Finder presented here will help you pull together the results of the self-assessment surveys of your preferences, interests, and abilities in terms of how your personality type fits with different "environments," academic majors, and technical training programs.

Holland describes the six basic worker personality types and environments in the following manner:

1. *Realistic people* like to work with their hands, are often athletic, and tend to enjoy working outdoors with animals, machines, or nature. They tend to be employed in skilled trades, technical areas, or a few service-related occupations.
2. *Investigative people* enjoy science-related activities in which they conduct research to test new ideas or develop products. They tend to enjoy the scientific fields and some technical specialties.
3. *Artistic people* enjoy expressing ideas and feelings through writing stories and poems, painting, photography, sculpture, and physical movement. Their academic and professional specialties are related to art, music, and literary occupations.
4. *Social people* find satisfaction in teaching, counseling, assisting, and informing others. Educational and social service occupations are attractive to such individuals.
5. *Enterprising people* like to persuade, supervise, or lead others toward common goals or to sell an idea or a product. Managerial or marketing-related specialties are representative of fields that attract enterprising types.
6. *Conventional people* like activities that allow them to organize data, attend to detail, and check results for accuracy. Secretaries and accounting clerks are examples of workers who fit this type.

According to Holland, people who have a wide variety of talents and interests may share qualities from all six types. He suggests, however, that the work personalities of most people are likely to reflect a combination of three types. For example, people whose personalities show a combination of the realistic, investigative, and artistic (RIA) types may share a common characteristic of using objects to produce, study, or represent an idea or product. The fields of study presented in the Majors Finder are organized according to the three types that best describe them. The initials of the types (RIASEC) are used to present each grouping or area of study. Thus, if you have completed the self-assessment inventories in Appendix B and found that your strongest types were social, enterprising, and conventional, you would look under SEC to locate majors that are consistent with your preferences, interests, and abilities. To broaden your list of potential areas of study, you should rotate your three-letter code—for example, ESC, CES, SCE, ECS. If you cannot find your three-letter code listed in the finder, use one or two letters to identify areas of study that are consistent with your type and investigate those areas.

To the right of each area of study, you will find a T, B, M, or D listed. The letter T indicates that a technical or two-year degree is offered at post-secondary institutions for persons interested in that field of study. The letters B, M, and D indicate a bachelor's degree, a master's degree, and a doctorate degree, respectively. This information will be helpful to you as you consider how far you want to go with your education, based on the time and resources you have available to complete your studies.

In addition to helping you identify potential areas of study, the Majors Finder can also suggest occupations for you to explore. This is particularly true of some technical, trade, and professional fields of study, such as computer science, engineering, bookkeeping, and social work, that are directly related to occupational specialties. Other areas, such as law, counseling, and some areas of medicine, which require advanced levels of study, may attract persons from a variety of undergraduate disciplines. You should seek the advice of a person who teaches or advises students in the particular field for suggestions about which area(s) of study best prepare students for entry into the profession or program of advanced study in which you are interested.

For a broader listing of occupations, classified according to the Holland types, consult J. L. Holland, *The Occupations Finder for Use with the Self-Directed Search* (Odessa, FL: Psychological Assessment Resources, 1985).

For an extensive listing of post-secondary institutions and the types of training and academic programs they provide, consult D. B. Biesel and E. B. Widdies (Eds.), *The College Blue Book: Degrees Offered by College and Subject*, 17th ed. (New York: Macmillan, 1979).

Three-letter code and areas of study	Degree levels	
"Realistic" Areas		
RIS		
Cabinetmaking technology	T	
Electronics engineering	T	B
Emergency medical technology	T	
	(continued)	

Three-letter code and areas of study	Degree levels		

"Realistic" Areas (continued)

RIS

Farm operations	T	B	
Industrial technology	T		
Landscape horticulture	T	B	
Mechanical engineering	B	M	
Tool and die design	T		

RIE

Agriculture	B	M	D
Aircraft mechanics	T		
Automotive body repair	T		
Aviation sciences and technology	T	B	
Biomedical equipment technology	T		
Electrical technician	T		
Engineering mechanics	B		
Horticulture	B	M	D
Industrial arts education	B		
Industrial design	B	M	
Laboratory technology	T		
Optical technology	T		
Petroleum engineering	B	M	D
Petroleum geology	B		
Prosthetics technology	T		
Welding	T		

RIC

Instrumentation technology	T		
Marine life technology	T		
Nuclear engineering	B	M	D
Nuclear technology	T	B	M
Optical technology	T		
Television technology	T		

RAS

Culinary arts	T		

RAE

Floral design	T		
Sound recording	T		

RAI

Sculpture	B	M	

(continued)

Three-letter code and areas of study	Degree levels		

"Realistic" Areas (continued)

RSE

Automotive technology	T		
Electrical appliance repair	T		
Electrician	T		
Law enforcement	T		
Photography	T	B	
Police science and administration	T	B	
Prosthetics and orthodontics	B	M	
Wildlife and conservation management	T	B	

RSI

Fire sciences and administration	T	B	
Forest management	T	B	M
Orthodontics assistant	T		
Radiologic technology	T		
Ultrasound technology	T		
Vocational agriculture education	B	M	D

REI

Carpentry	T		
Diesel mechanics	T		
Electrician	T		
Materials engineering	B		
Mining engineering	B		
Navigation, ship	T		
Optician	T		
Plumber	T		
Production management	B		
Television and radio repair	T		

REA

Culinary arts	T
Dental ceramics artist	T
Marine service management	T

RES

Animal breeding/training	T
Cement masonry	T
Costume design	T
Fish and game management	T
Locomotive engineer	T
Optical technician	T

(continued)

Three-letter code and areas of study	Degree levels			

"Realistic" Areas (continued)

    REC

Construction inspection	T			
Jewelry repair	T			
Large equipment operations	T			
Marine surveying	B			

    RCI

Architectural drafting	T			
Calibration laboratory technology	B			
Electrocardiograph technology	T			

    RCS

Electroencephalographic technology	T			
Energy technologies	T			
Oil well surveying	B			

    RCE

Camera repair	T			
Orthodontic technology	T			

"Investigative" Areas

    IAS

Economics	B	M	D	
Marketing	B	M	D	

    ISE

Actuarial science	B	M	D	
Drafting and design	T	B		
Nursing	B			
Photographic engineering	B			
Product safety engineering	B			

    ISC

Linguistics	B	M	D	
Mathematics education	B	M		
Public health technology and administration	T	B	M	D

    ISR

Airport engineering	B			
Audiology	B	M	D	

(*continued*)

Three-letter code and areas of study	Degree levels			

"Investigative" Areas (continued)

ISR (continued)

Biology	B	M	D	
Chiropractic	T	B	D	
Dentistry	B	M	D	
Dermatology	M	D		
Dietetics and nutrition	T	B	M	D
Food technology	T			
Mineralogy	B	M	D	
Natural sciences	T	B	M	
Ophthalmology	B	M	D	
Optometry	T	B	D	
Osteopathic medicine	D			
Paleontology	B	M	D	
Safety engineering	B			
Surgical technology	T			

ISA

Medical technology	T		
Medicine	D		
Nursing, practical	T	B	M
Physician's assistant	T		
Psychiatry	D		

IER

Geography	B	M	D
Marine surveys	B		
Pollution control and technology	T		
Psychology, educational	M	D	
Seismology	B	M	
Surveying	T	B	
Systems engineering and management	B	M	D

IEA

Medical technology	T	
Quality control management	B	
Surveying	T	B

IES

Electronics engineering	B	M	
Meteorology	T	B	M	D
Occupational safety	T	B	
Pharmaceutical sciences and technology	T	B	M	D

(continued)

Three-letter code and areas of study	Degree levels

"Investigative" Areas (continued)

IES (continued)

Public health administration	T	B	M	D
Sociology	T	B	M	D

IEC

Computer and information systems	T	B
Highway engineering	B	
Tissue technology	B	

ICR

Cytology and histology technology	T	B
Management science	B	

IRA

Surgery	D	
Veterinary medicine	T	B	D

IRS

Aeronautical engineering and science	T	B	M	D
Agronomy	B	M	D	
Anesthesiology	D			
Anthropology	T	B	M	D
Astronomy and physics	B	M	D	
Biochemistry	B	M	D	
Biomedical engineering	T	B	M	D
Biophysics	B	M	D	
Botany	B	M	D	
Cardiology	D			
Ceramic engineering	T	B	M	
Chemical engineering and technology	T	B	M	D
Chemistry	T	B	M	D
Civil engineering and technology	T	B	M	
Computer engineering	B	M	D	
Dairy science	T	B	M	D
Drafting	T	B		
Electrical engineering	T	B	M	D
Electronics technology	T			
Entomology	M	D		
Environmental engineering	B	M	D	
Genetics	M	D		
Geography	B	M	D	

(continued)

Three-letter code and areas of study	Degree levels			

"Investigative" Areas (continued)

IRS (continued)

Geology	T	B	M	D
Geophysics	M	D		
Laboratory assistant	T			
Marine engineering and technology	T	B		
Medical lab assistant	T			
Metallurgical engineering	B	M	D	
Meteorology	B			
Nuclear engineering	T	B	M	D
Pathology	B	M	D	
Pediatric medicine	D			
Pharmacology	M	D		
Physics	B	M	D	
Physiology	B	M	D	
Psychology, experimental	M	D		
Radiologic technology	T	D		
Soil science	B	M	D	
Statistics	B	M	D	
Systems engineering and management	B	M	D	
Veterinary medicine	B	M	D	

IRE

Agricultural engineering	B	M	D	
Anthropology	B	M	D	
Archaeology	M	D		
Astronomy	M	D		
Biology, aquatic	M	D		
Biomedical engineering	M			
Biophysics	M	D		
Ceramic engineering	M	D		
Chemical engineering	M	D		
Chemistry	M	D		
Civil engineering	B	M	D	
Computer engineering	M			
Dairy science	B	M		
Electronics technology	T			
Ethnology	M	D		
Geography	B	M	D	
Laser technology	T			
Marine engineering	B	M		
Medical lab technology	T			
Metallurgic science	B			

(continued)

Three-letter code and areas of study	Degree levels			
"Investigative" Areas (continued)				
IRE (continued)				
Nuclear engineering	M			
Periodontics	D			
Statistics	M	D		
IRC				
Aeronautical drafting	T			
Structural drafting	T			
"Artistic" Areas				
ASE				
Acting/theater	T	B	M	D
Art	B	M		
Creative writing	B	M	D	
Dance	T	B	M	
English	B	M	D	
Foreign languages	B	M	D	
Journalism	B	M		
Writing	B	M		
ASI				
Art	B	M		
Commercial art	B			
English education	B	M		
Music	B	M	D	
Philosophy	B	M	D	
Technical writing	B			
ASR				
Fashion design and retailing	T	B		
Fashion illustration	T	B	M	
AES				
Art	T	B	M	
Art education	B	M	D	
Commercial art and advertising	T	B		
Music	T	B	M	D
Technical writing	T	B	M	
AEC				
Journalism	B			
Photography	T	B	M	

(continued)

Three-letter code and areas of study	Degree levels			

"Artistic" Areas (continued)

AER

Cosmetology	T			
Dance	T	B	M	
Fashion design	B	M		
Sculpture	T	B	M	

AES

Art	B	M		
Audiovisual technology	T			
Dance	B			
Furniture design	T	B		
Graphic arts and design	T	B	M	
Industrial design	B	M		
Interior decorating and design	T	B	M	
Music	T	B	M	D
Photography	T	B	M	
Theater	B	M	D	
Writing	B	M		

ARI

Model making	T			

AIR

Architecture	T	B	M	D
Landscape architecture	B	M	D	

AIE

Medical illustration	T	B	M	
Stage design	B			

"Social" Areas

SEC

City management	B			
Education	T	B	M	D
Employee relations and personnel management	B	M		
Fire science	T	B		
Human resource management	B			
Motion pictures/cinema	T	B	M	
Paralegal assistant	T			
Probation and parole	B			
Psychiatric assistant	T			

(continued)

Three-letter code and areas of study	Degree levels			

"Social" Areas (continued)

　　SEC (continued)

Recreation education/leadership	T	B	M	
Social studies education	B	M	D	
Social work	B	M		
Student personnel services	B	M	D	

　　SER

Athletic administration	B	M		
Business management	T	B	M	
Correctional science	T			
Criminal justice administration	B	M		
Education, physical	B	M		
Hospital administration	M	D		
Industrial relations	T	B	M	
Law enforcement	T	B	M	
Library science	T	B	M	D
Police science	T	B		
Rehabilitation counseling	B	M	D	

　　SEI

Education administration	M	D		
Guidance counseling	M	D		
History	B	M	D	
Human resource administration	B	M		
Nursing	B	M	D	
Park and recreation leadership	T	B		
Political science	B	M	D	
Psychology	B	M	D	
School administration	M	D		

　　SEA

College student personnel	B	M	D	
Labor relations	B	M		
Public administration	B			
Religious education	B	M	D	
Social work, psychiatric	T	B	M	D
Special education	B	M	D	
Television production	T	B		

　　SCR

Library assistant	T			
Medical assistant	T			
Physical therapy assistant	T			

(continued)

Three-letter code and areas of study	Degree levels		

"Social" Areas (continued)

SCI

Medical records administration	T	B		
Nursing	T	B	M	D
Optometric assistant	T			

SCE

Air traffic control	B	
Guidance counseling	B	M
Occupational therapy assistant	T	
Real estate	T	

SRE

Athletic trainer	T	B	M
Cosmetology	T		
Dietetic technician	T		
Law enforcement	T		
Optometric technician	T		

SRC

Audiology	B	M	D
Radiologic technology	T	B	

SIA

Nursing	T	B	
Psychology: clinical, counseling, school	B	M	D
Rehabilitation counseling	B	M	D

SIE

Accounting	B	M	D
Corrections administration	T	B	
Dietetics	B	M	D
Education administration	M	D	
Medical records administration	T	B	
Nursing administration	B	M	
Physical therapy	T	B	M

SIR

Athletic administration	M
Inhalation therapy	T
Nursing	B

(continued)

Three-letter code and areas of study	Degree levels			
"Social" Areas (continued)				
SIR (continued)				
Occupational medicine	D			
Podiatry	B	M	D	
SAE				
Counseling and guidance	M	D		
Elementary education	B	M	D	
Home economics	T	B	M	D
Speech and hearing therapy	B	M	D	
Speech communication	B	M	D	
Vocational rehabilitation counseling	B	M	D	
SAC				
Beautician	T			
Cosmetology	T			
Hair styling	T			
Physical therapy aide	T			
SAI				
Dental assistant	T			
Dental hygiene	T			
Library sciences	T	B	M	D
Licensed practical nursing	T			
Minister, priest, rabbi	B	D		
Speech therapy	B	M	D	
"Enterprising" Areas				
ECR				
Executive housekeeper	T			
ECS				
Accounting	B	M	D	
Business administration	T	B	M	
Distribution management	T			
Occupational safety and health technology	T	B		
Travel agency management	T	B		
ERI				
Business management	T	B		
Criminal science	T			

(continued)

Three-letter code and areas of study	Degree levels			

"Enterprising" Areas (continued)

   ERA

Park administration	T	B		

   ERS

Business management, technical areas	T	B		
Construction administration	T	B		
Fire science technology and management	T	B		

   EIS

Dental laboratory technology	T			
Dietetics	T	B		
Laboratory science	T			

   EIC

Banking and finance	B	M	D	
Industrial engineering	T	B		
Production management	B	M		

   EIR

Business administration	T	B	M	D
Industrial engineering	B	M	D	
International business	B			

   EAR

Fire science management	T			

   EAI

Higher education administration	M	D		
Records management	T	B		

   EAS

Fashion merchandising	T	B		
Journalism	B	M		

   ESC

Administrative assistant	T	B		
Business management	T	B	M	
College student personnel administration	M	D		

(continued)

Three-letter code and areas of study	Degree levels			
"Enterprising" Areas (continued)				
ESC (continued)				
Insurance and real estate	T	B		
Travel administration	T	B		
ESR				
Athletic administration	B	M		
Banking and finance	B	M	D	
Barbering	T			
Business management	T	B	M	
Journalism	B	M		
Marketing	B	M	D	
Radio/television broadcasting	T	B	M	D
ESI				
Business administration	B	M	D	
Finance	B	M	D	
Law	B	M	D	
Purchasing management	T			
ESA				
Business administration	B	M	D	
College student personnel administration	M	D		
Flight attendant	T			
Guidance counseling	M	D		
International relations	B	M	D	
Law	B	M	D	
Marketing	B	M	D	
Outdoor recreation	B	M		
Photography	B	M	D	
Political science	B	M	D	
"Conventional" Areas				
CRI				
Computer and data processing	T	B		
Office administration/management	T	B		
Office machine technology	T			
CRS				
Bookkeeping	T	B		

(continued)

Three-letter code and areas of study	Degree levels			
"Conventional"Areas (continued)				
CRE				
Office machine technology	T			
CIS				
Accounting	T	B	M	
Bookkeeping	T			
CIE				
Building inspection	T			
CSE				
Accounting	T	B	M	
Business education	B	M	D	
Computer operator	T			
Court reporter	T			
Library assistant	T			
Medical records technology	T			
Personnel clerk	T			
Secretarial science	T	B		
CSR				
Orthodontics assistant	T			
Quality control technology	T			
CSI				
Finance	B	M	D	
CES				
Accounting	T	B	M	D
Electrical technology	T			
Medical secretary	T			

APPENDIX D

Conducting a Career Information Search

The following exercises represent different approaches to help you learn about gathering, organizing, and critically evaluating career information.

"Your Ideal Job Description" will guide you in using the exercises you have completed to pull together a concise *summary* of what you are looking for in an occupation. "Strategies for Gathering Information" presents ideas for doing some active, personal research on at least two of your ideal jobs. "P.L.A.C.E." gives you a format to help organize and evaluate occupational information against your ideal job requirements. "A Place for Your Values" is a framework for identifying some of your work values and comparing your ideal jobs with them. Finally, "Guidelines for Your Occupational Report" suggests steps for completing a written summary and comparing information about yourself and about the job(s) you find most interesting. This exercise allows you to see what your future in one of your ideal jobs might be like.

This set of exercises is designed to help you integrate what you know about your preferences, interests, and abilities with gathering in-depth information about a few occupations that seem to fit you well. This should help you learn some different ways of assessing and using career information, not just to narrow your list of choices, but to get current, accurate information about the occupations you are considering.

Your Ideal Job Description

To help you explore various occupations with a sense of direction and purpose, it is useful to have your own needs and priorities in mind before setting out to gather information. Imagine you have the opportunity to create a description of your ideal job, a job that fits the unique you and the way you want to live. Take several sheets of paper and, using the information you have gathered about yourself so far, create a *written sketch* of the way you would most like to spend your life in the future. You can do this by answering the five basic career-planning questions presented in Chapter 1.

1. *Who am I?* Start with the life stage that is most descriptive of where you are currently. What are the needs and pressures that affect you right now? How are you dealing with them? What choices will you be making during the next five years?

Next, recall the personal characteristics that seemed most descriptive of you in the self-assessment activities found in Chapters 3, 4, and 5 and in Appendix B. Identify three or more preferences, interests, and skills that you would like to express through work. Explain in several sentences why you selected these preferences, interests, and skills and how they fit into your career objectives.

From the exercise entitled "Exploring Your Personal Values" at the end of Chapter 4, identify three values that you want to express at work. Briefly explain the reasons you selected those values and discuss their implications for your future. Consider the type and amount of responsibility you want to take for decision making and supervision at work and the effect this will have on the level at which you choose to work.

2. *How do I want to live?* Describe the lifestyle you prefer. How would you ideally like to balance the time you spend at work, the time you spend at leisure and recreation, and the time you spend with family and friends? What kinds of things do you enjoy doing outside of work? What important needs will you be meeting through those activities? What salary will you need to support your lifestyle?

3. *Where do I want to live?* If you have a geographical preference, state it and explain what makes it ideal for you.

4. *What will I do for a living?* Avoid giving your job description a title such as "accountant" or "nurse," especially if you already have an idea about what you want to do. Try to look at the ideas you are including from a fresh perspective. Make the answer to this question a description of you doing what you want to do (and not doing what you don't want to do) rather than a description of a job you think is realistic and available. Make the component activities, pleasures, and problems clear and identifiable so that you can discover fields or settings where they might be used.

5. *Who will I be spending my time with* in my studies and work and in my leisure/recreational and social pursuits? Describe the kinds of people you will be taking classes with, working with, and engaging in leisure/recreational and social pursuits with. Describe these people in terms of what their interests and values would be like, the kinds of topics you would talk about, the things you would be doing together, their sex, age, and so on.

Strategies for Gathering Information

When you have completed the description of your ideal job, select at least two occupations that you would like to explore in depth. Be sure they are consistent with your three-letter Summary Profile code derived from the self-assessment inventories in Appendix B. Write the occupations in the spaces provided on the pages that follow and identify the informational resources you plan to draw on while exploring each occupation. You may wish to write to some professional associations for information. Addresses for a number of professional and trade associations are found in Appendix E. It will also be helpful to indicate when you plan on using those resources.

After you have identified the resources you will use to explore each occupation, turn to the P.L.A.C.E. activity in the next section for guidelines on

how to pull together the information you have gathered about the different occupations. By comparing your ideal job description with information about
specific occupations from the P.L.A.C.E. activity, you will begin to have a sense
of which occupations you are considering are most consistent with your needs
and preferences.

Occupation _____

I will *read* the following materials about this occupation by _____ .
                                                                    (date)

1. _____

2. _____

3. _____

I will *talk* to the following persons about this occupation by _____ .
                                                                    (date)

1. _____

2. _____

3. _____

I will *visit* the following places that employ people in this occupation by

_____ .
   (date)

1. _____

2. _____

3. _____

If possible, I will *volunteer* some time to work alongside someone in this occu-

pation. I will do this by _____ .
                             (date)

The person I will contact to see about volunteer opportunities is _____

_____ .

Occupation _____

I will *read* the following materials about this occupation by_____ .
                                                                        (date)

1. _____

2. _____

3. _____

I will *talk* to the following persons about this occupation by_____ .
                                                                        (date)

1. _____

2. _____

3. _____

I will *visit* the following places that employ people in this occupation by

_____ .
    (date)

1. _____

2. _____

3. _____

If possible, I will *volunteer* some time to work alongside someone in this oc-

cupation. I will do this by _____ .
                                (date)

The person I will contact to see about volunteer opportunities is _____

_____ .

Occupation _____

I will *read* the following materials about this occupation by_____ .

1. _____

2. _____

3. _____

I will *talk* to the following persons about this occupation by_____ .
(date)

1. _____

2. _____

3. _____

I will *visit* the following places that employ people in this occupation by

_____ .
(date)

1. _____

2. _____

3. _____

If possible, I will *volunteer* some time to work alongside someone in this oc-

cupation. I will do this by_____ .
(date)

The person I will contact to see about volunteer opportunities is _____

_____ .

P.L.A.C.E.: A Guide for Exploring and Evaluating an Occupation

As you explore different occupations, it will be useful to organize the information you gather so that the various alternatives can be assessed individually and compared with one another. This can be accomplished using the following format for organizing occupational information. This system requires that you look at each occupation in terms of its

P. Position description, including general duties, occupational level, and associated enterprises.

L. Location, including the geographical area and the physical environment where you will be working.

A. Advancement opportunities and job security.

C. Conditions of employment, including salary, benefits, hours, and special demands such as dress codes.

E. Entry requirements, including required educational and training experiences.

The following worksheets (pages 255–257) will help you pull together the P.L.A.C.E. information about each occupation you explore and to evaluate it in terms of how the occupation fits the description of your ideal job. Use the five P.L.A.C.E. boxes on the left side of the page to write notes about the occupation. The Comments section can be used to jot down your reactions to the occupation's characteristics. In making your comments, you may wish to focus on how the demands and rewards of the occupation will affect your leisure/recreation and kinship/friendship pursuits. You can indicate how much the occupation appeals to you by circling 1, 2, or 3 in the box across from each characteristic of the occupation according to the following criteria:

Circle "3" if the occupation has a definite or strong appeal for you.
Circle "2" if it has a moderate amount of appeal for you.
Circle "1" if it has little appeal for you.
Circle "0" if it has equally appealing positive and negative qualities or if you are indifferent to it.
Circle "–1" if you are turned off in a small way by the occupation.
Circle "–2" if its negative qualities turn you off in a moderate way.
Circle "–3" if its negative qualities completely turn you off.

After you have rated the occupation in each of the five areas, total the circled numbers and write the figure you obtained in the box at the bottom of the page next to "Total rating." This score, which can be positive or negative, will provide you with a sense of the occupation's overall appeal to you. You can later compare this figure with the totals you obtain from rating other occupations, to get an idea of which occupations you have explored appeal most to you.

A Place for Your Values

We have already explored how your personal values have emerged and changed over time and how they influence your decisions. This activity provides you with an opportunity to examine how well the different occupations you are currently exploring match your values. In completing the activity, you will be asked to identify values and to use them as criteria for assessing occupations. Worksheets (pages 260–262) are provided for comparing up to three occupations.

Occupational Evaluation Worksheet

Position Title _____

Characteristics of the occupation	Comments	Rating
P. Position description *Notes:*		−3 −2 −1 0 1 2 3
L. Location *Notes:*		−3 −2 −1 0 1 2 3
A. Advancement opportunities *Notes:*		−3 −2 −1 0 1 2 3
C. Conditions of employment *Notes:*		−3 −2 −1 0 1 2 3
E. Entry requirements *Notes:*		−3 −2 −1 0 1 2 3

Total rating =

Occupational Evaluation Worksheet

Position Title _____

Characteristics of the occupation	Comments	Rating
P. Position description *Notes:*		-3 -2 -1 0 1 2 3
L. Location *Notes:*		-3 -2 -1 0 1 2 3
A. Advancement opportunities *Notes:*		-3 -2 -1 0 1 2 3
C. Conditions of employment *Notes:*		-3 -2 -1 0 1 2 3
E. Entry requirements *Notes:*		-3 -2 -1 0 1 2 3

Total rating =

Occupational Evaluation Worksheet

Position Title _____

Characteristics of the occupation	Comments	Rating
P. Position description *Notes:*		-3 -2 -1 0 1 2 3
L. Location *Notes:*		-3 -2 -1 0 1 2 3
A. Advancement opportunities *Notes:*		-3 -2 -1 0 1 2 3
C. Conditions of employment *Notes:*		-3 -2 -1 0 1 2 3
E. Entry requirements *Notes:*		-3 -2 -1 0 1 2 3

Total rating =

Once you learn how to use this technique, you may find it useful in making other career decisions, such as selecting from among job possibilities or deciding on a promotion. The same approach can be used in other areas of your life, including decisions about a major purchase, about where you live, or about where you will vacation. The only information you need for each of these decisions is a list of your values and a list of alternate choices.

The format for this activity is basically the same as that of the P.L.A.C.E. activity, except that instead of looking at occupations in terms of position, location, and so on, you will be using your values as your criteria. The activity involves six steps.

Step 1. Identify Your Values

Read through the list of values below and check the boxes next to the values that are *most important* to you—the values that you must have the opportunity to express if you are to be happy with your major or work.

The ideal job would have to . . .

☐ provide me with *achievement, recognition, status,* or approval from others

☐ provide me with opportunities and time to appreciate *beauty* in people, art, and nature

☐ provide me with *challenging opportunities* to use my creativity, training, intelligence, and talents

☐ provide me with opportunities to experience *good health physically* and *mentally* by being free of anxiety and stress

☐ provide me with an opportunity to *improve my financial position* significantly

☐ provide me with *independence* to be free to do my own thing, independently of others

☐ provide me with time to devote to *close personal relationships* with my peers and family

☐ provide me with an opportunity to work in settings that agree with my *moral* or *religious standards*

☐ provide me with time for *pleasure* and *fun*

☐ provide me with opportunities to *influence* or *control* the activities of others

☐ provide me with *security* and *safety* from unexpected or unpleasant change

☐ provide me with opportunities for *personal development* by using my talents and interests; support me in my efforts to become more well rounded as a person

☐ provide me with opportunities to be of *service* to others

Step 2. List Your Values

From each of the values you checked, write down the italicized words representing the values that are most important to you in the column labeled "My most important values are" on page 255. Put one value in each box.

Step 3. Indicate the Occupation Being Considered

Write the name of the occupation you are considering in the space provided at the top of the page.

Step 4. Gather Information About the Occupation

Use the same procedures you used in the P.L.A.C.E. activity for gathering information about an occupation. Write your observations in the Comments section of the grid on page 255.

Step 5. Rate the Occupation

Rate the occupation according to the following scale. Circle the appropriate rating next to each value.

Circle "3" if the occupation is very consistent with your value.

Circle "2" if the occupation is generally consistent with your value.

Circle "1" if the occupation is somewhat consistent with your value.

Circle "0" if the occupation has some qualities that are consistent with your value and some that are not.

Circle " – 1" if the occupation is somewhat inconsistent with your value.

Circle " – 2" if the occupation is generally inconsistent with your value.

Circle " – 3" if the occupation is very inconsistent with your value.

Step 6. Total Value Rating

After you have rated the occupation for each of the values, total the circled numbers and write the figure you obtained in the space on page 255 labeled

Occupation Evaluation Worksheet—Values

Occupation _____

My most important values are	Comments	Rating
		-3 -2 -1 0 1 2 3
		-3 -2 -1 0 1 2 3
		-3 -2 -1 0 1 2 3
		-3 -2 -1 0 1 2 3
		-3 -2 -1 0 1 2 3
		-3 -2 -1 0 1 2 3
		-3 -2 -1 0 1 2 3

Total rating =

Occupation Evaluation Worksheet—Values

Occupation _____

My most important values are	Comments	Rating
		-3 -2 -1 0 1 2 3
		-3 -2 -1 0 1 2 3
		-3 -2 -1 0 1 2 3
		-3 -2 -1 0 1 2 3
		-3 -2 -1 0 1 2 3
		-3 -2 -1 0 1 2 3
		-3 -2 -1 0 1 2 3

Total rating =

Occupation Evaluation Worksheet—Values

Occupation _____

My most important values are	Comments	Rating
		−3 −2 −1 0 1 2 3
		−3 −2 −1 0 1 2 3
		−3 −2 −1 0 1 2 3
		−3 −2 −1 0 1 2 3
		−3 −2 −1 0 1 2 3
		−3 −2 −1 0 1 2 3
		−3 −2 −1 0 1 2 3

Total rating =

"Total rating." (In calculating your totals, remember that a minus is always subtracted from a plus.) This score, which can be positive or negative, will provide you with a sense of the occupation's value to you. You can later compare this figure with the totals you obtain from rating other occupations, to get a clear idea of which of the occupations you have explored appeal most to you.

Guidelines for Your Occupational Report

Prepare an "Occupational Report" to help you pull together and compare information you have generated about yourself with information you gather about an occupation or occupations that interest you.

Your description of your ideal job is the first important aspect of the Occupational Report. It helped you characterize your preferred lifestyle. The second step, the P.L.A.C.E. occupational rating activity, allowed you to compare a specific occupation or several occupations with these ideal requirements. The Occupational Report will allow you to summarize this information in narrative form and to project yourself into the future in the occupation that currently has most appeal to you.

Plan on covering five steps in preparing your Occupational Report:

1. Select one occupation from the P.L.A.C.E. activity that you would like to describe in depth.
2. Identify the resources you have used in exploring that occupation, including conversations you have had with others in the field (one instructor and one worker are required), places you have visited or done volunteer work in, and written materials you have read.
3. Compare the information you have obtained with the requirements of your ideal job. Indicate in what ways and how frequently the occupation would allow you to exercise your ideals. Also indicate the skills you would need to be successful in this occupation and how you would go about acquiring them.
4. Identify and briefly describe occupations that are related to the one you explored. Indicate which ones you would consider as alternatives to your primary occupation.
5. Pretend you have the ability to see the future clearly. Based on what you know about yourself now, the occupation you explored in your Occupational Report, and what you have learned about how individuals continue to develop over their adult years, write four "notes to yourself" in the future. The notes should portray what is important to you and the choices you will be making at the following points in time.

   a. The remainder of this year.
   b. Shortly after college graduation.

    c. Ten years from now.

    d. At retirement.

By completing these five steps in the Occupational Report, you will gain a clearer perspective on what is most important to you in your life and work, and you will be able to see how well each occupation you explore fits into your most preferred way of living.

APPENDIX E

A Selected Listing of Professional and Trade Associations

Listed here are the names and addresses of professional and trade associations you may wish to contact as you gather information about occupational fields that are consistent with your preferences, interests, abilities, and values. Use the references sources provided at the end of the list for a broader sample of the names and addresses of professional associations.

Occupation	Organization and address
Accountants	American Institute of Certified Public Accountants, 1211 Avenue of the Americas, New York, NY 10036
Actors and artists	Associated Actors and Artists of America, 165 W. 46th St., New York, NY 10036
Actuaries	Society of Actuaries, 208 S. LaSalle St., Chicago, IL 60604
Advertising workers	American Advertising Federation, 1225 Connecticut Ave., N.W., Washington, DC 20036
Aircraft industries	Aerospace Industries Association of America, 1725 DeSales St., N.W., Washington, DC 20036
Airline workers	Air Transport Association of America, 1000 Connecticut Ave., Washington, DC 20036
Architects	American Institute of Architects, 1735 New York Ave., N.W., Washington, DC 20036
Architects, landscape	American Society of Landscape Architects, 1750 Old Meadow Rd., McLean, VA 22101
Astronomers	American Astronomical Society, 211 Fitz Randolph Rd., Princeton, NJ 08540
Bakers	American Bakers Association, Suite 650, 1700 Pennsylvania Ave., N.W., Washington, DC 20006
Bankers	American Bankers Association, 90 Park Ave., New York, NY 10016
Barbers and beauty operators	Associated Master Barbers and Beauticians of America, 219 Greenwich Rd., P.O. Box 17782, Charlotte, NC 28211
Bricklayers	Structural Clay Products Institute, 1750 Old Meadow Rd., McLean, VA 22101
Broadcasters	National Association of Broadcasters, 1771 N St., N.W., Washington, DC 20036
Building trades	AFL and CIO Building and Construction Trades Dept., 815 16th St., N.W., Washington, DC 20006
Chemists	American Chemical Society, 1155 16th St., N.W., Washington, DC 20036
Chiropractors	International Chiropractors Association, 741 Brady St., Davenport, IA 52805
Coal mining	National Coal Association, 1130 17th St., N.W., Washington, DC 20036

Occupation	*Organization and address*
Compositors	Printing Industries of America, Inc., 5223 River Rd., N.W., Washington, DC 20016
Data processors	Data Processing Management Association, 505 Busse Hwy., Park Ridge, IL 60068
Decorators	American Institute of Interior Decorators, 730 Fifth Ave., New York, NY 10019
Dental assistants	American Dental Assistants Association, 211 E. Chicago Ave., Chicago, IL 60611
Dental hygienists	American Dental Assistants Association, 211 E. Chicago Ave., Chicago, IL 60611
Dental technicians	National Association of Certified Dental Laboratories, 1330 Massachusetts Ave., N.W., Washington, DC 20005
Dentists	American Dental Association, 211 E. Chicago Ave., Chicago, IL 60611
Dieticians	American Dietetic Association, 620 N. Michigan Ave., Chicago, IL 60611
Ecology workers	Ecological Society of America, Dept. of Botany, Southern Illinois University, Carbondale, IL 62901
Economists	American Economic Association, 1313 21st Ave., S., Nashville, TN 37212
Electrical workers	International Brotherhood of Electrical Workers, 1200 15th St., N.W., Washington, DC 20005
Engineers, aeronautical	American Institute of Aeronautics and Astronautics, 1290 Avenue of the Americas, New York, NY 10019
Engineers, agricultural	American Society of Agricultural Engineers, 2950 Niles Rd., St. Joseph, MI 49085
Engineers, ceramic	American Ceramic Society, 4055 N. High St., Columbus, OH 43214
Engineers, chemical	American Institute of Chemical Engineers, 345 E. 47th St., New York, NY 10017
Engineers, civil	American Society of Civil Engineers, 345 E. 47th St., New York, NY 10017
Engineers, electrical	Institute of Electrical and Electronics Engineers, 345 E. 47th St., New York, NY 10017
Engineers, industrial	American Institute of Industrial Engineers, 345 E. 47th St., New York, NY 10017
Engineers, marine	American Society of Naval Engineers, Inc., 1012 14th St., N.W., Suite 807, Washington, DC 20005
Engineers, mechanical	American Society of Mechanical Engineers, 345 E. 47th St., New York, NY 10017
Engineers, mining, metallurgical, and petroleum	American Institute of Mining, Metallurgical, and Petroleum Engineers, 345 E. 47th St., New York, NY 10017

Occupation	Organization and address
Engineers, radio	Institute of Electrical and Electronics Engineers, 345 E. 47th St., New York, NY 10017
Farmers	U.S. Dept. of Agriculture, Washington, DC 20250
Florists	Society of American Florists and Ornamental Horticulturalists, 901 N. Washington St., Alexandria, VA 22314
Foresters	Society of American Foresters, 1010 16th St., N.W., Washington, DC 20036
Forge shop workers	Forging Industry Association, 55 Public Square, Cleveland, OH 44113
Funeral directors and embalmers	National Funeral Directors Association of the U.S., 135 W. Wells St., Milwaukee, WI 53203
Geographers	Association of American Geographers, 1146 16th St., N.W., Washington, DC 20036
Geologists	American Geological Institute, 1444 North St., N.W., Washington, DC 20005
Hairdressers and cosmetologists	National Hairdressers and Cosmetologists Association, 175 Fifth Ave., New York, NY 10010
Home economists	American Home Economics Association, 1600 20th St., N.W., Washington, DC 20009
Hospital workers	American Hospital Association, 840 N. Lake Shore Dr., Chicago, IL 60611
Hotel workers	American Hotel and Motel Association, 221 W. 57th St., New York, NY 10019
Insurance agents	National Association of Insurance Agents, 96 Fulton St., New York, NY 10038
Jewelers and jewelry repairers	Retail Jewelers of America, 1025 Vermont Ave., N.W., Washington, DC 20005
Lawyers	American Bar Association, 1155 E. 60th St., Chicago, IL 60637
Librarians	American Library Association, 50 E. Huron St., Chicago, IL 60611
Machinists, all-around	International Association of Machinists, 1300 Connecticut Ave., Washington, DC 20036
Mathematicians	Mathematical Association of America, SUNY at Buffalo, Buffalo, NY 14214
Mechanics, refrigeration and air conditioning	United Association of Journeymen, Apprentices of Plumbing and Pipe Fitting Industries, 901 Massachusetts Ave., N.W., Washington, DC 20001
Medical laboratory technicians	Registry of Medical Technologists, American Society of Chemical Pathologists, P.O. Box 2544, Muncie, IN 47302

Occupation	*Organization and address*
Medical record librarians	American Medical Record Association, 875 N. Michigan Ave., Chicago, IL 60611
Medical X-ray technicians	American Society, Radiologic Technicians, 537 S. Main St., Fond Du Lac, WI 54935
Meteorologists	American Meteorological Society, 45 Beacon St., Boston, MA 02108
Microbiologists	American Society for Bacteriology, 1913 Eye St., N.W., Washington, DC 20006
Musicians	American Federation of Musicians, 641 Lexington Ave., New York, NY 10022
Nurses, practical	National Association for Practical Nurse Education and Service, Inc., 1465 Broadway, New York, NY 10036
Nurses, registered	National League for Nursing, 10 Columbus Circle, New York, NY 10018
Occupational therapists	American Occupational Therapy Association, 251 Park Ave. South, New York, NY 10010
Opticians	Optical Society of America, 2100 Pennsylvania Ave., N.W., Washington, DC 20037
Optometrists	American Optometric Association, 7000 Chippewa St., St. Louis, MO 63119
Osteopathic physicians	American Osteopathic Association, 212 E. Ohio St., Chicago, IL 60611
Petroleum workers	American Petroleum Institute, 1271 Avenue of the Americas, New York, NY 10020
Pharmacists	American Pharmaceutical Association, 2215 Constitution Ave., Washington, DC 20037
Photographers	Professional Photographers of America, 1090 Executive Way, Oak Leaf Commons, Des Plaines, IL 60018
Physical therapists	American Physical Therapy Association, 1790 Broadway, New York, NY 10019
Physicians	American Medical Association, 535 N. Dearborn St., Chicago, IL 60610
Physicists	American Institute of Physics, 335 E. 45th St., New York, NY 10017
Plastics workers	Society of the Plastics Industry, 250 Park Ave., New York, NY 10017
Plumbers and pipe fitters	United Association of Journeymen, Apprentices of Plumbing and Pipe Fitting Industries, 901 Massachusetts Ave., N.W., Washington, DC 20001
Podiatrists	American Podiatry Association, 20 Chevy Chase Circle, N.W., Washington, DC 20015
Psychologists	American Psychological Association, 1200 17th St., N.W., Washington, DC 20036

Occupation	Organization and address
Public relations	Public Relations Society of America, 845 Third Ave., New York, NY 10022
Railroad workers	Association of American Railroads, American Railroads Bldg., Washington, DC 20036
Real estate salesmen	National Association of Real Estate Boards, 155 E. Superior St., Chicago, IL 60611
Recreation workers	National Recreation and Park Association, 1700 Pennsylvania Ave., N.W., Washington, DC 20006
Restaurant workers	National Restaurant Association, 1530 N. Lake Shore Dr., Chicago, IL 60610
Retail grocers	National Association of Retail Grocers of the United States, 360 N. Michigan Ave., Chicago, IL 60601
Secretaries	National Secretaries Association, 616 E. 63rd St., Kansas City, MO 64110
Social workers	National Commission for Social Work Careers, 2 Park Ave., New York, NY 10016
Sociologists	American Sociological Association, 1772 N St. N.W., Washington, DC 20036
Speech therapists	American Speech and Hearing Association, 9030 Old Georgetown Road, Washington, DC 20014
Teachers	National Center for Information on Careers in Education, 1607 New Hampshire Ave., N.W., Washington, DC 20009
Television and radio workers	American Federation of Television and Radio Artists, 724 Fifth Ave., New York, NY 10022
Textile workers	American Textiles Association, 1501 Johnston St., Charlotte, NC 28202
Truckers	American Trucking Association, 1616 P St., N.W., Washington, DC 20036
Veterinarians	American Veterinary Medical Association, 600 S. Michigan Ave., Chicago, IL 60605
Welders	American Welding Society, 2501 N.W. 7th St., Miami, FL 33125

For additional listings, see *Career Guide to Professional Associations* (Cranston, RI: The Carroll Press, 1976) and *National Trade and Professional Associations of the United States and Canada and Labor Unions,* ed. C. Colgate, Jr., and G. J. Slagle (Washington, DC: Columbia Books, 1976).

Removing Barriers to Effective Career Planning

When Others Challenge Your Career Choice:
Strategies for Conflict Resolution
Removing Myths and Beliefs That Block Effective
    Career Decision Making
References and Resources

When Others Challenge Your Career Choice: Strategies for Conflict Resolution[1]

Goethe, the famous novelist, once observed that behavior is a mirror in which we display who we are and how we would like to be seen. We are also social detectives: with every important decision, we cast about for clues from others that reflect their viewpoints on the wisdom of our choice. As we do, we often find ourselves wondering or asking: What do you think of my choice? Does it fit my image? Is it the right one for me?

The choice of a major, a profession, or a job is no different from any other decision. We use our career choices as a mirror of who we are and hope that our choices will be supported by others who are important to us.

A well-planned career choice will recognize your need for feedback and support from others and will balance their views with your own wants and needs. Despite your best attempts to make a balanced choice, however, you will occasionally find that others may disagree with your plans or even resist them. This two-part module will help you understand why others disagree with your choice and will suggest ways that you can more effectively and positively present your point of view as you work toward resolving your differences with them.

Part One: Understanding Your Conflicts with Others

The following three steps will help you better understand how conflicts are created and perpetuated because of the way people think, feel, and act.

Step 1: Identify Your Expectations of Others   The imaginary news conference that follows is based on *A Transitions Fantasy*, created by Charles Seashore. It will help you become more attuned to your expectations about how things would go if you announced to others that you had changed your career plans.

To start the activity, find a private, quiet place to think and write. Make yourself comfortable and relax.

Imagine that you have made a significant career choice (a major, profession, or job) that you are going to announce in the form of a "news release" to a committee consisting of the four most important people in your life. Use the news release form on page 274 to describe in detail what your choice is, how you went about making it, how you feel about it, and how you plan to carry it out.

[1]Written by Clarke Carney, Ph.D., and Amy Reynolds, M.A. Copyright by Counseling and Consultation Service, The Ohio State University. Used with permission of the agency and authors.

When you finish writing the narrative of the news release, pick a time and place to share it. Put that information in the space provided at the bottom of the news release form. Describe your reason for choosing that particular time and place in the space provided. Such information can be helpful in planning a strategy for announcing your decision to others.

After you complete the news release, write the names of the people you want to share your news with on the committee roster on page 275. As you identify each person, think about the role he or she plays in your life and why you have selected that individual for your committee. Record this information about each person in the appropriate columns on the "Committee Roster."

Imagine next that it is time to meet with the committee at the place you have selected. You have arrived a few minutes early and are thinking about each of your guests. Record your thoughts about each person on the roster sheet in the space provided.

Fantasize now that your committee is gathering. You are standing at the entrance, greeting your guests as they enter. How do you react as you see each person? List your reactions on the committee roster.

The time has come for you to share your news release with your committee. Look at each person as you share your decision. What do you experience as you look at each person? How do they react as you talk? Who supports your choice? What do they say or do that indicates their agreement? Who challenges your choice? What do they say or do that suggests they disagree with you? Allow this imaginary dialogue to continue until each person has shared his or her point of view and you have had an opportunity to respond to it. Record your dialogue with each person on the committee roster sheet.

Finally, imagine that the discussion has ended and the committee is leaving. Each person walks past you to say goodbye. What do you say to each other? Take a few minutes to sift through your reactions to each person. Record your observations on the bottom of the committee roster sheet. In the sections that follow, you will be using this information to (a) examine the nature of any disagreements you may have with others over your choice and (b) identify ways of working through their resistance to your goals.

Step 2: Understand the Source of Your Disagreement   Before you begin to sort out the implications of your news conference, it may be helpful to understand how conflicts are started.

Our trust in others is based on their predictability. Just as a thermostat keeps our homes at a steady temperature, we expect others to conform to our standards for thinking and acting. Some regulations, such as laws and codes of conduct, are quite formal; others are less formal and are often implied in consistent patterns of behavior. Friends at a party, for example, learn to play different roles, such as "practical joker," "intellectual," "flirt," and "sports enthusiast." Somehow each person fits into his or her assigned role, and their friends encourage them to stay in it either by praising them or by somehow letting them know when they are "out of character." When the "practical joker" doesn't play that role, for example, we may find ourselves wondering "what's wrong"

Important

NEWS RELEASE

_____ announced to a selected committee
(your name)

of people in his or her life today that he or she has decided to

_____

_____

_____

_____ .

_____ indicated that he or she carefully
(your name)

considered this choice and engaged in the following activities in
making it: _____

_____

_____

_____ .

_____ also indicated that he or she feels
(your name)

_____ about the decision and plans to carry

it out by _____

_____

_____ .

Date and time: _____

Place: _____

Reasons for selecting this time and place:_____

Committee Roster

	Committee members			
	Name:	*Name:*	*Name:*	*Name:*
Relationship to me:				
Reasons for inviting this person:				
Reactions I have to this person as I wait for him or her to arrive:				
Reactions as I greet this person:				
Reactions I have to each person before I speak:				
How this person reacts to my choice:				
What I say or do in response to this person's reaction:				
Parting observations as the committee leaves:				

and looking for ways to prod that person back into being his or her "usual self" through teasing, coaxing, or expressions of concern such as "You seem out of sorts."

Families operate in much the same way. Each family member expects the others to fit into a family portrait that mirrors his or her image of what the family is or should be like. Family members may vary their roles as they grow and change—as, for example, when a child moves into adulthood—but a radical or rapid departure from the family norm (including a shift in career direction) may be cause for alarm among other family members, who may react with puzzlement, resistance, and anger. Thus, when a family member does not act in the way that others in the family expect, a conflict may occur.

Generally speaking, conflicts tend to arise when one person thinks that another has not acted appropriately or when one person has prevented another from meeting an important need. We'll call this violation of trust a "precipitating event." An example of a violation of an expectation would be a student failing to follow a family tradition of becoming a physician or a student dropping out of school after agreeing with his or her parents and adviser to complete the term. An example of a violation of a personal need would be a spouse who quits a job and leaves his or her family financially insecure and in need of food and shelter.

Regardless of how the violation has occurred, the person whose expectations or needs have not been met will make a judgment about the appropriateness of the actions of the other person. This in turn causes him or her to react in certain ways. The precipitating event that is created by one person's actions will thus set forth a chain reaction in the other person.

An example of such a chain reaction is shown on page 277, which describes the experiences of John, who has come into conflict with his parents over his career goals.

If you apply the flowchart that describes John's situation to yourself, you may observe that in examining your own conflict you should pay attention to (a) the event that precipitated the conflict; (b) the different interpretations that others may have of the event; (c) how others may feel about it because of what they think; and (d) how others may act because of what they think and feel. This knowledge can also be helpful in examining your own thoughts, feelings, and behaviors to see how you may be contributing to the conflict.

In Step 3, you will use an approach known as the ABCD method to help you analyze how others may react to your career decision.

Step 3: Analyze the Source of Your Disagreement in Detail   On page 279, you will find a Conflict Assessment Guide that will help you compare the reactions that the four people on your committee have to your news release. Put the name of the person who is likely to express the strongest disagreement with your announcement on the top of the left-hand column. Put the name of the person who is most likely to support your choice at the bottom of that column. The middle two boxes can be used to analyze the reactions of people who fall between these two extremes.

Precipitating event (Unmet expectation) →	Interpretation →	Feelings →	Actions →
John announces to his parents that he is changing his major from pre-med to psychology because he is doing poorly in required science classes.	John's parents are concerned that John is not living up to the family tradition in medicine and that he is not as "bright" as his brother and sister who have pursued careers in medicine.	His parents feel: disappointed hurt angry	His father *moralizes* with John and tells him how disappointed he is that John is not acting like a "member of the Smith family." His mother engages in *name calling* and says that John is "lazy." Both of his parents *order* him to stay in the pre-med program, and his father *warns* him that if John doesn't he will withdraw financial support for his education.

Precipitating event	Interpretation →	Feelings →	Actions →
His parents' actions become a precipitating event for John, to which he may react in one of two ways.	John thinks, "I have let my family down. I am lazy and inconsiderate. I had better study harder."	He feels: guilty foolish	John pursues a *self-defeating approach behavior*. He tries harder by studying more but is still not successful and his grades continue to decline.
	Interpretation →	Feelings →	Actions →
	John says to himself: "They really don't care about me. All they are concerned about is protecting the family tradition."	He feels: angry foolish hurt	John pursues a *self-defeating avoidant behavior*. He stops studying and gets involved in a social group that his parents don't accept. His grades decline and he eventually drops out of college.

After you have listed the names of your four committee members, consider how they may interpret your announcement. Listed below are a number of possible reasons why others may disagree with you. Pick the interpretation(s) that best fit(s) each person and write those interpretations in Box B next to that person's name on the Conflict Assessment Guide.

1. They lack information about you or your choice.
2. They believe that you are bucking an important family tradition.
3. They are afraid of losing you because you are becoming independent and are changing your views of life.
4. They believe that you should engage in only certain kinds of work because of your sex or ethnic background.
5. They are concerned about the costs associated with your choice because they are footing the bill for your education or training.
6. It doesn't fit their image of you.
7. They think they have a better understanding of you or the world of work than you do.
8. They're disappointed because they feel you're lowering your sights or are playing it safe.
9. Even though you've changed, they still view you the way you were before.
10. They are dependent on you financially and fear your plan will jeopardize their current way of living.

If this list does not fully describe a person's interpretation of your actions, feel free to write in other interpretations that he or she might have of your announcement.

Your next task is to identify how they may feel about your choice. Following is a list of negative feelings that people may have because they disagree with your choice. Try to identify the feelings that each person is likely to have about your choice and list those feelings in Box C on the Conflict Assessment Guide.

1. Angry or irritable
2. Anxious, worried, or fearful
3. Frustrated
4. Disappointed
9. Self-pitying
10. Worthless, inferior
11. Resentful
12. Foolish
13. Vulnerable

5. Guilty
6. Hopeless, depressed
7. Abandoned or alone
8. Inadequate
14. Rigid
15. Dependent
16. Cautious
17. Embarrassed

Now that you have listed the possible interpretations and feelings of others, your next task will be to identify how they will act when you inform them of your choice. Psychologist Thomas Gordon (1972) has identified 12 behaviors—the "dirty dozen"—that people tend to use as barriers when another person has not lived up to an expectation or need. These behaviors are listed below with examples. Pick the behavior(s) that best depict(s) the reactions of each person on your committee and list them next to the person's name under Column D

ABCD Conflict Assessment Guide

A *The precipitating event: my news release*	B *How he or she interprets my choice*	C *How he or she feels*	D *How he or she acts (roadblocks)*	*My reaction to this person*
The person who is *most upset* is: 1.				
2.				
3.				
The person who is *least upset* is: 4.				

on the Conflict Assessment Guide. If an individual is likely to engage in several behaviors, you may want to list them in the sequence in which they are apt to occur. For example, a person may start ordering and directing you, and if that doesn't work he or she may moralize or preach at you in order to get his or her way. If moralizing and preaching don't work, he or she might call you a name that gets your goat. Since people may use several strategies as they attempt to get their way, you may find yourself creating a fairly long list of behaviors for some individuals on your list.

1. *Ordering, Directing, Commanding*

   "I don't care what your counselor says. Do what I tell you to do because I know what's best for you."

2. *Warning, Threatening, Promising*

   "If you change your major, I'll stop paying your tuition."
   "If you do things my way, I'll send you on a special trip this summer."

3. *Moralizing, Preaching, Shoulds and Oughts*

"You shouldn't change directions because other people will think that you're immature and indecisive."

"You ought to major in engineering. It pays well and promises a secure future."

"You should respect our wishes. Look what we've done for you. How could you be so ungrateful?"

4. *Advising: Giving Solutions or Suggestions*

"Just wait a couple of years before deciding on a college/major. You'll know better what you want then."

"I'd suggest that you talk to your uncle about that. He's our accountant and knows more about the field than your adviser does."

5. *Teaching, Lecturing, Giving Logical Arguments*

"College can be the most wonderful experience you'll have. Just stick it out. You'll see what I mean by the end of the year."

"If you take responsibility and stick to your original plans, you'll be more marketable when you graduate."

"Let's look at the facts about the program."

"When I was your age, we didn't have the advantages you do now."

6. *Judging, Criticizing, Disagreeing, Blaming*

"You're not thinking clearly about this. Give it some more thought and you'll see what I mean."

"That's an immature and irresponsible way of acting."

"I couldn't be more disappointed in you."

7. *Praising, Agreeing*

"You've always been such a good student."

"I've always been proud of you."

8. *Name Calling, Labeling, Stereotyping*

   "You're spoiled and inconsiderate of others."

   "OK, you think you're so smart because you've had two years of college and I haven't."

   "What have you become, one of those — — —s?"

9. *Interpreting, Analyzing, Diagnosing*

   "You're just doing this to upset me."

   "You really don't know what you're doing."

   "You're not doing well because you're not trying hard enough."

10. *Reassuring, Sympathizing, Consoling, Supporting*

    "All students go through a phase like this. It will pass."

    "I used to feel that way too."

    "You can be an excellent student. You have great potential."

11. *Probing, Questioning, Interrogating*

    "When did you start to feel this way about your major?"

    "Why do you suppose you hate your job?"

    "Who put that idea in your head?"

    "What will you do if you don't go to college?"

12. *Withdrawing, Distracting, Sarcasm, Humoring, Diverting, Indirection*

    "Come on, let's talk about more pleasant things."

    "How's the college football team doing?"

    "Why don't you quit and hide in the mountains?"

    "We've been through this before."

Your last task in analyzing your conflict with others is to assess your own reactions to their behavior. Using the boxes provided at the right of the Conflict Assessment Guide, briefly note how you react to each person's behaviors. Pay particular attention to what you think, feel, and do in reacting to each person. What do you do in response to each person that indicates that you may be *approaching* your differences in a self-defeating way? What do you do that suggests that you may be *avoiding* the conflict in a self-defeating way? What do you do in response to other people that keeps communication open and supportive?

If you have not been as effective as you would like to be in discussing your ideas with your committee, you may find the following suggestions helpful in rethinking and changing the ways you present yourself to them.

Part Two: Constructive Ways of Managing Conflict

The following suggestions focus on what you can do to help resolve the possible conflicts that might arise because of your career decision. The first suggestion is to be as knowledgeable as you can be about yourself and the major or occupation you have selected.

1. *Know what you like to do, can do, and prize the most.* It will help you feel confident about what you are saying. The information others have concerning your career is dependent on what you've shared with them. If their response to your news release is based on faulty information—Interpretations 1, 3, 6, 8, and 9—you will need to show them how you've changed and grown. In doing so, you might contrast your past actions with present feelings, goals, hopes, and plans. Ask that they expand their views of you to include how you see yourself now. Conflicts here may also have to do with ways in which you're not "living up" to their expectations or meeting their needs. Discuss those expectations and needs openly.

2. *Be sure the career information you use is the best available.* Use accurate, current, and unbiased facts to back up your decision. Make a list of resources you used in making your decision. You may want to call on it when you present your choice to others.

With Interpretations 1, 4, 5, and 10, you may also want to share occupational information, such as job prospects, salary information, advancement opportunities, and so on. Answer any questions that may have to do with the time it will take to achieve your goal, how much it will cost, and the effects it will have on them. You will gain their confidence if you present them with thorough and factual career information and demonstrate how planful you have been in making your decision.

The second suggestion is to examine how effective you are in dealing with others. Concentrate on how effectively you express yourself, how well you listen to others, and how you respond to them. The following suggestions can help you strengthen your communication and conflicting-resolution skills.

1. *Select a comfortable place to discuss your plan.* A public setting such as a park or a restaurant can be a great place to share your decision. It can help you feel relaxed, create the atmosphere of a special occasion, and encourage a sense of mutual understanding.

2. *Be positive, clear, and precise in presenting your choice.* Your news release can be used as a script to help you prepare for your news conference. Read it out loud to yourself. Does it effectively present the information that you used in making your choice? If it is not as clear as you would like it to be, edit it so it effectively reflects your views. Role-play your news conference with someone such as a friend or counselor who is unbiased and from whom you are open to receiving feedback. Effective communication with others in a conflict that can be refined with practice and role-playing will allow you the opportunity to practice and feel more confident in the actual situation.

3. *Be open to learn from what others say.* Invite their reactions without losing sight of your own objectives. Be willing to change your mind if you find that you have not seen things as fully or clearly as you had first thought.

4. *Be willing to listen to others.* Acknowledge the feelings and interpretations before challenging them. Put yourself in the other person's frame of mind and let the person know that you are trying to understand his or her point of view without compromising your own objectives.

5. *Be patient.* It may take a while for the other person to change his or her views. Plant a seed of thought and nourish it over time with additional facts and observations. Remember too that some people will engage in several "dirty dozen" behaviors before they accept your ideas. Knowing their habitual ways of behaving can help you withstand their challenge until they are willing to see your side.

6. *Build on your commonalities* and agreements *and minimize your differences.* This is best done honestly and openly, not in a shallow, camouflaging way. Show that you are not in total disagreement about everything.

7. *Accept responsibility for your part of the conflict.* Avoid tapping into the list of the "dirty dozen" behaviors yourself. If conflict arises, don't blame or placate others—talk about it instead.

8. *Act assertively.* Express your needs and feelings in a nonjudgmental, responsible way. Identify the source(s) of disagreement (probably where interpretations differ) and discuss strategies for moving beyond them. For example, with Interpretation 2 it's quite possible that the pressure to "live up to a family tradition" would make you feel angry and disappointed. Stating what you feel and what causes you to feel that way and asking that they not have such fixed expectations of you is an assertive way of dealing with the situation. Another assertive technique is to keep the discussion focused on the choice to be made rather than letting it drift into an argument about each other's personalities or your past disagreements.

Expressing your feelings about yourself, the other person, and your relationship is important when dealing with others. It may mean sharing your anger,

A	B	C	D
Precipitating event	*John's interpretation of his parents' reactions*	*John's feelings*	*John's actions*
John's parents reject his choice of a major in psychology.	My family cares for me but doesn't know how to express it without attempting to control me. I'll need to acknowledge their caring, but stand my ground by being persistent in presenting my choice. I'll also need to make sure that they understand how I gathered information about my interests and abilities and how strong the job prospects are for someone who is well prepared in the field. It will also be helpful for them to learn how closely linked psychology and medicine are with sports psychology and behavioral medicine.	Confident Planful Independent Guilt-free	He announces his choice to his parents and fully informs them about how he went about making it. He patiently listens and acknowledges his parents' disappointment, but reminds them that he has to do what is best for him. He points out the strong relationship between psychology and medicine and invites them to talk with his new adviser in psychology about the field.

hurt, disappointment, frustration, or whatever else you might be feeling about the changes to come and how you hope/expect it to affect you and your relationship. Ask for his or her understanding and support during the change process.

The flowchart above shows how John, the student described earlier, used some of these tips to change his behavior and produce a more positive solution to his differences with his parents. A similar chart is provided for your own use on page 285.

Since we will all grow and change during our lives, we must expect that the important changes we go through will affect our relationships with others in some way. It is hoped that suggestions offered here will give you some effective strategies to work successfully through your differences with others as they arise.

Removing Myths and Beliefs That Block Effective Career Decision Making[2]

Conventional wisdom tells us that we get what we expect from our lives. It is easy to find many examples of this in our everyday decisions and actions. If we

[2]This activity was adapted from "Removing Attitudinal Blocks to Career Decision Making: A Self-Directed Module" by Clarke Carney, 1978, *Counseling and Human Development*, 2(4). Copyright 1978 by Love Publishing Company. Adapted by permission.

A Describe the precipitating event	B Reinterpret the stiuation in a more positive light	C List the positive feelings that your new view of the event creates in you	D Describe the positive behaviors that you will engage in to reduce your conflict with the other person

are preoccupied with failure, we may make hasty and uninformed decisions and create disasters for ourselves. These may include freezing on an exam, making plans to be at two places at once, or ruining a social activity by putting our worst foot forward.

Many of these stressful events are caused by myths or beliefs we hold that may lead us to exaggerate a situation, misinterpret circumstances, or otherwise cause us not to get the best outcomes from our efforts. Psychologist Albert Ellis suggests that such beliefs hinder us from taking an objective and realistic view of a situation. He observed that beliefs are often tied to the notions we have about success and failure—what we think we should or shouldn't be doing with our lives. When we accept such beliefs without checking their accuracy, we can become inflexible in our thinking and keep ourselves from finding creative ways of dealing with new situations.

Much of the discomfort that students experience in making career decisions is caused by myths or beliefs about career planning that are out of date or not accurate. We have seen that our ideas about what we should be doing in our careers are shaped by the ever-changing nature of society. Sometimes changes come so rapidly that it takes a while for individual beliefs and standards to catch up, especially if we learned them from an older generation.

For example, our society offers students many options and encourages them to make their own choices. Thus, while students know that they have a number of personal career options, many are still influenced by the old myth that the choice of a vocation will last a lifetime. As a result, they may feel anxious about making a career decision because they believe they have to come up with the one "right" and permanent occupation. The activity that follows identifies this and other inaccurate myths or beliefs that can operate in career decisions and make choosing an educational or vocational objective a distressing problem.

This activity presents the rational/emotive, or ABCD, method of problem analysis developed by Donald Tosi[3] to help people who want to change behaviors they are uncomfortable with. It is based on the premise that when an environmental event occurs, people filter it through a series of myths and beliefs that in turn generate a series of positive or negative feelings. These feelings cause people to make a choice and act in ways that move them either toward or away from an appropriate or effective response. The cycle completes itself when their behavior confirms their original interpretation of the situation and they do indeed get what they expect. An example of the ABCD paradigm is shown in Figure F-1.

The first part of the activity will teach you how to identify faulty myths or beliefs that can affect your career planning. The second part will teach you how to correct them and alter your decisions and behaviors toward more rewarding directions.

Part One: The ABCD Problem-Creating Career-Planning Sequence

The first four steps are designed to help you determine the personal sources of discomfort or conflict that affect your career planning.

Step 1: Possible Activating Events   Career decision making and career planning involve a series of steps, from early exploration, to commitment, and finally to action. Each step may serve as an activating event that invites problem-creating decision making. Some of these events appear in the following list. No doubt you will discover others as you work through your career plans. Spaces are provided so you can lengthen or modify this list. Choose three activating events from the list below that apply to you. Rank them from most upsetting to least upsetting and write them under "A" (Activating events) in Figure F-2.

1. Graduating from high school and being faced with the choice between college and work.
2. Graduating from high school and having to decide between colleges.
3. Being asked to declare a major on the college application form.
4. Seeing the results of a national college admissions exam and realizing how you compare with other college-bound individuals in your major.

---

[3]Adapted from "Self-Directed Behavior Change in the Cognitive, Affective, and Behavioral Motoric Domains: A Rational-Emotive Approach" by Donald J. Tosi, 1973, *Focus on Guidance*, 6, pp. 6–10. Copyright 1973 by Love Publishing Company. Adapted by permission.

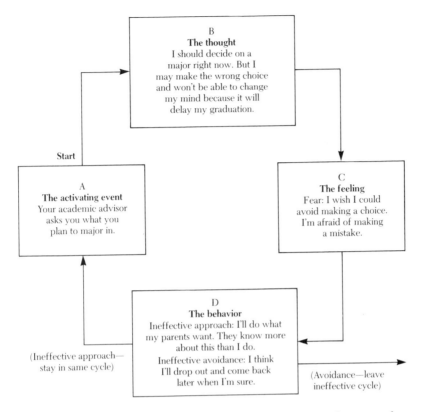

FIGURE F-1   Example of a problem-creating ABCD decision-making episode.

5. Being asked to declare a major in order to register for another term.
6. Being asked what you plan to do with the rest of your life.
7. Having to plan a class schedule.

Step 2: Undesirable Emotional or Affective States   The following is a partial list of emotional states that people often associate with career decision making. Try to identify the feelings you experience accompanying the activating events (A's) that have influenced your current career decision making. Record these under "C" (Undesirable emotions) in Figure F-2.

1. I feel angry or irritable.
2. I feel anxious, worried, and fearful.
3. I feel bored or dull.
4. I feel like I've failed.
5. I feel frustrated.
6. I feel guilty or self-condemning.
7. I feel hopeless or depressed.
8. I feel all alone.
9. I feel helpless or inadequate.

10. I feel self-pity.
11. I feel worthless or inferior.
12. I feel resentful.
13. I feel lazy.
14. I feel vulnerable.
15. I feel foolish.
16. I feel rigid or stuck.
17. I feel dependent.
18. I feel cautious.

	Least emotionally upsetting		Most emotionally upsetting
A. Activating events (A's)			
B. Problem- creating beliefs (B's)			
C. Undesirable emotions (C's)			
D. Undesirable behaviors (D's)			

FIGURE F-2   ABCD Problem Analysis, Part One. Complete by following the steps in Part One.

Step 3: Undesirable Behaviors, Actions, or Habits   The following behaviors tend to be self-defeating and inappropriate for effective career planning, especially if they appear with great intensity or regularity. From this list, select behaviors that you are likely to engage in as a consequence of the activating events (A's) you specified and the undesirable emotions (C's) you identified in Figure F-2. Record these under undesirable behaviors (D's) on Figure F-2. Describe your behavior as specifically as you can.

1. I avoid responsibility for the choice.
2. I procrastinate or postpone the choice.
3. I withdraw.
4. I do not gather the necessary information for making a decision.
5. I gather information but do not have any criteria for evaluating its relevance to me.
6. I allow others to make the choice for me.
7. I get stomachaches or show other signs of anxiety.
8. I declare a choice without fully exploring it.
9. I make up a class schedule without seeing my adviser.
10. I do not study or prepare.

11. I go on unemployment.
12. I put myself down in front of others.
13. I act guilty.
14. I frequently change my mind.
15. I stay in the undecided curriculum until an adviser pushes for a decision.
16. I explore excessively without deciding.
17. I choose a major or a job that is beyond my abilities.
18. I choose a major or a job that is below my abilities.
19. I frequently drop classes.
20. I become a professional student.
21. I ask a counselor for a test that will tell me what to do with my life.
22. I do not prepare a resumé or cover letter.
23. I slap together a resumé or cover letter with little thought.
24. I do not use the placement office to locate job possibilities.
25. I avoid employment interviews.
26. I perform poorly during an interview.
27. I stay in a job or family situation even though I am dissatisfied.
28. I set myself up to fail.
29. I do not really try, so I can't really fail.

Step 4: The Problem-Creating Myths or Beliefs   A great number of myths and beliefs operate to cause undesirable actions in career planning. The following is a partial list of some of the more commonly held beliefs that college students have about the process of career planning. From this list, select those myths and beliefs (B's) that occur between the activating events (A's) and the undesirable emotions (C's) you experience in your own career decision making. List them in the space provided under Problem-creating beliefs (B's) in Figure F-2.

1. The choice of a major or occupation is irreversible. Once you make it you cannot change your mind.
2. There is a single "right" career for everyone.
3. It is not okay to be undecided because being undecided is a sign of immaturity.
4. Nobody else is undecided. I'm all alone.
5. Somewhere there is a test that can tell me what to do with the rest of my life.
6. I know other people who have known what they wanted to be since childhood. Something's wrong with me because I can't be that way.
7. Others know what's best for me.
8. Somewhere there is an expert who can tell me what to do.
9. Everyone must climb the ladder of success even if it means doing things that are not interesting.
10. If you can find out what you are interested in, you'll automatically do well at it.
11. You must thoroughly analyze all aspects of a choice before you implement it; otherwise, you're not really prepared.

12. People are either successful or complete failures in their career pursuits. There's no in-between.
13. If I get away from the pressure to decide—if I take a year or two off from college—I'll make a better decision.
14. Go where the money is, regardless of what kind of work it involves.
15. The world of work is changing so rapidly that you really can't plan for the future.
16. We should respect tradition and maintain different types of work for men and women.
17. If things don't go the way I expect, it means that I'm a failure.
18. In order to have a feeling of worth, I should be and must be thoroughly competent, adequate, intelligent, and achieving in all possible respects.
19. Work is the only real way to personal fulfillment.
20. If I say no to what others expect of me, I'll be insensitive and unlovable.
21. I'm unhappy when I think about selecting a career goal because things external to me make me that way.
22. A person should be in total control of his or her career.
23. I must choose between really having a career and having a family.
24. Women shouldn't compete with men for jobs, especially jobs that involve creativity, managing others, and decision making. Since they are passive, emotional, and respond to things intuitively, women just aren't equipped to handle such situations.
25. If I lose a job to a woman, it means I'm inadequate as a male.
26. If my spouse has to go to work, it means I've failed as a husband.
27. Life is always fair.
28. Life is always unfair.

Part Two: The Reconstruction Process

The central theme of the rational/emotive change theory is that our beliefs dictate our feelings and behaviors. The theory also suggests that by becoming aware of problem-creating patterns of thought and challenging them, we can replace them with more realistic forms of thinking, more positive feelings, and more constructive behaviors. Based on this idea, this part will (1) attempt to help you correct any problem-creating ideas you may have about career planning and (2) help you find more satisfying ways of thinking, feeling, and acting as you pursue a career objective.

Step 1: Developing More Constructive Beliefs   The following section groups the problem-creating myths and beliefs of the Part One activities according to their common themes, points out evidence that contradicts them, and provides alternative constructive beliefs. Read through the problem-creating myths and beliefs and the evidence that contradicts them, and the more constructive beliefs, presented below. Use section B of Figure F-3 (Constructive ideas) to record the beliefs you wish to substitute for the problem-creating beliefs you listed in Figure F-2.

	Least emotionally upsetting		Most emotionally upsetting
A. Activating events (A's)			
B. Constructive ideas (B's)			
C. Desirable emotions (C's)			
D. Desirable behaviors (D's)			

FIGURE F-3   ABCD Problem Analysis, Part Two. Complete by following the steps in Part Two.

1. PROBLEM-CREATING BELIEF   The choice of a major or occupation is irreversible. Once you make it, you cannot or should not change your mind.

The Facts. Several surveys of college students have shown that from 30 to 50 percent of an entering freshman class will change majors at least once by graduation. Thus, changing one's mind is common in the student population. The belief that choices are irreversible stems from the idea that because most academic programs have lockstep requirements, a person will lose time and credits if he or she gets out of step with other students in the program. True, one does risk losing time and having to make up credits, and it does cost money to postpone graduating. However, the hidden costs of not leaving a major or occupation one is uncomfortable with are also great in terms of job dissatisfaction, personal stress, and poor performance. Thus, short-term avoidance of inconvenience can lead to long-range heartaches.

A More Constructive Belief. Regardless of how carefully I plan an occupation or academic choice, there is always some risk of dissatisfaction because I cannot know all the consequences of a choice. Therefore, I'll need to study the prospects carefully, bearing in mind my own needs and strengths. I'll follow the belief that commitment and action are better than inaction, and I'll prepare to review and perhaps renegotiate my decision at a later time.

2. PROBLEM-CREATING BELIEF   There is a single right career choice for everyone.

The Facts. The belief that there is an ideal occupation for everyone originated with the notion that one's choice of a vocation demonstrated a calling from God. However, the U.S. Department of Labor's *Dictionary of Occupational Titles* lists some 20,000 occupations grouped according to skill requirements, and a cursory examination of these occupations indicates that certain groups share common skills. Thus, a given individual may have the talents and interests to perform well at a variety of occupations. Although large numbers of people perform the same work throughout their lives, statistics show that most people try out several occupations or work settings during their careers. Trial lawyers have become teachers, social service administrators, and artists. Engineers have become physicians and psychologists.

A More Constructive Belief. Choosing an occupation is but one step in a career that I'll be able to review with certainty only at the end of my working life. Part of the enjoyment of my own growth will be recognizing my need to change as I develop new skills and interests and try new things through work, including changing my original occupational goals.

3. PROBLEM-CREATING BELIEF   It is not okay to be undecided. Being undecided is a sign of immaturity. A variation on this theme: Nobody else is undecided. I'm all alone. A third variation on this theme: Other people have known what they want to do since childhood. Something's wrong with me because I can't be that way.

The Facts. As we noted above, 30 to 50 percent of the students in a college class will change majors at least once—many more than it seems on the surface. In reality, undecidedness is natural for most of us, irrespective of age or academic status. All of this shows that the process of living and growing is one of continued exploration, decision, and redecision. Not to decide is nonetheless a decision and is perhaps the wisest decision a person can make under certain circumstances.

A More Constructive Belief. Immaturity and undecidedness are not the same thing. It's okay to be undecided; many of my peers are. The important thing is that I make the best use of the available resources so I can make the proper kind of decision when I'm ready to.

4. PROBLEM-CREATING BELIEF   Somewhere there is a test or an expert who can tell me what to do with the rest of my life. This theme has other variations: Others know what is best for me. If I say no to what others expect of me, I'll be demonstrating that I'm insensitive and unlovable.

The Facts. Again, the *Dictionary of Occupational Titles* lists as many as 20,000 occupations, and most interest and aptitude inventories sample no more than 200 of these 20,000 occupations. Thus, tests can suggest general areas to explore but should not be construed as the last word. In fact, statistics show that the best indicator of what a person will do occupationally is what the person says he or she will do, not what tests say. This suggests that even the experts have their limits and are best able to help you find trends in your occupational personal style and teach you how to gather current and accurate information so you can make up your own mind. You need not be viewed as uncaring if you elect to do something different from what others advise, including well-intentioned family and friends who would like to think that they know more than the experts when it comes to planning your future.

A More Constructive Belief. What I do with my life will always be my choice. I'll solicit feedback about my interests and talents from others and from tests to get some ideas for exploration, but what I do with that information is really up to me.

5. PROBLEM-CREATING BELIEF   If you find out what you are interested in, you'll automatically do well at it.

The Facts. This belief treats one's interests (what you would like to do) and aptitudes (what you can do) as though they were the same. It implies that motivation generated by interests can compensate for deficiencies in one's abilities. While the motivation to do well in a given area can overcome deficiencies, the connection between the two is not one-to-one. Being good at something doesn't necessarily mean that you enjoy it, and liking something doesn't mean you will do well at it.

A More Constructive Belief. In my search for an educational or occupational goal I must keep in mind that the most satisfying choice will combine the best aspects of my interests and talents. Using either alone as a criterion for choice can invite frustration later.

6. PROBLEM-CREATING BELIEF   A number of problem-creating beliefs play on a theme of personal control: You must thoroughly analyze all aspects of a choice before you implement it; otherwise, you're not really prepared. People are either successful or complete failures in their careers. There's no in-between. If things don't go the way I expect, it means I'm a failure. In order to feel worthwhile, I must be thoroughly competent, adequate, intelligent, and achieving in all possible respects. A person should be in total control of his or her career.

The Facts. Even the most advanced sciences admit errors in prediction. Ours is a probabilistic world that cannot be totally predicted or controlled. At best we can only guess what the future will be like, based on the information we have available now. Success in this sense is relative; it recognizes that errors will be made and admits to shades of grey. The odds are that we all will have some successes and some failures—it's a matter of degree, not of kind.

A More Constructive Belief. Although I cannot fully control the future, I can increase the odds that my best guesses will be more accurate. I'm likely to be wrong sometimes, but I've got to guess about possible alternatives and their consequences. If I hang myself up on the idea of being perfect, I'll never do anything.

7. PROBLEM-CREATING BELIEF The world of work is changing so rapidly that you really can't plan the future. I'm unhappy when I think about selecting a career goal, because things external to me make me that way. Life is either always fair or unfair.

The Facts. Unlike the problem-creating beliefs discussed under 6 above (which focus on the issue of personal control), these beliefs focus on external events as the controlling forces. Taken in the extreme, both sets of beliefs are problem creating. While we do not have total control over our futures, we do have some control. We take on more control in our lives when we look for continuity in change. Even though some jobs may become obsolete, the structure of the world of work remains basically the same. The best prediction for the immediate future is that which we observe now. Again, we are playing with probability, not certainty. We can increase the odds in our favor by staying on top of labor trends.

A More Constructive Belief. Informed action is better than passive inaction or reaction. Keeping abreast of labor trends and changes in myself, I can better prepare for and accommodate changes while still utilizing my natural talents and interests.

8. PROBLEM-CREATING BELIEF If I get away from the pressure to decide—if I "stop out" and take a year or two off from college—I'll make a better decision.

The Facts. While taking time away from a problem can sometimes provide added clarity, the mere passage of time will not produce a solution. What time can provide is opportunity for planful self- and occupational exploration.

A More Constructive Belief. My time away from the pressures of a decision can be well spent if I plan for ways of getting the new information I need to make the decision. Before I decide to "stop out," I had better identify exactly what information I need and see if leaving college is the best way to obtain it.

9. PROBLEM-CREATING BELIEF Work as the major source of personal fulfillment gets played as a theme in several ways. Everyone must climb the ladder of success, even if it means doing things that are not interesting. Go where the money is, regardless of what you are doing—at least you'll be secure. Work is the only way to personal fulfillment.

The Facts. Work means many things to different people. For some it is indeed the benchmark of personal success, but for others it supports a personal lifestyle and thus has secondary importance to leisure and interpersonal pursuits. The value of work for each individual is a matter of personal choice. Thus, success is a relative notion that each individual defines according to his or her life goals and lifestyle preference.

A More Constructive Belief. Before I decide what type of work I want to do and how high I want to climb on the career ladder, I should decide what lifestyle I prefer and what it will take to achieve it financially.

10. PROBLEM-CREATING BELIEF We should respect tradition and maintain different types of work for men and women. I must choose between really

having a career and having a family. Women shouldn't compete with men for jobs, especially jobs that involve creativity, managing others, and decision making. Since they are passive, emotional, and respond to things intuitively, women aren't equipped to handle such situations. If I lose a job to a woman, it means I'm inadequate as a male. If my spouse has to go to work, it means I've failed as a husband.

The Facts. While it is true that certain physical limitations can restrict the performance of some men and women at some jobs, many of society's beliefs about a person's place are based on misinformation and stereotypes. Fortunately, equal-rights legislation has done a great deal to level some of these false beliefs by providing opportunities based on merit and skill, not on bias. Even given such legislation, it will be important for each individual to carefully check out his or her biases before rejecting any occupation from consideration.

A More Constructive Belief. Before I reject any occupation as unsuitable for me, I should check out my own biases and those within my environment for possible inaccuracies in the information I have obtained or in my own beliefs.

Step 2: Positive Emotions   The following list consists of positive or desirable emotions that can vary according to frequency, intensity, and duration. They share the self-enhancing quality of making an individual feel good and reinforcing the positive aspects of decision making. Imagine what it would be like to experience each emotion on the list, and try to identify which are most likely to be associated with the constructive beliefs (B) that follow the activating events (A) you recorded in Figure F-3. Record your choices under C (Desirable emotions) in Figure F-3.

1. Relaxed	12. Dependable
2. Joyful	13. Independent
3. Worthwhile	14. Planful
4. Happy	15. Able
5. Confident	16. Patient
6. Guiltless	17. Trusting
7. Hopeful	18. Satisfied
8. Shameless	19. Stable
9. Elated	20. Knowledgeable
10. Energetic	21. Active
11. Cheerful	22. Competent

Step 3: Desirable Behavior, Actions, or Habits   The behaviors listed below are generally described as desirable, growth producing, and self-enhancing. People who engage in these behaviors tend to see themselves as confident, competent, independent, and on top of their careers. Select the behaviors from the list that you believe are likely to occur as a consequence of using more rational ways of thinking about the activating events of Figure F-3 and the feelings they produce. Record them under D (Desirable behaviors) on Figure F-3. Imagine what it would be like for you to engage in these desirable behaviors.

1. Making decisions on my own.
2. Gathering and assessing occupational information by using a self-determined set of criteria.
3. Preparing for an exam with time to spare.
4. Talking through my educational and vocational plans with my adviser or counselor.
5. Volunteering or working part-time in an area related to my career objectives.
6. Taking courses that are consistent with my abilities.
7. Taking courses that will build up my skills.
8. Declaring a major.
9. Preparing a one-year plan to continue exploring or building on a choice.
10. Acting confidently about my goals for future exploration should I elect to "decide not to decide."
11. Talking through my educational and vocational plans with my family.
12. Establishing a long-range plan for exploring career possibilities should I decide to stop out.
13. Planning and preparing a resumé and cover letter, perhaps with the assistance of the placement office.
14. Attending a job interviewing skills workshop.
15. Preparing an effective job-search campaign.

Step 4: New Action Steps   Use the space below to list the thoughts, emotions, and behaviors related to your career planning that you would like to change after completing this exercise.

_____

_____

_____

_____

_____

Now list the strategies or solutions you will use to help you achieve more desirable thoughts, feelings, and actions in your career planning:

What I can do right now:

1. _____

2. _____

3. _____

4. _____

What I can do by a week from today:

1. _____

2. _____

3. _____

4. _____

What I can do in a month:

1. _____

2. _____

3. _____

4. _____

What I can do when I graduate from or leave college:

1. _____

2. _____

References and Resources

Gordon, T. (1972). *Teacher effectiveness training: Supplement to the instructor's outline.* Pasadena, CA: Effectiveness Training Associates.

Seashore, C. *A transitions fantasy.* Source unknown.

Tosi, D. (1973). Self-directed behavior change in the cognitive, affective, and behavioral motoric domains: A rational-emotive approach. *Focus on Guidance, 6,* 6–10.

Index

TO THE OWNER OF THIS BOOK:

We hope that you have found *Discover the Career within You, Third Edition,* useful. So that this book can be improved in a future edition, would you take the time to complete this sheet and return it? Thank you.

School and address: _____

Department: _____

Instructor's name: _____

1. What I like most about this book is: _____

_____

2. What I like least about this book is: _____

_____

3. My general reaction to this book is: _____

_____

4. The name of the course in which I used this book is: _____

_____

5. Were all of the chapters of the book assigned for you to read? _____

   If not, which ones weren't? _____

_____

6. In the space below, or on a separate sheet of paper, please write specific suggestions for improving this book and anything else you'd care to share about your experience in using the book.

_____

_____

_____

_____

_____

Optional:

Your name: _____ Date: _____

May Brooks/Cole quote you, either in promotion for *Discover the Career within You, Third Edition*, or in future publishing ventures?

Yes:

Since

Clar
Cind

DATE DUE

FOLD HERE

B U

FIRS

POSTA

ATT:

Broo
511
Paci

DEMCO

FOLD HERE